THE INVALID MARRIAGE

Lawrence G. Wrenn

Canon Law Society of America
Washington, D.C. 20064

Copyright 1998 by Canon Law Society of America
All rights reserved
ISBN: 0-943616-78-6
SAN: 237-6296

Matrimonium invalidum absque ullo dubio
est aliquid seu non est mera matrimonii negatio:
non est idem ac nullum matrimonium

L. Bender, O.P.
1941

CONTENTS

PREFACE

This is the same old book that used to be called "Annulments" but with a new title and one new appendix (Appendix One) that explains the title change.

Basically I have become convinced that the term "annulment" confuses people by conveying the inaccurate notion that when a marriage is declared to have been invalid it means that it was null. In Appendix One I try to explain the difference between invalidity and nullity, but the *fact* that there *is* a difference has perhaps never been more succinctly stated than in the line from Father Bender quoted on page ii as an introduction to this book.

Appendixes Two and Three, incidentally, are reprinted in this volume exactly as they first apeared in 1984 and 1986 respectively (in *The Jurist* and *CLSAP*), despite the fact that they contain occasional language that would now be considered dated.

Lawrence G. Wrenn

Hartford
June 26, 1998

PREFACE TO THE SECOND PRINTING

Since the first printing of *The Invalid Marriage*, it has occurred to me that the reader might welcome, right up front, a brief explanation of the difference between the terms "invalid" and "null." First of all it must be conceded that, *in common parlance,* even among canon lawyers, indeed even in the Code of Canon Law itself, the two terms have long been used interchangeably. At the same time, however, it is important to note that at least as far back as the great Cardinal Gasparri, surely the most influential canonist of the twentieth century, it has been generally understood by the authors that, *strictly and properly speaking,* the two terms are not synonymous, and that, properly speaking, we should not be calling invalid marriages "null."

The difference between an invalid marriage and a null marriage lies in this: that in an *invalid* marriage there is a reciprocal, external act of a man and a woman which is, per se, a manifestation of matrimonial consent, whereas in a *null* marriage that act is missing. In a null marriage, there may be some act. There may even be a reciprocal, external act between a man and a woman, but not one that is, per se, a manifestation of matrimonial consent, that is, one which the ordinary bystander would conclude was a marriage.

Perhaps an example would help. One day in 1865 the forty year old Angelo Bordoni was sitting on a wall near the parish church in a small town in Italy. He was employed in the selling and delivery of oil but was known by all the townsfolk as the town jester. He was chatting this day with a certain Livia who told him that he could never get a woman to marry him because he smelled of oil. As Angelo and Livia were debating this issue, the beautiful twenty year old Anna Campitelli happened to walk by, whereupon Livia said to Angelo, "Well, let's see who's right. There's Anna. See if she'll marry you." Angelo accepted the challenge, begged Anna, in his usual humourous way, to marry him and to accompany him, then and there, to the rectory. Anna, caught up in the spirit of fun, agreed. So Angelo and Anna went to the rectory, caught the pastor and two other people off guard, and quickly recited the marriage formula, all the time laughing and joking. The pastor regarded the whole thing as a mockery and as ludicrous and refused to regard it as a marriage or to enter it into the marriage register. The form of marriage, of course, has been observed; it was not until more than forty years later that the Church, in the decree *Ne Temere,* eliminated the "surprise marriage" by shifting the role of the priest from a passive to an active one, and requiring him to "request and receive the consent." Back in 1865, however, it was only required that the couple express their consent before the priest, and Angelo and Anna did that. But the marriage was nevertheless truly *null,* not just invalid but null, because even though there was an external, reciprocal act of a man and a woman, it was not one that was, per se, a manifestation of matrimonial consent, since no one who would have witnessed it would have seriously regarded it as a marriage. (See *Acta Sanctae Sedis* 22 (1889-1890) 529 - 546, and Gasparri, *De Matrimonio,* 1932 edition, par. 831.)

Contrast this with another case. In 1904 Nicia and Varo married in a Catholic ceremony. Within two weeks, however, Varo was seeing a prostitute and after two and a half years he abandoned his wife and child. Nicia eventually petitioned to have the marriage declared invalid and, during the course of the proceedings, it was demonstrated that Varo, a lawyer, was a "free-thinker" and of the opinion that marriage was repugnant to human freedom and did not give rise to any bond. It was further proved that, much like Angelo and Anna regarding their marriage, Varo regarded his wedding ceremony with Nicia to have been "a joke and a comedy" that did not entail any obligations. The marriage was clearly *invalid* and was found to have been so on the ground that Varo simulated marriage (today the ground might have been determining error - c. 1099). It was not, however, null because the wedding ceremony involved a reciprocal, external act of a man and a woman which was, per se, a manifestation of matrimonial consent. Unlike the wedding of Angelo and Anna, in other words, the ordinary bystander or attendant at this wedding would have had no reason to conclude that a marriage was not taking place. (For the case of Nicia and Varo, See *SRRD* 3 (1911) 15-29 and 460-473.)

It seems to me that many of us have, over the years, failed to appreciate the great wisdom of Cardinal Gasparri when he pointed out that, properly speaking, the term "null" should be reserved for those marriages that lack the *species seu figura matrimonii,* the appearance or configuration of a marriage. And were Gasparri writing today, he would, I'm sure, see the marriage of Angelo and Anna as truly *null* because it lacked the configuration of a marriage; whereas the marriage of Nicia and Varo, since it had the appearance of a marriage, he would regard as *invalid* but not null.

Appendix I attempts to provide an historical context as well as a rationale for the distinction between nullity and invalidity, but perhaps the two cases of Angelo and Anna and Nicia and Varo will provide a practical context for a better understanding of the issue.

Lawrence G. Wrenn

Hartford
January 6, 1999

INTRODUCTION

NOTES ON CANONICAL JURISPRUDENCE

A. The Meaning Of Canonical Jurisprudence

1. Definition

    Canonical jurisprudence is the science and art of utilizing, interpreting, and supplying for the codified law by rescript and by judicial sentence.

2. Explanation of Definition

    a. *Utilizing* means the fitting of a clear law to a corresponding situation. An example might be the fitting of c. 1101 §2 (which says, among other things, that excluding perpetuity by a "positive act of the will" vitiates marriage) to a case where one party positively intended to obtain a divorce if the marriage proved unhappy.

    b. *Interpreting* means explaining the sense of a law that is obscure, at least as it applies to a particular situation. An example would be extending c. 1101 §2 to a case where one party believed so firmly in the dissolubility of marriage (error pervicax seu radicatus) that the error itself would inevitably be applied to a particular marriage and would therefore, in practice, be tantamount to (since it would certainly lead to) a positive exclusion of perpetuity.

    c. *Supplying* means creating a new norm where there is no express law. One example would be declaring a marriage invalid on the grounds that an essential property of marriage was excluded not by a positive act of the will but by an inadequate commitment. Another, much more successful example of supplementation, was the pre-Code development of the notion of lack of due competence which finally culminated in c. 1095, 3⁰.

3. Significance of Definition

    The general significance of defining jurisprudence as an art is that it gives to the local judge a degree of autonomy. One that must be used responsibly, of course, but still, it lifts the judge above the level of a mere enforcement officer. The local judge is not one who merely applies the judicial principles determined by higher courts. More specifically:

    a. *Utilization* - Occasionally a perfectly clear law goes unutilized. The old c. 1134 (like the present c. 1157), for example, said that, in a convalidation ceremony, the parties must personally recognize the former ceremony as invalid. It is only recently, however, that this law has been widely utilized in the United States to declare invalid ceremonies where a party viewed the convalidation as a mere blessing of an already valid marriage.

b. *Interpretation* - C. 16 points out that there are two interpreters of law: the legislator and the judge. When the legislator officially interprets a law, the interpretation has the same force as the law itself but when a judge interprets a law it does not have the force of law and affects only the parties involved in the case.

This is true per se. But per accidens, namely by the force of consuetudinary law, the interpretations of judges can become the law. If, in other words, all judges hand down like decisions over a period of thirty years, the interpretation is then tantamount to law (c. 26). Or, to put it another way, the original law, at that point, may no longer be regarded as obscure. Later judges should view it as a clear law to be utilized according to the generally accepted sense.

The Code (c.17) recommends that, in interpreting a law, the judge should look to various sources: other similar laws, the purpose of the law, the circumstances, and the mind of the legislator. Interestingly, it does not recommend that he look to the interpretations of other judges, even rotal judges.

c. *Supplementation* - When there is a lacuna or deficiency in the law, the Code views this situation as somewhat more urgent and delicate than it does an unclear law that needs interpreting. To fill the lacuna c. 19 suggests four sources, one of which is "the jurisprudence and practice of the Roman Curia," which, for the most part, means rotal jurisprudence.

Rotal supplementation does not, of course, have legal force but only suppletive force. A Rotal supplementation, in other words, is a priori recommended as safe. It has something more than its own intrinsic wisdom (which is all a supplementation by any other court has) to recommend it. This "Goodchurchkeeping Seal of Approval" awards a certain dignity to the Rota. On the other hand, it should not rob the local court of its independence, or make it excessively reliant on the Rota, because ultimately the real value of jurisprudence is not extrinsic (based on authority) but intrinsic (based on the merits of the legal argument).

There would seem to be only one occasion where a Rotal supplementation would be binding on a lower court and that would be when the following three conditions are verified: 1) some suppletory norm is required, 2) the lower court, using the other sources mentioned in c. 19, cannot supply its own norm and 3) the lower court cannot disprove the legitimacy of the Rota's norm.

B.   The Development Of Canonical Jurisprudence

1.   Like any other science, jurisprudence is dynamic and always evolving. It does this in the following ways:

a.   *Utilization,* i.e. by newly utilizing forgotten laws. The 1917 Code, for example, required, as noted above, that both parties in a convalidation 1) recognize the invalidity of the first ceremony and therefore 2) give a new exchange of consent at the time of the validation. It was not, however, until after the decision of January 2, 1969 coram Rogers that Tribunals began to investigate the possibility of declaring marriages invalid on this basis.

b.   *Application,* i.e. by finding new applications (because the cultural conditions or circumstances change) for old laws. It has, for example, always been understood that an intention against perpetuity is invalidating. In recent years, however, the prevalence of the divorce mentality in our culture has made for much broader applications of that source of invalidity than was true in the past.

c.   *Restoration,* i.e. by restoring old laws or principles that were not included in the Code. Both Peter Lombard and Thomas Aquinas, for example, held that when a couple consents to marry, their consent is not simply to sexual intercourse but to a broader interpersonal relationship as well. That principle was not incorporated in the 1917 Code but was, through jurisprudence, restored, and was finally incorporated in the 1983 Code.

d.   *Expansion,* i.e. by expanding the sense of a principle to include new situations. Substantial error, for example, has always been regarded as a ground of invalidity. In the 1917 Code, however, and for many years thereafter, error was, in practice, considered to be invalidating only when it involved mistaking one physical person for another (e.g. Leah for Rachel). In recent decades, however, that notion was expanded to include the situation where a person enters marriage directly and principally intending a quality which he or she erroneously thinks is present in the other person.

e.   *Contraction,* i.e. by giving a more restrictive interpretation to a law than had been previously given. Prior to 1977, for example, the marriage of a doubly vasectomized man was considered invalid by Church courts. After the decree of May 13, 1977, however, vasectomy was, in itself, no longer considered a source of marital invalidity.

2.   In recent years there have been two major influences on the development of jurisprudence. The first major influence was the Second Vatican Council,with its insight into the nature of the marriage covenant.

3

The second was the mental health sciences, with their insights into psychic disorders and the effect of these disorders on the consensual and functional capabilities of people.

C. The Roman Rota

1. Title

The Roman Wheel, as this great Tribunal is called, is most likely referred to as "The Wheel" either because the judges originally sat in a circle, or because there was a circle on the chamber floor at Avignon where the title is first known to have been used (circa A.D. 1350), or because the cases under consideration were moved from judge to judge on a bookstand which was on wheels. At any rate, the Rota has not only retained the name but still uses the wheel as its logo.

2. History of the Rota and Its Auditors

The Rota dates back at least to the twelfth century, though in those days the auditors, who were the Pope's chaplains, were only auditors and not judges as they are today. In the early days, in other words, the Pope's chaplains sat in an auditorium and took or audited the testimony, but only the Pope judged the cases. Today a judge on the Rota is still referred to as an auditor, but he has, of course, full judicial power.

There are nineteen such auditors today. Eight are from Italy; there are two from Spain, France, and the United States and there is one from each of the following countries: Germany, Ireland, Poland, Lebanon and the Slovak Republic. They are listed in the *Annuario Pontificio* according to the date of their Rotal appointment and are, in theory, assigned cases according to that listing in turns or boards of three in such a way that what might be called the first case would be heard by the three senior auditors, the next case by the second, third and fourth auditors and so on. The senior man on each turn is the Ponens or Commissioner and the sentence is frequently cited by referring to him: one might, for example, refer to a case "before Wynen" or "coram Wynen."

In 1870 when the Italian army invaded Rome the doors of the Rota were closed and they did not open again until 1908 when the Rota was revived by Pope Pius X. This marks, as it were, the beginning of the Rota's modern era.

3. Published Sentences

a. Enumeration of the Volumes

Volume I of the Rota's published sentences contains the decisions of 1909, the year following the Rota's revival. Each volume number, therefore, always lags eight numbers behind the year, so that volume 50, for example, contains the decisions for the year 1958.

b. The Work Load

A general idea of the Rota's case load over the years can be seen in the following table:

Year	Cases Decided
1912	42
1922	40
1932	59
1942	81
1952	188
1962	131
1972	306
1982	182
1992	120

c. Citing a Rotal Decision

The year 1954 introduced a new way of citing rotal decisions. Up to 1953 the decisions were numbered in Roman numerals both in the Table of Contents and in the text, and a citation would include the volume number, the decision number and the page number. In 1954, however, the decision number was dropped altogether from the text, and received an Arabic number in the Table of Contents. Since it was dropped from the text it has also commonly been dropped from the citation and a sentence formerly referred to as XX, XXXV, 323 is now generally cited simply as 20, 323. In formal citations, the numbers are preceded by SRRD (Sacrae Romanae Rotae Decisiones) or, since 1985, by ARRT Dec. (Apostolicum Rotae Romanae Tribunal Decisiones).

4. Value

The Rota is certainly the chief source of canonical jurisprudence for all other courts. It has set the tone and established virtually singlehandedly the traditional jurisprudence to which all other tribunals turn. And it has done so with masterly finesse and thoroughness, especially in the area of utilizing the law.

In the areas of interpreting and supplying, Rotal auditors, as might be expected, often take divergent positions on a given question. Generally, however, they are thorough, excellent theoreticians, and, especially considering their distance from the people involved, remarkably empathetic. Local judges, on the other hand, though sometimes inferior as theoreticians, nevertheless

5

have their own pragmatic strengths. Their understanding of the capacities of people, an understanding gained from broad, clinical experience, seems especially acute and real; and they have a high awareness and sensitivity to local conditions and their importance.

The challenge, at any rate, is the same for all judges, both rotal and local. They must know their own culture and their own times. They must be able to perceive, and to weigh, and to create suitable, enlightened norms by which justice can be rendered. They must avoid the extremes of being insensitive on the one hand, and pandering on the other; of being too theoretical on the one hand, and too intuitive on the other. They must be neither too legalistic nor too romantic, neither too demanding nor too excusing. They must, above all, show forth the ability of the Church to treat people as individual persons of the community and not just as cases or stereotypes. Only in this way can jurisprudence continue to be the "ars boni et aequi" for each succeeding generation.

MALE IMPOTENCE

A. The Pertinent Canon

C. 1084 - CCEO, c. 801 - §1 - Antecedent and perpetual impotence to have intercourse, whether on the part of the man or woman, which is either absolute or relative, of its very nature invalidates marriage.

§2 - If the impediment of impotence is doubtful, either by reason of a doubt of law or a doubt of fact, a marriage is neither to be impeded nor is it to be declared null as long as the doubt exists.

§3 - Sterility neither prohibits nor invalidates marriage, with due regard for the prescription of canon 1098.

B. Impotence As An Impediment

1. Impotence is regarded in the law as a diriment impediment. C. 1084 is found in Chapter III - "On Specific Diriment Impediments." A diriment impediment, according to c. 1073, renders a person ineligible (inhabilem) for contracting marriage validly.

2. A diriment impediment, understood in the strict sense, is a "lex inhabilitans," a law which disqualifies a person, who is per se capable, from entering a marriage. The diriment impediments of disparity of cult, sacred orders, public vow, etc., as found in canons 1086-1094, are all diriment impediments taken in this strict sense.

3. Some canonists have noted that impotence is not really an impediment in the strict sense, because the impotent person is not per se capable of marriage. The impotent person is incapable of assuming the essential obligations of marriage and is therefore incapable of placing the object of marital consent and is therefore incapable of marriage. See Navarrete, Urbano, "'Incapacitas Assumendi Onera' Uti Caput Autonomum Nullitatis Matrimonii" in *Periodica,* 1972, 1, p. 78-80.

4. Impotence, therefore, is a diriment impediment in a somewhat wider sense. The fact is, however, that, in canon law, impotence is regarded not as a defect of consent but as a diriment impediment.

5. Incompetence (lack of due competence) has much in common with impotence, not just phonetically but really. Taxonomically, however, they differ. Impotence is classified as an impediment; incompetence as a defect of consent. See the chapter entitled "Lack of Due Competence - General Remarks."

C. Definition Of The Impediment Of Impotence

1. The diriment impediment of impotence may be defined as the antecedent and perpetual incapacity of a man or woman to have physical intercourse in a human manner.

2. Three notions in this definition merit comment: a) the meaning of intercourse, b) that the impediment be antecedent, and c) that it be perpetual.

   a. *Intercourse*

   For the man to be capable of intercourse, three elements must be present; erection, penetration, and ejaculation during intercourse.

   Whether the man, to be potent, must be capable of ejaculating *within the vagina* is somewhat questionable (*Communicationes,* 1974, 2, pp. 177-196 and 1975, 1, pp. 58-60). Therefore, in view of c. 1084 §2, a man who can ejaculate during intercourse, but not within the vagina, would be regarded not as impotent but only as sterile. This would apply particularly to the man afflicted with either hypospadias (where the opening of the urethra is on the undersurface of the penis) or epispadias (on the dorsal surface) where these conditions might prevent depositing semen within the vagina. The man, however, who is incapable of any real, i.e. antegrade ejaculation must be regarded as not just sterile but impotent (see the Dublin decision in *Monitor Ecclesiasticus,* 1987, IV, pp. 485-495).

   b. *Antecedent*

   Although impotence, to be invalidating, must be antecedent (on the obvious grounds that no supervenient factor can affect validity), it is not required that the impotence should have manifested itself beforehand. It is not required that the impotence be actual or dynamic at the time of marriage, but only that it be virtual or causal. It is necessary and it suffices that the proximate disposition to impotence and the proximate causes of its onset be present at the time of marriage. This could be verified, for example, in the case of a homosexual but not in the case of a heterosexual who found himself impotent after marriage because he found his wife's obnoxious personal habits repulsive.

   c. *Perpetual*

   Impotence is considered to be perpetual when, at least relative to the marriage in question, it is incurable or when it is curable only by 1) a miracle, 2) illicit means, 3) probable danger to one's life, 4) serious harm to one's health or 5) doubtfully successful means. Or, to put it another way, impotence is perpetual when, at least relative to the marriage in question, it is irremediable except by extraordinary means. It should be noted, however, that to be invalidating, the impotence must be perpetual at the time of the marriage and not simply become so later. It is possible, in other words, that a man was de facto impotent at the time of marriage, but that he was not suffering from the impediment of impotence at that time, since it was then curable. Perhaps the impotence later became incurable but that does not affect validity. Nevertheless, if the experts can testify as regards *absolute* impotence (where the man is impotent in respect to women in general) that the very form of impotence from which the man suffers is incurable, or was at the time of marriage; and as regards *relative* impotence (where the man is impotent in respect to a particular woman) that he could at no stage of the marriage have been cured in respect to his wife, then the marriage would be considered invalid.

D. Causes Of Impotence

Impotence can be either organic or functional. *Organic* impotence arises from the fact that the sexual organs themselves are physically, anatomically or organically defective whereas in *functional* impotence the organs themselves are organically perfect but for one reason or another (either neurophysiological or psychical) they function imperfectly.

E. Forms Of Impotence

1. Organic

    a. Absence of the penis.
    b. Abnormal size or shape of the penis preventing vaginal intromission.
    c. Retrograde ejaculation (could also be Functional).

2. Functional
    a. Physical

    Paraplegia (a paralysis of the lower extremities of the body resulting from disease or injury to the central nervous system) and other similar infirmities when this does in fact render intercourse impossible. Brenkle notes that in fact about 70% of paraplegics are capable of erection but only about 10% of them are capable of ejaculation. (Brenkle, John, *The Impediment of Male Impotence with Special Application to Paraplegia,* Washington, D.C., CUA Press, 1963, pp. 156-157).

    b. Psychic

    1) Inability to obtain or sustain an erection (anaphrodisia).
    2) Excessive excitability resulting in premature ejaculation (aphrodisia).
    3) Ejaculatory Incompetence, also called Male Orgasmic Disorder, which is the opposite of premature ejaculation, namely the inability of the man to ejaculate during intercourse. See *Human Sexual*

Inadequacy, Masters and Johnson, pp. 116-136 and DSM IV, pp. 507-509.

4) Dyspareunia
  a) The Syndrome

  Although the term dyspareunia, that is, painful intercourse, has traditionally referred to coital distress in women, it can in fact, also refer to men (see DSM IV, p. 511 and Masters and Johnson, *Human Sexual Inadequacy,* pp. 288-294).

  b) The Juridic Principle

  The juridic principle is clearly stated (though in terms of female rather than male impotence) in the following remarks from the decision coram Bruno of April 3, 1987 (LS, 19-20):

  > It is to be noted, furthermore, that there are decisions handed down in our Apostolic Tribunal which, not without merit, are quite progressive in this area.
  >
  > In one decision, for example, Heard says "Finally it is to be noted that for the validity of the contract it is required that intercourse take place in a natural and human way. Consequently the depositing of seed within the vagina through the violence of a man, notwithstanding the resistance and intolerable pain of the woman, is not sufficient. For such an inhuman way of acting, even if it results in the physical consummation of the marriage, would not rule out the impediment of impotence; for just as no one is legally bound to undergo a surgical operation which would endanger one's life, so no one is legally bound to have intercourse which would necessarily involve intolerable pain " (the decision in a Milan case coram Heard, dated December 30, 1949; as regards nonconsummation see the decision in the Roman case coram Mattioli of October 17, 1951, ARRT Dec., vol. XLIII, p. 640, n. 2).
  >
  > The teaching enunciated in this decision coram Heard may be said to have been received into the new Code when in Canon 1061 §1 a marriage is called ratified and consummated "if the parties have performed between themselves in a human manner the conjugal act which is per se suitable for the generation of children, to which marriage is ordered by its very nature and by which the spouses become one flesh."

Consequently in a case where the marriage lasted for many years, and where the spouses, because of the woman's vaginismus, had sex only once or twice in all those years (and then only through violence or the use of aphrodisiacs) then the impotence of the woman should be recognized. For in this case the couple did not become one flesh in a human way and the impotence of the woman for placing, in a human way, a conjugal act which is per se apt for the generation of offspring, remains confirmed.

See also Keating, pp. 181-182.

F. Proof Of Impotence

In regard to organic impotence and functional-physical impotence, the proofs will consist almost entirely of medical reports. In regard to functional-psychic impotence, the Court must depend on the declarations of the parties, affidavits and testimony of witnesses, etc. (for the canons on this type of proof, see the chapters on simulation). When impotence results from a psychological cause, however, it is usually symptomatic of a more pervasive syndrome and can often be viewed more easily and more accurately under the heading of lack of due competence.

G. The Decree Of May 13, 1977

1. The jurisprudence outlined above reflects the tenor of the Decree of the Congregation of the Doctrine of the Faith, approved by the Pope on May 13, 1977. See Appendix Six on p. 231.

2. Prior to that decree jurisprudence recognized more forms of impotence (see Section E) than it does at present. Men, for example, who had been doubly vasectomized, even though they were entirely capable of erection, penetration and ejaculation, were regarded as impotent before the decree.

3. After the decree, *some* canonists were of the opinion that the decree was not retroactive. This was a well founded opinion based on seeing the decree as an authentic interpretation of what had been a dubious law. C. 16 §2 (c. 17 §2 in the 1917 Code) specifically states that such a decree is not retroactive. *Other* canonists, however, were of the opinion that the decree simply declared the true meaning of impotence, which meaning had always been intrinsically certain (in se certa) even though not properly understood by everyone. C. 16 §2 states that such a decree *is* retroactive. This position was also well founded.

4. Because of these two well founded but conflicting opinions a doubt of law remained regarding the retroactivity of the decree. According to the first

opinion there were more forms of impotence before the effective date of the decree than there were afterwards. This, however, was only a probable opinion. Therefore the "extra forms" of impotence, e.g. vasectomy, that were accepted by many prior to the decree were, in fact, only doubtful impediments. According to c. 1084 §2, however, a doubtful impediment is no impediment. In practice, therefore, it would seem that the jurisprudence as outlined in sections A to E above was the proper jurisprudence to apply to all marriages of whatever date.

5. This, indeed, became the accepted position following the decision of January 27, 1986, signed by nine judges, coram Serrano. The eighteen page law section of that sentence began with the words, "After the decree of May 13, 1977 of the S. Congregation for the Doctrine of the Faith, it can no longer be doubted which male impotence invalidates marriage. All judges, therefore, must accept this position and hold to it with religious obsequium, especially in view of Pope Paul VI's allocution to this Tribunal of January 28, 1978".

A. The Pertinent Canon

C. 1084 - CCEO, c. 801 - §1 - Antecedent and perpetual impotence to have intercourse, whether on the part of the man or the woman, which is either absolute or relative, of its very nature invalidates marriage.

§2 - If the impediment of impotence is doubtful, either by reason of a doubt of law or a doubt of fact, a marriage is neither to be impeded nor is it to be declared null as long as the doubt exists.

§3 - Sterility neither prohibits nor invalidates marriage, with due regard for the prescription of canon 1098.

B. Impotence As An Impediment

1. Impotence is regarded in the law as a diriment impediment. C. 1084 is found in Chapter III - "On Specific Diriment Impediments." A diriment impediment, according to c. 1073, renders a person ineligible (inhabilem) for contracting marriage validly.

2. A diriment impediment understood in the strict sense, is a "lex inhabilitans," a law which disqualifies a person, who is per se capable, from entering a marriage. The diriment impediments of disparity of cult, sacred orders, public vow, etc., as found in canons 1086-1094, are all diriment impediments taken in this strict sense.

3. Some canonists have noted that impotence is not really an impediment in the strict sense, because the impotent person is not per se capable of marriage. The impotent person is incapable of assuming the essential obligations of marriage and is therefore incapable of placing the object of marital consent and is therefore incapable of marriage. See Navarrete, Urbano, "'Incapacitas Assumendi Onera' Uti Caput Autonomum Nullitatis Matrimonii" in *Periodica*, 1972, 1, p. 78-80.

4. Impotence, therefore, is a diriment impediment in a somewhat wider sense. The fact is, however, that, in canon law, impotence is regarded not as a defect of consent but as a diriment impediment.

5. Incompetence (lack of due competence) has much in common with impotence, not just phonetically but really. Taxonomically, however, they differ. Impotence is classified as an impediment; incompetence as a defect of consent. See the chapter entitled "Lack of Due Competence - General Remarks."

C. Definition Of The Impediment Of Impotence

1. The diriment impediment of impotence may be defined as the antecedent and perpetual incapacity of a man or woman to have physical intercourse in a human manner.

2. Three notions in this definition merit comment: a) the meaning of intercourse, b) that the impediment be antecedent, and c) that it be perpetual.

   a. *Intercourse*

   For a woman to be organically capable of intercourse, she must have a vagina that is capable of receiving the erect male member. The vagina need not be natural. Even an artificial vagina would suffice. See the decision coram Raad of October 16, 1980 in D2, pp. 5-8.

   b. *Antecedent*

   Although impotence, to be invalidating, must be antecedent (on the obvious grounds that no supervenient factor can affect validity) it is not required that the impotence should have manifested itself beforehand. It is not required that the impotence be actual or dynamic at the time of marriage, but only that it be virtual or causal. It is necessary and it suffices that the proximate disposition to impotence and the proximate causes of its onset be present at the time of the marriage. This would be verified, for example, when the woman finds after marriage that she suffers from vaginismus due to a previous traumatic experience.

   c. *Perpetual*

   Impotence is considered to be perpetual when, at least relative to the marriage in question, it is incurable or when it is curable only by 1) a miracle, 2) illicit means, 3) probable danger to one's life, 4) serious harm to one's health or 5) doubtfully successful means. Or, to put it another way, impotence is perpetual when, at least relative to the marriage in question, it is irremediable except by extraordinary means.

   It should be noted, however, that, to be invalidating, the impotence must be perpetual at the time of the marriage, and not simply become so later. It is possible, in other words, that a woman was de facto impotent at the time of marriage, but that she was not suffering from the impediment of impotence at that time, since it was then curable. Perhaps the impotence later became incurable but that does not affect validity. Nevertheless, if the experts can testify as regards *absolute* impotence (where the woman is impotent in respect to men in general) that the very form of impotence from which the woman suffers is incurable, or was at the time of marriage; and as regards *relative* impotence (where the woman is impotent in respect to a particular man) that she could at no stage of the marriage have been cured in respect to her husband, then the marriage would be considered invalid.

D. Causes Of Impotence

Impotence can be either organic or functional. *Organic* impotence arises from the fact that the sexual organs themselves are physically, anatomically or organically defective whereas in *functional* impotence the organs themselves are organically perfect but for one reason or another (either physical or psychical) they function imperfectly.

E. Forms Of Impotence

1. Organic

A woman is considered organically impotent when she lacks a vagina (whether natural or artificial) of sufficient width and length to receive the erect male member.

2. Functional

A woman is considered functionally impotent when intercourse is either impossible due to vaginismus or intolerably painful due to Female Sexual Arousal Disorder or Dyspareunia.

a. *Vaginismus*

In a decision of October 9, 1964 (56, 682) Sabattani discussed the legal aspects of vaginismus. It may be summarized as follows:

1) *Definition* - Vaginismus may be defined as the painful spasm of all the muscles surrounding and supporting the vagina, which happens when intercourse is attempted or even when the area is merely touched and which renders intercourse impossible.

2) *Division*

a) Schema

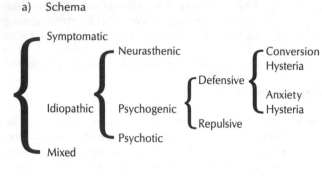

b) Discussion

Vaginismus is called *symptomatic* when there are present pathologic, inflammatory lesions of the urogenital structures due either to immoderate or violent attempts at intercourse or to hypersensitivity or to some injury or infection. It is called *idiopathic* when the vaginal contraction is caused by neurological or psychological factors only, without there being present any anatomic factors. It is called *mixed* when both factors are present.

Idiopathic vaginismus is called *neurasthenic* when it is of a temporary, passing nature. It is called *psychogenic* when it is a more permanent, constitutional problem. It is called *psychotic* when it is existing concomitantly with and probably as a symptom of an underlying psychosis.

Psychogenic vaginismus is called *defensive* whenever it is merely a subconscious defense mechanism against pain or against a hated husband. It is called *repulsive* when it creates in the woman an abhorrence for sexual relations.

Defensive vaginismus is manifested in an *anxiety hysteria* where it results from a real or suspected violent or inhuman approach by the man, and by a *conversion hysteria* where it results not from a faulty approach but from a pathological fear of pain resulting from the insertion of the penis. In this case, the woman, in effect, "converts" this fear of pain into a real pain, namely that resulting from the vaginal contraction.

3) *Presumptions Regarding Antecedence and Perpetuity*

a) *Symptomatic* vaginismus is not presumed to be either antecedent or supervenient. In a given case, however, it could be proved to have been antecedent. It is only considered perpetual when its organic basis can be proved incurable. Otherwise it is presumed to be temporary.

b) *Neurasthenic* vaginismus is not presumed to be either antecedent or perpetual.

c) The *conversion hysteria* type of defensive vaginismus is presumed to be antecedent if it is present on the first attempt at intercourse. As for perpetuity, there is no presumption favoring perpetuity because it can ordinarily be cured by psychotherapy.

d) The *anxiety hysteria* type follows the same general presumptions but it should be noted that in this case the woman could well be relatively impotent, that is, she could be impotent towards the man who originally approached her in an insensitive way.

e) *Repulsive* vaginismus is presumed antecedent if it is present on the first attempt at intercourse. It is also presumed perpetual - because it is extremely serious and because therapy is not usually successful. There is always the possibility of an operation of course. But if this is just a hymenal operation like a hymenectomy, it will not really cure the vaginismus, and if it is an operation on the nervous system, then it would have to be considered an extraordinary means.

f) *Psychotic* vaginismus is presumed antecedent if present on the first attempt at intercourse and is also presumed perpetual.

g) *Mixed* vaginismus depends for its ruling presumptions on the prevailing aspect, either symptomatic or idiopathic.

4) *Criteria For Judging Circumstantial Evidence*

The following criteria might be helpful in confirming the presence of an invalidating vaginismus. If most of these are present in a given case without being contravened by other evidence the marriage should certainly be declared invalid.

a) Objective Criteria - if the medical examination (preferably extrajudicial tolerated by the woman for the sake of a cure rather than at the request of the court) reveals immediate, obvious and intense spasms and if, because of the woman's abhorrence and sensitivity, the examination is finally conducted only with great difficulty.

17

b) Subjective Criteria - if the woman, although truly in love with her husband, becomes extremely agitated and even hysterical on the wedding night and if she honestly but vainly tries to submit to intercourse in order to save the marriage.

c) Psycho-Physical Criteria - if the vaginismus is accompanied by serious hypoplasia (inadequate evolution of the female organs), if the woman has a neuropsychopathic constitution, if she cries out in pain and even becomes convulsive during attempts at intercourse, and if she speaks of or actually attempts suicide.

d) Temporal Criteria - if the couple remained in love and stayed together for a long time and if the woman was diagnosed as suffering from severe vaginismus on many occasions all through her life, even after the separation, with no cure ever effected.

b. *Female Sexual Arousal Disorder and Dyspareunia*

1) The Syndromes
DSM IV (pp. 500 - 502 and 511 - 513) briefly describes these two disorders. The former involves a persistent or recurrent partial or complete failure to attain or maintain the lubrication-swelling response of sexual excitement until completion of the sexual activity. The latter involves recurrent or persistent pain before, during or after sexual intercourse. Both disorders can conceivably involve intolerable pain for the woman whenever intercourse is engaged in.

2) The Juridic Principle

The juridic principle is clearly stated in the following remarks from the decision coram Bruno of April 3, 1987 (LS, 19-20):

It is to be noted, furthermore, that there are decisions handed down in our Apostolic Tribunal which, not without merit, are quite progressive in this area.

In one decision, for example, Heard says "Finally it is to be noted that for the validity of the contract it is required that intercourse take place in a natural and human way. Consequently the depositing of seed within the vagina through the violence of a man, notwithstanding the resistance and intolerable pain of the woman, is not sufficient. For such an inhuman way of acting, even if it results in the physical consummation of the marriage, would not rule out the impediment of impotence; for just as no one is legally bound to undergo a surgical operation which would endanger one's life, so no one is legally bound to have intercourse which would necessarily involve intolerable pain " (the decision in a Milan case coram Heard, dated December 30, 1949; as regards nonconsummation see the decision in the Roman case coram Mattioli of October 17, 1951, ARRT Dec., vol. XLIII, p. 640, n. 2).

The teaching enunciated in this decision coram Heard may be said to have been received into the new Code when in Canon 1061 §1 a marriage is called ratified and consummated "if the parties have performed between themselves in a human manner the conjugal act which is per se suitable for the generation of children, to which marriage is ordered by its very nature and by which the spouses become one flesh."

Consequently in a case where the marriage lasted for many years, and where the spouses, because of the woman's vaginismus, had sex only once or twice in all those years (and then only through violence or the use of aphrodisiacs) then the impotence of the woman should be recognized. For in this case the couple did not become one flesh in a human way and the impotence of the woman for placing, in a human way, a conjugal act which is per se apt for the generation of offspring, remains confirmed.

See also Keating, pp. 181-182.

F.   Proof Of Impotence

Proof of organic impotence will consist almost entirely in medical reports. Proof of functional impotence will often include the declarations of the parties, affidavits and testimony of witnesses, etc. (for the canons on this type of proof, see the chapters on simulation). It should be noted, too, that functional impotence often involves deep-seated psychological problems on the part of the woman, in which case a report from a psychiatric expert is useful. See the Tern-Kapaun case in D1, pp. 5-7. And finally it should be noted that when the perpetuity of the disorder cannot be proved, as is often the case, especially with Female Sexual Arousal Disorder and Dyspareunia, then the case can often, in practice, be handled more easily on the grounds of incompetence (c. 1095, 3[0]) than on the grounds of impotence (c. 1084).

G. The Decree Of May 13, 1977

1. The jurisprudence outlined above reflects the tenor, as applied to the woman, of the Decree of the Congregation of the Doctrine of the Faith, approved by the Pope on May 13, 1977. See Appendix Six on p. 231.

2. Prior to that decree jurisprudence recognized more forms of impotence (see Section E) than it does at present. Women, for example, who had an artificial vagina at the time of marriage, even though it was quite capable of receiving the erect male member, were regarded as impotent before the decree.

3. After the decree, *some* canonists were of the opinion that the decree was not retroactive. This was a well founded opinion based on seeing the decree as an authentic interpretation of what had been a dubious law. C. 16 §2 (c. 17 §2 in the 1917 Code) specifically states that such a decree is not retroactive. *Other* canonists, however, were of the opinion that the decree simply declared the true meaning of impotence, which meaning had always been intrinsically certain (in se certa) even though not properly understood by everyone. C. 16 §2 states that such a decree *is* retroactive. This position was also well founded.

4. Because of these two well founded but conflicting opinions a doubt of law remained regarding the retroactivity of the decree. According to the first opinion there were more forms of impotence before the effective date of the decree than there were afterwards. This, however, was only a probable opinion. Therefore the "extra forms" of impotence, e.g. absence of a natural vagina, that were accepted by many prior to the decree were, in fact, only doubtful impediments. According to c. 1084 §2, however, a doubtful impediment is no impediment. In practice, therefore, it would seem that the jurisprudence as outlined in sections A to E above was the proper jurisprudence to apply to all marriages of whatever date.

5. This, indeed, became the accepted position following the decision of January 27, 1986, signed by nine judges, coram Serrano. The eighteen page law section of that sentence began with the words, "After the decree of May 13, 1977 of the S. Congregation for the Doctrine of the Faith, it can no longer be doubted which male impotence invalidates marriage. All judges, therefore, must accept this position and hold to it with religious obsequium, especially in view of Pope Paul VI's allocution to this Tribunal of January 28, 1978".

LACK OF DUE REASON

A. The Pertinent Canon

C. 1095 - CCEO, c. 818 - They are incapable of contracting marriage
   1^0 - who lack the sufficient use of reason.

B. The Context Of The Canon

This 1^0 of c. 1095 (on lack of due *reason*) is perhaps best understood in conjunction with 2^0 (on lack of due *discretion*) and 3^0(on lack of due *competence*). These read as follows:

C. 1095 - They are incapable of contracting marriage
   2^0 - who suffer from grave lack of discretion of judgment concerning essential matrimonial rights and duties which are to be mutually given and accepted;
   3^0 - who are not strong enough to assume the essential obligations of matrimony due to causes of a psychic nature.

C. The Meaning Of Lack Of Due Reason

1. When c. 1095 1^0 speaks of a lack of *sufficient* use of reason, it is not, of course, referring to a *simple* use of reason. It is not suggesting, in other words, that once one has attained the use of reason and can place a human act, he or she is capable of marriage. It is, rather, saying that, in order to be capable of marriage, one must have arrived at a degree of reasoning ability sufficient to understand that, in marrying, "a man and a woman give and receive each other by an irrevocable covenant to constitute...a partnership of the spouses' entire life, a partnership ordered, by its nature, to the good of the spouses and the procreation and education of children" (cc. 1057 § 2 and 1055 § 2).

2. When compared with 2^0 of this canon, however, 1^0 seems to be referring to a fairly primitive, conceptual understanding of the nature of marriage, whereas 2^0 is referring to a more mature, sophisticated, evaluative judgment regarding the rights and duties to be handed over.In a sense, therefore, 1^0 is superfluous. The two numbers together are rather like saying: 1) one may not join the army before the age of 10, 2) one may not join the army before the age of 18.

   Nevertheless, this number one of c. 1095 does have the advantage of reflecting the historical background of the canon and may even be put to use in cases where sufficient use of reason is, in fact, lacking. See D2 pp. 10-15 and 37-39.

D. The Cause Of Lack Of Due Reason

In order for an adult to be deprived of something as basic as the sufficient use of reason, he or she would have to be affected by a fairly serious condition. Traditionally such conditions have been divided into transitory and habitual (see 58, 180 and A1 and A2, pp. 20 and 21 respectively.) The 1980 draft of this canon retained that division by noting that lack of sufficient reason could be caused either by a disturbance (transitory) or by a disorder (habitual).

Although the Code itself has eliminated any reference to the causality of the lack of sufficient reason, the traditional distinction remains of some use in jurisprudence. Examples of an *habitual* disorder that would deprive a person of the sufficient use of reason would be schizophrenia (see D2, pp. 10-15) and profound mental retardation. Examples of a *transitory* disturbance that would produce the same effect would be alcoholic intoxication and an epileptic ictal twilight state.

E. The Result Of Lack Of Due Reason

When a person lacks due reason, the result is that that person cannot give consent (nil volitum nisi praecognitum). Ultimately it is this inability to give consent that invalidates the marriage, as is clear from the fact that this canon is located in Chapter IV which is entitled "On Matrimonial Consent".

This is appropriate. It is, after all, consent that makes marriage (consensus facit nuptias). As c. 1057 § 1 says, "Marriage is brought about through the consent of the parties, legitimately manifested between persons who are capable according to law of giving consent; no human power can replace this consent."

F. Proof Of Lack Of Due Reason

1. *Parties, Affiants and Witnesses*

In cases involving an alleged lack of due reason every effort should be made to obtain testimony from the respondent (usually the party whose lack of due reason is alleged). Sometimes the petitioner has lost touch with the respondent and cannot provide an address but usually, with a little effort, the respondent can be located.

The declarations of the parties and the affidavits and testimony of others are extremely important in these cases since they provide the data on which a judgment can be made. For the canons pertaining to the evaluation of this evidence, see one of the chapters on simulation in the section on proof.

2. Experts

    a.   *The Law*

C. 1680 reads as follows: In cases of impotence or of defect of consent due to a mental illness the judge is to use the services of one or more experts unless it is obvious from the circumstances that this would be useless; in other cases the prescription of c. 1574 is to be observed.

C. 1574 says: The services of experts must be used whenever their examination and opinion, based on the laws of art or science, are required in order to establish some fact or to clarify the true nature of some thing by reason of a prescription of the law or a judge.

    b.   *An Observation*

It is clear, first of all, as noted under E, that this ground does involve a "defect of consent." Taken together, therefore, the two canons seem to be saying that when the cause of the lack of due reason is some *habitual* disorder, the services of an expert are (unless they would be clearly superfluous) required, whereas, when the cause is of a *transitory* nature, their use is at the discretion of the judge.

    c.   *Selection of Experts*

In his 1987 allocution to the Rota Pope John Paul II spoke of the importance of the judge and the expert sharing a common anthropology and a common understanding of marriage that recognizes that a conjugal union is achieved only through the mutual self giving, renunciation and sacrifice of the spouses. Specifically, the Pope said:

> According to some psychological trends the vision of marriage is such that it reduces the meaning of the marriage union simply to a means of gratification or of self-fulfillment or of psychological release.

> Consequently, for the experts who take their inspiration from such tendencies every obstacle which requires effort, commitment or renunciation, and still more, every failure in fact of a marriage union, easily becomes proof of the inability of the presumed spouses to understand correctly and to succeed in their marriage.

> Expert examinations carried out on the bases of such a reductionist anthropology do not in practice take into consideration the duty, arising from a conscious undertaking on the part of the

spouses, to overcome even at the cost of sacrifice and renunciation the obstacles that interfere with the success of their marriage.
Hence they regard every tension as a negative sign, an indication
of weakness, and an incapacity to live out their marriage.
(Woestman, p. 193)

While all of this is true, it is also true that comments on the validity or
invalidity of a marriage are not part of the expert's function. As Pope
John Paul II said in the same allocution:

The judge cannot and ought not to expect from the expert a
judgment on the nullity of marriage, and still less must he feel
bound by any such judgment which the expert may have expressed.
It is for the judge and for him alone to consider the nullity of marriage. The task of the expert is only that of providing the elements
of information which have to do with his specific competence,
that is, the nature and extent of the psychic and psychiatric realities on grounds of which the nullity of the marriage has been alleged. (Woestman, pg. 194-195)

It is indeed only in regard to the "specific competence" of the expert
that the expert's report enjoys any probative force.

d.   *The Probative Force*

C. 1579 § 1 says that the judge is to weigh attentively not only the
conclusions of the experts but also the other circumstances of the case.
This is a reminder that the judge is the *peritus peritorum* and that besides the report of the expert, the judge must also be concerned with
such questions as whether the data on which the conclusions of the
expert are based are truly proved by the evidence. It is in this sense
that the *dicta peritorum cribranda sunt,* i.e., that the report of the expert should be "sifted". At the same time, however, *peritis in arte
credendum est* and, as Parisella noted, "When it comes to evaluating
the weight and importance of the expert's report, the Rota has many
times (see the decisions of 10/21/59 coram Lamas, of 8/5/54 coram
Pinna, of 11/6/56 coram Mattioli, of 2/26/52 and 4/6/54 coram Felici)
taught that it is wrong for the judge to depart from the conclusions of
the experts except for very weighty contrary arguments." (60, 564-565).

LACK OF DUE DISCRETION

GENERAL REMARKS

A. **The Pertinent Canon**

C. 1095, CCEO, c. 818 - They are incapable of contracting marriage
2^0 -who suffer from grave lack of discretion of judgment concerning essential matrimonial rights and duties which are to be mutually given and accepted.

B. **The Context Of The Canon**

This 2^0 of c. 1095 (on lack of due *discretion*) is perhaps best understood in conjunction with 1^0 (on lack of due *reason*) and 3^0 (on lack of due *competence*). These read as follows:

C. 1095 - They are incapable of contracting marriage
1^0 - who lack the sufficient use of reason
3^0 - who are not strong enough to assume the essential obligations of matrimony due to causes of a psychic nature.

C. **The Meaning Of Discretion**

To some readers the word "discretion," and a fortiori the term "discretion of judgment," sound as though they refer exclusively to the intellect. This, however, is not the case. The truth is that, in jurisprudence, the term refers to both the intellect and the will. What is required for discretion is that 1) the intellect make a mature evaluation and 2) the will make a free choice.

The inclusion of both intellect and will under the umbrella of discretion was clearly the mind of the legislator in drafting c. 1095 2^0. The present wording of the canon is, except for the insertion of the word "essential," exactly the same as in the 1980 draft of the Code (the number of the canon was then 1048 2^0). In preparation for the October 1981 meeting of the Commissioners, however, one of the Commissioners suggested that the canon be changed to read, "They are incapable of contracting marriage who labor under a severe and abnormal defect of judgmental discretion to such an extent that they are unable to understand even the necessary elements of marriage." The Secretary and the Consultors, however, successfully urged that the 1980 wording be retained because, they said: "what is at issue here is not cognition or perception of the intellectual order but rather a defect of judgmental discretion" (*Communicationes,* 1983, 2, p. 231). The 1980 wording, it was noted, reflected rotal jurisprudence. And rotal jurisprudence, it might be added, has consistently understood the term discretion to include a proper functioning of both intellect and will. See, for example, D2, pp. 22-23 and 33-34.

D. The Meaning Of Due Discretion

1. Although the canon does not contain the word "due", the word was used by Gasparri, who pioneered the concept (see the Index of the 1932 edition of his *De Matrimonio*), and is frequently used in rotal decisions (see, for example, D2, pp. 38-39 and 60, 193; 63, 763 and 69, 233). It simply means that, in performing any action, the agent should enjoy the degree of discretion that is due or proportionate to that action. As regards the amount of discretion due marriage, Sabattani noted in his decision of February 24, 1961 (53, 118):

> The doctrine on discretionary judgment...can be summed up in these words of Jullien, 'since marriage is a very serious contract which is not only future oriented but actually indissoluble, in order to enter it validly a greater degree of discretion is required than would be necessary to consent to some action which only concerned the present, as, for example, the amount of discretion required to commit a mortal sin' (27,79).

> Indeed, since marriage is 'a covenant filled with responsibilities in which the gift of one's whole life and being is pledged' (as Wynen said, 35, 171) then clearly 'greater freedom and deliberation is required for marriage than for other contracts' (from a decision of Grazioli 18, 111).

> And let it be remembered that a mere *cognoscitive* faculty, which consists in the simple mental apprehension of something, is not sufficient but that there is further required a *critical* faculty, which is the ability to judge and reason and so order one's judgments that new judgments can be deduced from them (see the December 3, 1957 decision of Felici and Lamas' sentence of October 21, 1959).

> A marriage, in short, is only valid when a person, using that critical faculty, can deliberately form judgments with the mind and freely choose actions with the will.

2. In order to consent to a valid marriage, in other words, the decision should be informed with a certain fundamental prudence. It should include, therefore, such qualities as good advice (eubulia), insight (synesis), a sense of the situation (gnome), deliberation, foresight, circumspection, appreciation, sound judgment and clear reasoning that enables the person to draw rational inferences from his or her insights and experiences.

More specifically, contractants must be able to make at least a rudimentary assessment of the capacities of themselves and their spouse, and to decide freely that they wish to establish a perpetual and exclusive community of life with this person, a community that will involve a lifetime of fundamentally faithful caring and sharing.

E. The Meaning Of Lack Of Discretion

Canon 1095, 2° is stated not positively but negatively - "They are incapable of contracting marriage who suffer from a grave lack of discretion". Regarding this grave lack of discretion Pope John Paul II noted in his 1987 allocution to the Rota:

> For the canonist the principle must remain clear that only *incapacity* and not *difficulty* in giving consent and in realizing a true community of life and love invalidates a marriage. Moreover, the breakdown of a marriage union is never in itself proof of such incapacity on the part of the contracting parties. They may have neglected or used badly the means, both natural and supernatural, at their disposal; or they may have failed to accept the inevitable limitations and burdens of married life, either because of blocks of an unconscious nature or because of slight pathological disturbances which leave substantially intact human freedom, or finally because of failures of a moral order. The hypothesis of real incapacity is to be considered only when an anomaly of a serious nature is present, which, however it may be defined, must substantially vitiate the capacity of the individual to understand and/or to will. (Woestman, p. 194).

F. The Object Of Discretion

Canon 1095, 2° implies that the object of discretion includes both a general element ("the essential matrimonial rights and duties") and a specific element ("which are to be mutually given and accepted").

1. General

In order to enter a valid marriage the thing about which one must exercise due discretion is "the essential matrimonial rights and duties". These essential rights and duties, according to Bruno (LS 25) and Stankiewicz (81, 282- 283) among others, include not only the bona prolis, fidei and sacramenti but also the bonum coniugum.

2. Specific

It is not, however, just matrimonial rights and duties in general that one must appreciate. It is, rather, those essential matrimonial rights which are to be mutually exchanged by these two people here and now.

As regards the bonum coniugum, these rights and duties would include 1) being truthful with one's spouse, i.e. letting one's spouse know one's true identity (self revelation), 2) appreciating one's spouse as a separate, independent person (understanding), and 3) sharing a mutual affection with one's spouse (loving). If, therefore, a person radically fails to appreciate these "rights and duties," he or she lacks due discretion.

G. The Cause Of Lack Of Discretion

Lack of due discretion is most often caused by a combination of factors, some intrinsic, some extrinsic. Among the *intrinsic* factors one frequently finds that the parties are quite young, have at least a moderately severe personality disorder or suffer from severe immaturity.

Regarding the latter, Civili noted in a decision of July 10, 1990 (82, 597): "Psycho-affective immaturity is rather frequently included among the causes which can bring about a grave lack of discretion of judgment regarding matrimonial rights and obligations...Psychic immaturity results from the abnormal evolution of the personality of one who has achieved a sufficient age but lacks the maturity of intellect and will that is proportionate to marital consent, so that the evolution of the critical faculty and therefore the harmonious cooperation of these higher faculties are impeded (see the decision of DiFelice dated February 16, 1985, n. 3)...The nullity of a marriage results, however, only when it is clearly proved that the psychic immaturity of one or the other party had been the cause of a grave lack of discretion of judgment regarding the essential matrimonial rights and duties".

For more on the subject of immaturity see the estimable decision of April 9, 1992 coram Doran (84, 171-181).

Among the *extrinsic* factors, one often finds a premarital pregnancy or abortion, an unhappy, burdensome life in the parental home with a desire to escape, a brief courtship, belated reluctance to marry, family pressure, fear of embarrassment or perhaps membership in some thoroughly antisocial group or subculture. See, for example, the decision of March 20, 1985 coram Davino (78, 180 - 188).

Taken at least in constellation, at any rate, these factors, both intrinsic and extrinsic, must, according to Pope John Paul II, constitute "an anomaly of a serious nature...however it may be defined" (see E. above) in order to be invalidating.

For some examples of specific causes, see the chapters immediately following. For examples of causes seen in constellation, see D2, pp. 16-45.

H. The Result Of Lack Of Discretion

When a person lacks due discretion, the net result is that the person is deprived of the ability to consent. This is clear from the fact that this canon is found under the general rubric (Chapter IV) of Matrimonial Consent.

I. Giving Consent vs. Expressing Consent

At the time of the marriage ceremony the parties *express* their consent. Presumably they gave their consent, i.e. actually consented to marry some time prior to that. At the time of the ceremony, besides expressing their consent, they may but need not actually renew their consent. It suffices if their consent previously given virtually perdures and is expressed at the time of the ceremony.

In order merely to express consent already given one does not need due discretion or a critical faculty or prudence. It suffices if one can simply place a human act. It would, therefore, be very difficult to prove a marriage invalid simply because one of the parties was, for example, drunk at the time of the ceremony. Because at the time of the ceremony one does not have to place a *prudent* act (consenting) but simply a *human* act (expressing consent).

When, therefore, a Court investigates the matter of due discretion, the investigation does not confine itself to the moment of the ceremony but rather concerns itself with the whole period of time during which the person decided to and consented to marry.

J. Proof Of Lack Of Due Discretion

1. *Parties, Affiants and Witnesses*

In cases involving an alleged lack of due discretion every effort should be made to obtain testimony from the respondent. Sometimes the petitioner has lost touch with the respondent, and cannot provide an address, but usually, with a little effort, the respondent can be located.

The declarations of the parties and the affidavits and testimony of others are extremely important in these cases since they provide the data on which a judgment can be made. For the canons pertaining to the evaluation of this evidence, see one of the chapters on simulation in the section on proof.

2. *Experts*

a. *The Law*

C. 1680 reads as follows: In cases of impotence or defect of consent due to mental illness, the judge is to use the services of one or more experts unless it is obvious from the circumstances that this would be useless; in other cases the prescription of c. 1574 is to be observed.

C. 1574 says: The services of experts must be used whenever their examination and opinion, based on the laws of art or science, are required in order to establish some fact or to clarify the true nature of some thing by reason of a prescription of the law or a judge.

b. *An Observation*

C. 1680 notes that an expert is called when 1) there is a defect of consent and 2) there is a mentis morbus.

Lack of due discretion, as noted under H, does involve a defect of consent. The term "mentis morbus" is here translated "mental illness" or "mental disorder" because, since the first edition of the *Diagnostic and Statistical Manual* in 1952, the American Psychiatric Association has referred to all psychopathology as Mental Disorders. For practical purposes here in America, therefore, the term may be regarded as co-extensive with the disorders listed in DSM IV.

A lack of due discretion case, as noted under G, does not always involve a mental disorder. Sometimes the indiscretion is caused by predominantly extrinsic causes coupled with immaturity. In such cases the services of an expert would be at the discretion of the judge. It is only when a true disorder is present that a perital report is required.

c. *Selection of Experts*

In his 1987 allocution to the Rota Pope John Paul II spoke of the importance of the judge and the expert sharing a common anthropology and a common understanding of marriage that recognizes that a conjugal union is achieved only through the mutual self giving, renunciation and sacrifice of the spouses. Specifically, the Pope said:

>   According to some psychological trends the vision of marriage is such that it reduces the meaning of the marriage union simply to a means of gratification or of self-fulfillment or of psychological release.

>   Consequently, for the experts who take their inspiration from such tendencies every obstacle which requires effort, commitment or renunciation, and still more, every failure in fact of a marriage union, easily becomes proof of the inability of the presumed spouses to understand correctly and to succeed in their marriage.

>   Expert examinations carried out on the bases of such a reductionist anthropology do not in practice take into consideration the duty, arising from a conscious undertaking on the part of the spouses, to overcome even at the cost of sacrifice and renunciation the obstacles that interfere with the success of their marriage. Hence they regard every tension as a negative sign, an indication

of weakness, and an incapacity to live out their marriage.(Woestman, p. 193)

While all of this is true, it is also true that comments on the validity or invalidity of a marriage are not part of the expert's function. As Pope John Paul II said in the same allocution:

> The judge cannot and ought not to expect from the expert a judgment on the nullity of marriage, and still less must he feel bound by any such judgment which the expert may have expressed. It is for the judge and for him alone to consider the nullity of marriage. The task of the expert is only that of providing the elements of information which have to do with his specific competence, that is, the nature and extent of the psychic and psychiatric realities on grounds of which the nullity of the marriage has been alleged. (Woestman, pp. 194-195)

It is indeed only in regard to this "specific competence" of the expert that the expert's report enjoys any probative force.

d.   *The Probative Force*

C. 1579 § 1 says that the judge is to weigh attentively not only the conclusions of the experts but also the other circumstances of the case. This is a reminder that the judge is the *peritus peritorum* and that besides the report of the expert, the judge must also be concerned with such questions as whether the data on which the conclusions of the expert are based are truly proved by the evidence. It is in this sense that the *dicta peritorum cribranda sunt,* i.e., that the report of the expert should be "sifted". At the same time, however, *peritis in arte credendum est* and, as Parisella noted, "When it comes to evaluating the weight and importance of the expert's report, the Rota has many times (see the decisions of 10/21/59 coram Lamas, of 8/5/54 coram Pinna, of 11/6/56 coram Mattioli, of 2/26/52 and 4/6/54 coram Felici) taught that it is wrong for the judge to depart from the conclusions of the experts except for very weighty contrary arguments." (60, 564-565).

K.   Use Of The Ground

It often happens that a person lacks both due discretion and due competence. In such a case a tribunal is free to select the ground on the basis of the particular circumstances. It may happen, for example, that the woman in a case is diagnosed by the expert as suffering from a Narcissistic Personality Disorder.

If the woman was twenty-five years old at the time of the marriage and was married after a two year courtship, the court would be inclined to judge the case on the grounds of lack of due *competence*. If however the woman was sixteen and pregnant and married after a five month courtship, the court would be inclined to judge the case on the ground of lack of due *discretion*. The same is true of other disorders. Anxiety Disorders, Mood Disorders and Schizophrenia, for example, are often heard as Lack of Due Discretion rather than Lack of Due Competence cases, depending on the circumstances as well as on the jurisprudential convictions of the judge. See also D2, p. 65.

A. Description Of Mental Retardation

Mental retardation is a condition manifested by a significantly subaverage general intellectual functioning resulting in, or associated with, deficits or impairments in adaptive behavior, with onset before the age of 18.

B. Subtypes Of Mental Retardation

1. DSM IV (pp. 39 - 46) lists four subtypes of mental retardation depending on intelligence quotient (IQ).

Mild	50-55 to approx. 70
Moderate	35-40 to 50-55
Severe	20-25 to 35-40
Profound	Below 20 or 25

2. These four subtypes are described by DSM IV as follows:

   a. *Mild Mental Retardation*

   Mild Mental Retardation is roughly equivalent to what used to be referred to as the educational category of "educable." This group constitutes the largest segment (about 85%) of those with the disorder. As a group, people with this level of Mental Retardation typically develop social and communication skills during the preschool years (ages 0-5 years), have minimal impairment in sensorimotor areas, and often are not distinguishable from children without Mental Retardation until a later age. By their late teens, they can acquire academic skills up to approximately the sixth-grade level. During their adult years, they usually achieve social and vocational skills adequate for minimum self-support, but may need supervision, guidance, and assistance, especially when under unusual social or economic stress. With appropriate supports, individuals with Mild Mental Retardation can usually live succcessfully in the community, either independently or in supervised settings.

   b. *Moderate Mental Retardation*

   Moderate Mental Retardation is roughly equivalent to what used to be referred to as the educational category of "trainable." This outdated term should not be used because it wrongly implies that people with Moderate Mental Retardation cannot benefit from educational programs. This group constitutes about 10% of the entire population of people with Mental Retardation. Most of the individuals with this level of Mental Retardation acquire communication skills during early childhood years. They profit from vocational training and, with moderate supervision, can attend to their personal care. They can also benefit from training in social and occupational skills but are unlikely to progress beyond the second-grade level in academic subjects. They may learn to travel independently in familiar places. During adolescence, their difficulties in recognizing social conventions may interfere with peer relationships. In their adult years, the majority are able to perform unskilled or semiskilled work under supervision in sheltered workshops or in the general work force. They adapt well to life in the community, usually in supervised settings.

c. *Severe Mental Retardation*

The group with Severe Mental Retardation constitutes 3%-4% of individuals with Mental Retardation. During the early childhood years, they acquire little or no communicative speech. During the school-age period, they may learn to talk and can be trained in elementary self-care skills. They profit to only a limited extent from instruction in pre-academic subjects, such as familiarity with the alphabet and simple counting, but can master skills such as learning sight reading of some "survival" words. In their adult years, they may be able to perform simple tasks in closely supervised settings. Most adapt well to life in the community, in group homes or with their families, unless they have an associated handicap that requires specialized nursing or other care.

d. *Profound Mental Retardation*

The group with Profound Mental Retardation constitutes approximately 1%-2% of people with Mental Retardation. Most individuals with this diagnosis have an identified neurological condition that accounts for their Mental Retardation. During the early childhood years, they display considerable impairments in sensorimotor functioning. Optimal development may occur in a highly structured environment with constant aid and supervision and an individualized relationship with a caregiver. Motor development and self-care and communication skills may improve if appropriate training is provided. Some can perform simple tasks in closely supervised and sheltered settings.

C. A Jurisprudence

Two things, first of all, should be observed regarding the classification of the subtypes of mental retardation: that other factors besides IQ are important in determining retardation, and that the IQ itself of a person may differ by as much as twenty points depending on how the person feels when tested. Any rule of thumb in this matter will, therefore, be just that - an approximation.

With that caveat noted, however, it may be said that when a marriage involving a retarded person, even a mildly retarded person, ends in divorce and is presented to a tribunal for adjudication, that marriage may be declared invalid on the ground of lack of due discretion.

Indeed, according to a decision coram Rogers of January 31, 1970, not only the retarded person but any person with an IQ below 80 is considered to lack the degree of discretion required for a valid marriage. In that decision, the Rota endorsed the observation of the expert who noted that "an IQ below the 70-80 range is indicative of a pathological condition of mental insufficiency which renders the individual incapable of intending and willing, of administrating one's estate and of conducting business affairs...Substandard intelligence below an IQ of 80 inevitably entails an incapacity to contract marriage." (62, 116-117).

EPILEPSY

A. **The Syndrome**

1. Definition

    Epilepsy may be defined as disordered regulation of energy release within the brain entailing the periodic appearance of a recurring pattern of short-lived disturbances of consciousness, typically accompanied by unrestrained motor activity.

    These paroxysmal energy releases or brain storms are called cerebral dysrhythmia and can be measured by an electroencephalogram.

2. Causal and Precipitating Factors

    The dysrhythmia is caused by some brain injury or chemical derangement. It is precipitated by various factors such as alcoholic intake, emotionally charged situations, periods of stress or fatigue, sleep and drowsiness, flickering lights and certain types or tempos of music.

3. Some Specific Epileptic Disorders

    a. The *Grand Mal Seizure* - a major convulsive attack originating in the central integrating system of the higher brain stem. There are four stages in the grand mal seizure:

        1) The Warning Stage - called "auras," involving mood and motor disturbances and visceral sensations and lasting anywhere from a few seconds to a few days.

        2) The Tonic Stage - the period of rigidity lasting less than a minute.

        3) The Clonic Stage - the period of alternating rigidity and relaxation lasting a minute or less.

        4) The Postictal Twilight Stage - the period of automatism lasting anywhere from a few minutes to several days. During this period the subject does not fully regain consciousness, performs automatically and has little or no memory.

    b. The *Ictal Twilight States* - when the brain storms not only originate in the centrencephalic system but also substantially remain there we have an ictal state, sometimes called a psychomotor seizure. Such seizures are of two basic types:

1) Shorter - lasting for five or ten minutes during which the subject is disoriented and almost totally unaware of his surroundings.

2) Longer - lasting several hours or even days during which the subject can mechanically continue previous activities and can appear normal to the casual observer but is, in fact, in a state of automatism or what amounts to a state of unconsciousness.

c. *The Petit Mal Seizure* - a brief attack of impaired consciousness associated with one or more of the following: strong rhythmic blinking of the eyes, nodding of the head, jerking of the arms, sudden loss of posture and staring.

d. *Circumscribed Seizures* - these are motor seizures (eye rolling, masticatory movements, etc.) or sensory seizures (numbness, tingling, buzzing sounds, disagreeable odors, etc.) which do not involve a clouding or loss of consciousness.

e. *Episodic Psychoses* - some epileptics show an extremely variable psychotic symptomatology such as hallucinations, anxiety, ideas of reference, catatonic states, etc. An electroencephalograph, however, can demonstrate that the correct diagnosis is an epileptic episodic psychosis. Furthermore the attacks are generally characterized by some loss of consciousness and by amnesia.

f. *Episodic Psychiatric Changes* - periods of irritableness, depression, mental dullness, lack of initiative, etc. which precede or follow a seizure.

g. *Behavior Disorders* - these are permanent behavioral deviations like emotional rigidity, egoism, hypochondriasis, verbosity, tendencies to violence, etc. which occur in some epileptics as the result of the same cerebral disorders that cause the convulsions.

B. The Jurisprudence

Besides noting that the typical wedding day (involving fatigue from the preparations, emotional stress of embarking on a new life, extra cocktails, early morning drowsiness, flickering lights and music) is a veritable potpourri of the precipitating factors of epilepsy, few generalizations can be made.

But if we examine the specific epileptic disorders individually, it is clear that some would not be likely to invalidate a marriage while others would.

1. Among the non invalidating types some are too mild, some too severe and some too brief to be sources of invalidity.

a.   *Too mild* - this would include the warning stage of grand mal seizures, circumscribed seizures, episodic psychiatric changes and most behavior disorders since these latter are normally curable by efficient medication.

b.   *Too severe* - in this category should be listed the tonic and clonic stage of a grand mal which render the person completely unconscious and therefore rule out going through the ceremony.

c.   *Too brief* - the petit mal seizure.

2.   The following three disorders, on the other hand, can easily invalidate a marriage because they rob the subjects of the ability even to manifest or express consent since in these states they could not realistically be held accountable for their actions. They are, in short, incapable of placing a human act.

a.   *Episodic Psychoses*

These psychoses, even though episodic, may still be considered permanent since the underlying cerebal disorder presumably remains. Even apart from the episodes themselves, therefore, the person is considered psychotic and consequently incapable of marriage.

b.   *The postictal twilight stage of grand mal*

This stage, as we have seen, can last for several days. During this time, even though the person may appear calm, he or she is in fact acting automatically and is not truly in control of, does not truly have dominion over his or her actions. Any apparent expression of consent would therefore not really express anything deliberate or human.

c.   *The ictal twilight state*

This state is, of course, very similar to the postictal stage of the grand mal seizure, particularly in that it is characterized by loss of consciousness and automatism. Furthermore, because this state is not immediately preceded by any seizure that might cause a cancellation of the scheduled marriage and because it can last for several days and also because it can go unnoticed by the casual observer, this ictal state is the epileptic disorder which is most likely to be operative in and indeed invalidating of a marriage.

In fact on April 26, 1967, Monsignor Pinna of the Rota gave an affirmative decision in the following case: Julia and George met in school and fell in love. While on an excursion in the Appenine mountains in February of 1948 there was an automobile accident. George was driving and

38

Julia was a passenger along with her brother and two sisters. Julia's head hit the windshield and although her convalescence was brief there were obvious psychic aftereffects. Her personality changed and she began to experience some mind blurring and forgetfulness. In January of 1949 she suffered a blank-spell, and in October of 1949, a complete grand mal seizure, followed by several minor disturbances. Despite this, George had relations with her and Julia became pregnant. Then, largely for the sake of the family reputations, they planned to marry in the spring of 1952. According to Julia herself the approaching marriage aggravated her psychic problem, and her memory of the events around the time of the marriage was very hazy. Her mother testified that Julia looked pale while putting on the wedding gown, that she had to lie down for a while and that she looked extremely pale during the ceremony. Other witnesses agreed that she looked foggy and confused.

The marriage proved unhappy. In the spring of 1953 Julia suffered a second grand mal seizure and in November 1954 she fell off a bicycle, apparently during an ictal twilight state.

The couple divorced and George petitioned the Tribunal of Bologna to declare the marriage invalid. A negative decision was given in the Bologna court and the case eventually went to the Rota.

Several factors are of particular note in this case: that the circumstances preceding and during the wedding tended to trigger or exacerbate Julia's epileptic condition, that Julia underwent a personality change not untypical of the epileptic, that the two grand mal seizures were long before and long after the wedding but that there were apparently rather frequent twilight states in between.

The case was heard "ex automatismo ab epilepsia temporanea" and Pinna concluded that "a sufficient use of reason is removed not only during the ictal stage of a grand mal seizure but in the postictal stage as well and indeed likewise during the ictal twilight state or, as they say, in the state of automatism, because during those periods the mind is beclouded at best and freedom of will reduced practically to zero." (59, 282)

ALCOHOLIC INTOXICATION

A. Factors In Intoxication

Basically the degree of intoxication depends on the percentage of alcohol in the bloodstream which, in turn, depends on several factors. Among these factors are:

1. *Intake Duration*

   Some alcohol is eliminated in the urine and by perspiration but most of it, about 90% of it, must be oxidized or burned off in the liver. The liver, however, can only burn alcohol at a fixed rate of something less than one ounce per hour of 100 proof liquor so if a person consumes a great deal of alcohol in a short period of time the alcohol accumulates in the blood.

2. *Absorption*

   The bloodstream absorbs from the intestines more quickly than it does from the stomach so that if the stomach is filled with food the absorption of alcohol is delayed. Furthermore, wine and beer contain food elements within themselves and are therefore more slowly absorbed than other alcoholic beverages.

3. *Tolerance*

   Exhaustion, emotional stress and other factors can lower one's tolerance to alcohol and besides, some people seem to have a kind of psychological tolerance to alcohol which permits them to ingest fairly large amounts of alcohol without becoming intoxicated.

4. *Weight*

   The size and weight of a person is a considerable factor in intoxication. Generally speaking, a 200 pound person can drink twice as much as a 100 pound person before reaching the same blood alcohol level.

5. *Amount of Alcohol*

   This obviously is the principal factor in intoxication. Recognizing that the factors mentioned above can modify the results, the following table, based on a 160 pound person drinking 90 proof whiskey, is, nevertheless, generally reliable.

   a. Two ounces dulls the top layers of the brain, causes some diminution in inhibition and in recognizing conventional courtesy and results in a blood alcohol level (bal) of .05%.

b. Four ounces affects the moral and physical control centers, often motivates the person to take certain liberties and results in a bal of .10%,
recognized by many states in the U.S. as constituting legal drunkenness.

c. Six ounces causes blurred speech and unsteady gait, slows reflexes,
causes carelessness, overconfidence and impulsive behavior and results in a bal of .15%, recognized by all states as constituting legal
drunkenness.

d. Eight ounces affects the lower motor and sensory areas of the brain,
causes double vision and drowsiness and results in a bal of .20%.

e. Ten ounces causes increasingly slower reflexes, poorer judgment and
results in a bal of .25%.

f. Twelve ounces results in lurching unsteadiness during which the person needs help to walk or undress and tends to fall asleep. Results in a
bal of .30%.

g. Fourteen ounces affects the more primitive areas of the brain, causes
the person to lose practically all consciousness and fall into a stupor.
bal - .35% or more.

B.   A Jurisprudence

1. In general, where the person both consents to marry and also actually goes
through the marriage ceremony during the period of intoxication, then *imperfect* drunkenness suffices to invalidate the marriage. But *perfect* drunkenness is required to invalidate the marriage when the person has already
consented and agreed to marry but gets drunk on the day of the wedding in
order to get through the ceremony itself (see "Giving Consent vs. Expressing Consent" on p. 29, and Keating, pp. 101 - 108).

2. More specifically, the standard commentators on moral theology customar-
ily defined the signs of *perfect* drunkenness as an inability to distinguish
right from wrong, an inability to remember the major events of the preceding day and an entirely unaccustomed mode of behavior; whereas the signs
of *imperfect* drunkenness were such things as double vision, unsteady gait,
dizziness and vomiting (Noldin-Schmidt, 1, 339).

3. In terms of percentage of alcohol in the blood stream, this means that a
blood alcohol level of from .15% to .20% would constitute *imperfect* drunkenness and would incapacitate a person for *giving* consent. And a blood
alcohol level of .25% to .30% would constitute *perfect* drunkenness and
incapacitate the person for *expressing* consent.

41

4. The court should, moreover, be alert to the possibility, where a person was heavily intoxicated at the time of the ceremony, of other sources of invalidity. The person, for example, might have become intoxicated in order to get through a ceremony which he or she was thoroughly unwilling to enter anyway and which might have involved force or simulation.

The law on force and fear is well known. In order to be invalidating it must be grave, extrinsic, and causative.

Over the years some authors have suggested that the requirement of extrinsicality is excessive, and that fear should be regarded as invalidating even when there is no extrinsic force. Given the human condition, they say, the source of the fear, i.e. whether it be extrinsic or intrinsic, is not all that important. Intrinsic fear can be just as severe and just as paralyzing as extrinsic fear.

Generally, however, jurists have seen wisdom in the traditional approach. The ground of "vis et metus" is designed for application to a specific situation, namely one where there is not only "metus" but also "vis," that is to say, some extrinsic force. Where such a situation is not verified, one should look to another ground.

This seems fair enough. Particularly considering the fact that the adjacent ground of lack of due discretion picks up exactly where force and fear leaves off. Where, in other words, the fear is present to such a degree that it disturbs the subject's faculties and disables him or her from making a sound judgment and a free choice, then, even though the fear is intrinsic, the marriage is nevertheless invalid, not on the ground of force and fear but on the ground of lack of due discretion.

Given sufficient pressures, even mature, experienced people can make stupid, disastrous mistakes. The ship's captain, for example, when suddenly faced with another ship bearing down on him from out of the fog, and with only a split second to make a decision, turns port instead of starboard. The ships collide and lives are lost. He might spend the rest of his life wondering why he failed to make the obvious and traditional turn to starboard, but the fact is that the pressure was so great that it robbed him of his wits.

Lesser pressure has the same effect on lesser people. Immature, inexperienced people can be robbed of their wits by a circumstance that would be quite manageable for the average person.

When all of this is applied to marriage, it can be said that, given sufficient pressure on a sufficiently immature person, the faculties of intellect and will can be so diminished as to render marital consent defective and the marriage invalid. To be more specific, it is entirely conceivable, and surely recognized by the principles of our jurisprudence, that when a young, immature girl discovers that she is pregnant, given certain attitudes on her part, and a certain attachment to her family, and given a certain amount of pressure, which may fall short of the "vis" required in a force and fear case, and given, on the one hand, a certain time limit within which to make a decision, and, on the other hand, a protraction of the pressure, it is, I repeat, entirely conceivable that such a girl could, so to speak, turn port into marriage rather than starboard away from it. She could, in other words, be robbed of her wits, temporarily deprived of due discretion and thus enter marriage irresponsibly and invalidly.

LACK OF DUE COMPETENCE
GENERAL REMARKS

A. The Pertinent Canon

C. 1095 - CCEO, c. 818 - They are incapable of contracting marriage
    3° - who are not strong enough to assume the essential obligations of matrimony due to causes of a psychic nature.

B. The Context Of The Canon

This 3° of C. 1095 (on lack of due *competence*) is perhaps best understood in conjunction with 1° (on lack of due *reason*) and 2° (on lack of due *discretion*). These read as follows:

C. 1095 - They are incapable of contracting marriage
    1° - who lack the sufficient use of reason
    2° - who suffer from grave lack of discretion of judgment concerning essential matrimonial rights and duties which are to be mutually given and accepted.

C. The Meaning Of Incompetence

1. Lack of due competence (sometimes referred to as "marital incompetence" or simply "incompetence") is the disability for assuming the essential obligations of marriage.

2. The canon notes that this disability must be the result of "causes of a psychic nature." The source of the disability or incapacity, in other words, must not be either extrinsic circumstances (e.g. exile or imprisonment) or some physical factor (e.g. a severe physical handicap or illness) but must rather reside in the psychological constitution of the person.

3. The canon further notes that the impairment involves an inability to *assume* the essential obligations of marriage. The question arises, however: how does one decide whether a person is unable to *assume* obligations? In practice, a judge usually investigates the matter indirectly. The direct, immediate object of the judge's investigation is the ability or inability of the party to *fulfill* the obligations of marriage. The judge looks to the behavior, the performance of the person before and after marriage. If the conclusion is reached that the person *did not fulfill* essential responsibilities and indeed *could not*, the judge then goes on to conclude that the person was unable to *assume* those obligations, since it is axiomatic that one cannot *assume* what one cannot *fulfill*.

4. Why, then, does the Code speak about the indirect question (the inability to *assume*) rather than the direct question (the inability to *fulfill*)? It does so,

partly at least, because it wishes to emphasize that the fundamental defect, even in a lack of due competence case, is a consensual one. This too is why c. 1095 is positioned where it is, in Chapter IV - On Matrimonial Consent.

5. In practice, therefore, a judicial investigation tends to focus on the *matrimonium in facto esse* (the relationship) but, in theory, the invalidating factor devolves to the *matrimonium in fieri* (the covenanting). See 68, 387 and D2, p. 64.

6. Along these same lines, Navarrete (in *Periodica,* 1972, p. 53) made a useful distinction in pointing out that, unlike the lack of due reason and discretion case, which involves a true incapacity for placing consent (*incapacitas praestandi consensum),* the lack of due competence case is more a matter of an incapacity for placing the object of consent (*incapacitas praestandi objectum consensus).*

D. The Object Of Incompetence

1. The object of incompetence is the essential obligations of marriage. It is when a person is disabled from assuming these obligations that he or she is incapable of contracting marriage.

2. These obligations stem, of course, from the nature of marriage as a "covenant by which a man and a woman establish between them a partnership of their entire lives, a partnership which is, by its very nature, ordered to the good of the spouses and to the procreation and education of children" (C. 1055 §1).

3. These essential obligations of marriage are basically twofold: procreational and personalist.

When a person is incapable of assuming the *procreational* obligations of marriage he or she is generally regarded as impotent rather than as incompetent.

As regards the *personalist* obligations, these are those actions which are required in order to sustain the marital partnership "which is, by its very nature, ordered to the good of the spouses." As c. 1135 says, "Each of the spouses has equal obligations and rights to those things which pertain to the partnership of conjugal life."

These essential personalist obligations may be said to reside in the bonum prolis, bonum fidei, bonum sacramenti and the bonum coniugum (81, 282 - 283). More specifically the obligations residing in the bonum coniugum consist in:

a. *Self Revelation* - a person must first of all enjoy a basic ego identity. A man, for example, must see himself as one fairly consistent person, have a reasonable degree of respect for that person, and convey a knowledge of himself to his spouse.

b. *Understanding* - a person must see one's spouse as a separate person, and appreciate the spouse's way of feeling and thinking, without distorting it excessively by his or her own attitudes, needs or insecurities.

c. *Loving* - a person must be capable of being a loving person to one's spouse. A woman, for example, must be able to give to her spouse and to receive from him an affection that bonds them as a couple.

Both spouses, furthermore, must have the ability to perform these same three acts towards any children that might be born of the marriage, since marriage "by its very nature, is ordered to the procreation and education of children."

When a person lacks the ability to perform those acts, and therefore lacks the ability to assume those obligations, he or she is said to lack the due competence for marriage, as marriage is understood in the Catholic community. (For more on the bonum coniugum see pp. 141-147 and 184-218).

For a valid marriage, it is not necessary that spouses actually perform those acts, but it is necessary that they have the capacity to perform those acts and that they exchange the perpetual right to them.

E.   The Term Incompetence

Incapacity for assuming the essential obligations of marriage is a genus of which there are two species: 1) *impotence,* the incapacity for the procreational obligations of marriage and 2) *incompetence,* the incapacity for the personalist obligations of marriage.

Some judges refer to the ground of invalidity described in c. 1095, 3° as "incapacity for assuming the essential obligations of marriage." To this author, however, it seems more precise to use the specific rather than the generic term, that is, to call this ground incompetence (or lack of due competence) rather than incapacity.

While the terms "incompetence" and "lack of due competence" (like the terms "contra bonum prolis", "contra bonum fidei", "contra bonum sacramenti", "simulation", "partial simulation" and "total simulation") are not found in the Code of Canon Law, they do, it seems, have the merit of briefly and adequately describing and distinguishing a specific ground of invalidity.

F. The Causes Of Incompetence

1. C. 1095, unlike earlier drafts of the canon, does not concern itself with specific causes of the various defects. It says nothing at all about the causes behind lack of due reason and lack of due discretion, and regarding lack of due competence, it merely notes that some psychological reasons (causae naturae psychicae) would bring it about.

2. The phrase "psychological reasons" is, obviously, extremely broad and would include psychoses, neuroses, personality disorders and even homosexuality, which the American Psychiatric Association does not regard as a disorder unless it happens to be ego-dystonic, i.e. unless the person is experiencing persistent and marked distress about his or her sexual orientation. The phrase could also include the situation where neither party to the marriage suffers from a true disorder but they still remain truly incapable of establishing a marital relationship with each other. See the decision of April 5, 1973 coram Serrano, paragraph 7 in D1, p. 12.

3. For further specifics regarding the causes of incompetence, see Section H on the areas of investigation.

G. The Result Of Incompetence

As noted in Section C, 4,5 and 6, lack of due competence is *au fond,* a defect of consent. Unlike impotence, therefore, incompetence is regarded in law not as an impediment but rather as an inability to elicit consent. See Section B in the chapters on Impotence.

H. Areas Of Investigation

When investigating lack of due competence, four areas deserve particular attention: severity, antecedence, perpetuity and relativity.

1. *Severity.* The "psychological reasons" of which the canon speaks must be, to some extent, disabling, i.e. incapacitating. They must, in other words, bring it about that the party or parties were not strong enough (non valent - for a somewhat similar use of the term see c. 689 §3) to assume the essential obligations of marriage. This implies some degree of severity. Generally speaking, therefore, "mild characterological disturbances," as DiFelice noted (D2, p. 65) would not be regarded as disabling. Some rotal auditors, as a matter of fact, consider it a rule of thumb that only an incurable disorder can be considered serious enough to be invalidating. See McGrath, Aidan "On the Gravity of Causes of a Psychological Nature in the Proof of Inability to Assume the Essential Obligations of Marriage," *Studia Canonica* 22/1, 1988, pp. 71-72.

2. *Antecedence.* The disability in question is that of *assuming* the obligations

of marriage. One, of course, assumes these obligations at the moment of marriage. To be invalidating, in other words, the disability must exist at the moment of marriage, that is to say, it must be antecedent to (or at least concomitant with) the consent to marry.

This is not to say, however, that the incompetence should have manifested itself beforehand. It is not required that the incompetence be actual or dynamic at the time of marriage, but only that it be virtual or causal. It is necessary and it suffices that the proximate disposition to incompetence and the proximate causes of its onset be present at the time of marriage.

For example, a woman with a severe Personality Disorder enters marriage. For a time she functions adequately in marriage but after six months or a year the disorder surfaces, severely impairs her ability to meet her obligations, and destroys the marriage. Such a woman would be regarded as virtually or causally incompetent because a Personality Disorder, by its nature as a pervasive personality pattern, is *present* from childhood or at least adolescence, even though it might not be *apparent* at the time of marriage.

3. *Perpetuity*. Since perpetuity is one of the essential properties of marriage (CC. 1056 and 1134), it follows that the essential obligations of marriage are lifelong obligations. In order to enter a valid marriage, therefore, it is not enough that a person has the capacity to assume the obligations for a month or a year or a decade; it is, rather, required that one have the capacity, at the time of marriage, to assume the perpetual obligations involved in marriage.

Clearly this is quite different from the perpetuity that must be proved in an impotence case.

In a case of impotence it is the incapacity which must be perpetual. In order to be invalidating, in other words, the impotence must exist throughout the entire marriage, from beginning to end and even beyond. If, therefore, a man lived in a marriage for five years and was capable of intercourse only for the first year, say, or only for the last, that marriage could not be proved invalid on the ground of impotence because the impotence was not perpetual. Temporary impotence is not invalidating. In the case of impotence, therefore, the requirement of perpetuity makes it harder to prove invalidity. The requirement of perpetuity favors validity.

In the case of incompetence, however, it is quite different. Here it is not the incapacity but the obligations that are perpetual. Unlike impotence, incompetence can invalidate even though it is not perpetual. Consider again the woman who enters marriage with a severe Personality Disorder. She functions reasonably well for, say, a year but then the Disorder surfaces and destroys the marriage over the next three or four years. Or perhaps the Disorder causes destructive behavior right from the beginning and the husband finds it intolerable after a year and leaves; had he stayed for three or four years it is possible that the woman could have entered therapy and modified her behavior but in fact the Disorder destroyed the marriage before the Disorder could be controlled. In both cases the marriage can be declared invalid because in both cases the woman was incapable of assuming the perpetual obligations of marriage. In the case of incompetence, therefore, the requirement of perpetuity (that is, the fact that the obligations undertaken are perpetual) makes it easier to prove invalidity. The requirement of perpetuity favors invalidity in the sense that perpetual obligations are more demanding than temporary obligations.

The position taken by the author on this point (namely that perpetuity refers not to the incapacity but to the obligations) is but one of several positions taken by jurists over the last several years. For a brief discussion of these positions see Fellhauer, David *The New Code of Canon Law, Proceedings of the 5th International Congress,* II, pp. 1036-37 and *CLSA Proceedings, 1986,* pp. 111-112. See also 84, 326, n. 9.

It should be noted, however, that for a marriage to be considered invalid, the spouse in question must truly be incompetent at the time of marriage and not just become so later on. It might happen, for example, that at the time of marriage, a man suffers from a mild or moderate Personality Disorder. At the time he is aware of the value and need of therapy but neglects to avail himself of it. Unattended, the disorder is exacerbated by the stresses of marriage and becomes severe and destructive. Since it was curable, that is to say, controllable at the time of marriage, the man would not be regarded as incompetent.

4. *Relativity.* Sometimes incompetence is *absolute* (where the person would be incapable of marrying anyone), but sometimes it is *relative* (where the person is judged incapable of entering a relationship with the particular partner chosen as his or her spouse). It is important, therefore, that a person's competence always be judged relative to the marriage in question and not just in general. It may even happen in a given instance that the only identifiable, diagnosable disorder present consists in the inability of the person to engage in the marital relationship in question. But since every marriage is essentially a relationship, where there is no capacity for the relationship there is no valid marriage. See the Serrano decision of 4/5/73 as found in D1, p. 8.

This position, it should be noted, is not endorsed by all jurists. Pompedda, for example, denies that there is any genuine foundation in jurisprudence for the notion of relative incapacity. See Pompedda, Mario, "Incapacity to Assume the Essential Obligations of Marriage" in *Incapacity For Marriage,* Third Gregorian Colloquium, Robert Sable, coordinator and editor, Rome, 1987, pp. 205 - 206. See also 84, 326 - 327.

I.   Proof Of Lack Of Due Competence

1.   *Parties, Affiants and Witnesses*

In cases involving an alleged lack of due competence every effort should be made to obtain testimony from the respondent (usually the party whose incompetence is alleged). Sometimes the petitioner has lost touch with the respondent, and cannot provide an address, but usually, with a little effort, the respondent can be located.

The declarations of the parties and the affidavits and testimony of others are extremely important in these cases since they provide the data on which a judgment can be made. For the canons pertaining to the evaluation of this evidence, see one of the chapters on simulation in the section on proof.

2.   *Experts*

   a.   *The Law*

C. 1680 reads as follows: In cases of impotence or defect of consent due to mental illness, the judge is to use the services of one or more experts unless it is obvious from the circumstances that this would be useless; in other cases the prescription of c. 1574 is to be observed.

C. 1574 says: The services of experts must be used whenever their examination and opinion, based on the laws of art or science, are required in order to establish some fact or to clarify the true nature of some thing by reason of a prescription of the law or a judge.

   b.   *An Observation*

C. 1680 notes that an expert is called when 1) there is a defect of consent and 2) there is a mentis morbus.

Lack of due competence, as noted under G, does involve a defect of consent. The term "mentis morbus" is here translated "mental illness" or "mental disorder" because, since the first edition of the *Diagnostic and Statistical Manual* in 1952, the American Psychiatric Association has referred to all psychopathology as Mental Disorders. For practical purposes here in America, therefore, the term may be regarded as coextensive with the disorders listed in DSM IV.

A lack of due competence case, as noted in F, does not always involve a mental disorder. Sometimes, for example, the incompetence is caused by homosexuality (which is not per se, a disorder) or by a non-pathological incapacity for the particular relationship in question. In such cases the services of an expert would be at the discretion of the judge. In accord with c. 1680 it is only when a true mental illness or disorder is present that a perital report is required.

c. *Selection of Experts*

In his 1987 allocution to the Rota Pope John Paul II spoke of the importance of the judge and the expert sharing a common anthropology and a common understanding of marriage that recognizes that a conjugal union is achieved only through the mutual self giving, renunciation and sacrifice of the spouses. Specifically, the Pope said:

> According to some psychological trends the vision of marriage is such that it reduces the meaning of the marriage union simply to a means of gratification or of self-fulfillment or of psychological release.

> Consequently, for the experts who take their inspiration from such tendencies every obstacle which requires effort, commitment or renunciation, and still more, every failure in fact of a marriage union, easily becomes proof of the inability of the presumed spouses to understand correctly and to succeed in their marriage.

> Expert examinations carried out on the bases of such a reductionist anthropology do not in practice take into consideration the duty, arising from a conscious undertaking on the part of the spouses, to overcome even at the cost of sacrifice and renunciation the obstacles that interfere with the success of their marriage. Hence they regard every tension as a negative sign, an indication of weakness, and an incapacity to live out their marriage.(Woestman, p. 193)

While all of this is true, it is also true that comments on the validity or invalidity of a marriage are not part of the expert's function. As Pope John Paul II said in the same allocution:

> The judge cannot and ought not to expect from the expert a judgment on the nullity of marriage, and still less must he feel bound by any such judgment which the expert may have expressed. It is for the judge and for him alone to consider the nullity of marriage. The task of the expert is only that of providing the elements of information which have to do with his specific competence, that is, the nature and extent of the psychic and psychiatric realities on grounds of which the nullity of the marriage has been alleged. (Woestman, pg. 194-195)

It is indeed only in regard to the "specific competence" of the expert that the expert's report enjoys any probative force.

d. *The Probative Force*

C. 1579 § 1 says that the judge is to weigh attentively not only the conclusions of the experts but also the other circumstances of the case. This is a reminder that the judge is the *peritus peritorum* and that besides the report of the expert, the judge must also be concerned with such questions as whether the data on which the conclusions of the expert are based are truly proved by the evidence. It is in this sense that the *dicta peritorum cribranda sunt,* i.e., that the report of the expert should be "sifted". At the same time, however, *peritis in arte credendum est* and, as Parisella noted, "When it comes to evaluating the weight and importance of the expert's report, the Rota has many times (see the decisions of 10/21/59 coram Lamas, of 8/5/54 coram Pinna, of 11/6/56 coram Mattioli, of 2/26/52 and 4/6/54 coram Felici) taught that it is wrong for the judge to depart from the conclusions of the experts except for very weighty contrary arguments." (60, 564-565).

J. Use Of The Ground

It often happens that a person lacks both due competence and due discretion. In such a case a tribunal is free to select the ground on the basis of the particular circumstances. It may happen, for example, that the woman in a case is diagnosed by the expert as suffering from a Narcissistic Personality Disorder. If the woman was twenty-five years old at the time of the marriage and was married after a two year courtship, the court would be inclined to judge the case on the grounds of lack of due *competence.* If, however, the woman was sixteen and pregnant and married after a five month courtship, the court would be inclined to judge the case on the ground of lack of due *discretion.* The same is true of other disorders. Anxiety Disorders, Mood Disorders and Schizophrenia, for example, are often heard as Lack of Due Discretion rather than Lack of Due Competence cases, depending on the circumstances as well as on the jurisprudential convictions of the judge. See also D2, p. 65.

PERSONALITY DISORDERS

A. Personality Disorders In General

DSM IV describes Personality Disorder as follows:

> The essential feature of a Personality Disorder is an enduring pattern of inner experience and behavior that deviates markedly from the expectations of the individual's culture and is manifested in at least two of the following areas: cognition, affectivity, interpersonal functioning, or impulse control. This enduring pattern is inflexible and pervasive across a broad range of personal and social situations and leads to clinically significant distress or impairment in social, occupational, or other important areas of functioning. The pattern is stable and of long duration, and its onset can be traced back at least to adolescence or early adulthood. The pattern is not better accounted for as a manifestation or consequence of another mental disorder and is not due to the direct physiological effects of a substance (e.g., a drug of abuse, a medication, exposure to a toxin) or a general medical condition (e.g., head trauma).

> *Personality traits* are enduring patterns of perceiving, relating to, and thinking about the environment and oneself that are exhibited in a wide range of social and personal contexts. Only when personality traits are inflexible and maladaptive and cause significant functional impairment or subjective distress do they constitute Personality Disorders.

B. Personality Disorders In Particular

DSM IV has grouped Personality Disorders into three clusters. The first cluster, referred to as cluster A, includes Paranoid, Schizoid, and Schizotypal Personality Disorders. People with these disorders often appear odd or eccentric. Cluster B includes Antisocial, Borderline, Histrionic, and Narcissistic Personality Disorders. People with these disorders often appear dramatic, emotional, or erratic. Cluster C includes Avoidant, Dependent and Obsessive-Compulsive Personality Disorders. People with these disorders often appear anxious or fearful. Finally, there is a residual category, Personality Disorder Not Otherwise Specified, that can be used for other specific Personality Disorders or for mixed conditions that do not qualify as any of the ten specific Personality Disorders described below.

1. Cluster A (Odd or Eccentric)

    a. Paranoid

       1) Diagnostic Features

          The essential feature of Paranoid Personality Disorder is a pattern of pervasive distrust and suspiciousness of others such that their motives are interpreted as malevolent. This pattern begins by early adulthood and is present in a variety of contexts.

Individuals with this disorder assume that other people will exploit, harm, or deceive them, even if no evidence exists to support this expectation. They suspect on the basis of little or no evidence that others are plotting against them and may attack them suddenly, at any time and without reason. They often feel that they have been deeply and irreversibly injured by another person or persons even when there is no objective evidence for this. They are preoccupied with unjustified doubts about the loyalty or trustworthiness of their friends and associates, whose actions are minutely scrutinized for evidence of hostile intentions. Any perceived deviation from trustworthiness or loyalty serves to support their underlying assumptions. They are so amazed when a friend or associate shows loyalty that they cannot trust or believe it. If they get into trouble, they expect that friends and associates will either attack or ignore them.

Individuals with this disorder are reluctant to confide in or become close to others because they fear that the information they share will be used against them. They may refuse to answer personal questions, saying that the information is "nobody's business." They read hidden meanings that are demeaning and threatening into benign remarks or events. For example, an individual with this disorder may misinterpret an honest mistake by a store clerk as a deliberate attempt to shortchange or may view a casual humorous remark by a co-worker as a serious character attack. Compliments are often misinterpreted (e.g., a compliment on a new acquisition is misinterpreted as a criticism for selfishness; a compliment on an accomplishment is misinterpreted as an attempt to coerce more and better performance). They may view an offer of help as a criticism that they are not doing well enough on their own.

Individuals with this disorder persistently bear grudges and are unwilling to forgive the insults, injuries, or slights that they think they have received. Minor slights arouse major hostility, and the hostile feelings persist for a long time. Because they are constantly vigilant to the harmful intentions of others, they very often feel that their character or reputation has been attacked or that they have been slighted in some other way. They are quick to counterattack and react with anger to perceived insults. Individuals with this disorder may be pathologically jealous, often suspecting that their spouse or sexual partner is unfaithful without any adequate justification. They may gather trivial and circumstantial "evidence" to support their jealous beliefs. They want to maintain complete control of intimate relationships to avoid being betrayed and may constantly question and challenge the whereabouts, actions, intentions, and fidelity of their spouse or partner.

2) Associated Features

Individuals with Paranoid Personality Disorder are generally difficult to get along with and often have problems with close relationships. Their excessive suspiciousness and hostility may be expressed
in overt argumentativeness, in recurrent complaining, or by quiet,
apparently hostile aloofness. Because they are hypervigilant for
potential threats, they may act in a guarded, secretive, or devious
manner and appear to be "cold" and lacking in tender feelings.
Although they may appear to be objective, rational, and
unemotional,they more often display a labile range of affect, with
hostile, stubborn, and sarcastic expressions predominating. Their
combative and suspicious nature may elicit a hostile response in
others, which then serves to confirm their original expectations.

Because individuals with Paranoid Personality Disorder lack trust
in others, they have an excessive need to be self-sufficient and a
strong sense of autonomy. They also need to have a high degree
of control over those around them. They are often rigid, critical of
others, and unable to collaborate, although they have great difficulty accepting criticism themselves. They may blame others for
their own shortcomings. Because of their quickness to counterattack in response to the threats they perceive around them, they
may be litigious and frequently become involved in legal disputes.
Individuals with this disorder seek to confirm their preconceived
negative notions regarding people or situations they encounter,
attributing malevolent motivations to others that are projections
of their own fears. They may exhibit thinly hidden, unrealistic grandiose fantasies, are often attuned to issues of power and rank, and
tend to develop negative stereotypes of others, particularly those
from population groups distinct from their own. Attracted by sim-
plistic formulations of the world, they are often wary of ambiguous situations. They may be perceived as "fanatics" and form tightly
knit "cults" or groups with others who share their paranoid belief
systems.

b. Schizoid

1) Diagnostic Features

The essential feature of Schizoid Personality Disorder is a pervasive pattern of detachment from social relationships and a restricted
range of expression of emotions in interpersonal settings. This pattern begins by early adulthood and is present in a variety of contexts.

Individuals with Schizoid Personality Disorder appear to lack a desire for intimacy, seem indifferent to opportunities to develop close relationships, and do not seem to derive much satisfaction from being part of a family or other social group. They prefer spending time by themselves, rather than being with other people. They often appear to be socially isolated or "loners" and almost always choose solitary activities or hobbies that do not include interaction with others. They prefer mechanical or abstract tasks, such as computer or mathematical games. They may have very little interest in having sexual experiences with another person and take pleasure in few, if any, activities. There is usually a reduced experience of pleasure from sensory, bodily, or interpersonal experiences, such as walking on a beach at sunset or having sex. These individuals have no close friends or confidants, except possibly a first-degree relative.

Individuals with Schizoid Personality Disorder often seem indifferent to the approval or criticism of others and do not appear to be bothered by what others may think of them. They may be oblivious to the normal subtleties of social interaction and often do not respond appropriately to social cues so that they seem socially inept or superficial and self-absorbed. They usually display a "bland" exterior without visible emotional reactivity and rarely reciprocate gestures or facial expressions, such as smiles or nods. They claim that they rarely experience strong emotions such as anger and joy. They often display a constricted affect and appear cold and aloof. However, in those very unusual circumstances in which these individuals become at least temporarily comfortable in revealing themselves, they may acknowledge having painful feelings, particularly related to social interactions.

2) Associated Features

Individuals with Schizoid Personality Disorder may have particular difficulty expressing anger, even in response to direct provocation, which contributes to the impression that they lack emotion. Their lives sometimes seem directionless, and they may appear to "drift" in their goals. Such individuals often react passively to adverse circumstances and have difficulty responding appropriately to important life events. Because of their lack of social skills and lack of desire for sexual experiences, individuals with this disorder have few friendships, date infrequently, and often do not marry. Occupational functioning may be impaired, particularly if interpersonal involvement is required, but individuals with this disorder may do well when they work under conditions of social isolation.

c. Schizotypal

1) Diagnostic Features

The essential feature of Schizotypal Personality Disorder is a pervasive pattern of social and interpersonal deficits marked by acute discomfort with, and reduced capacity for, close relationships as well as by cognitive or perceptual distortions and eccentricities of behavior. This pattern begins by early adulthood and is present in a variety of contexts.

Individuals with Schizotypal Personality Disorder often have ideas of reference (i.e., incorrect interpretations of casual incidents and external events as having a particular and unusual meaning specifically for the person). These should be distinguished from delusions of reference, in which the beliefs are held with delusional conviction. These individuals may be superstitious or preoccupied with paranormal phenomena that are outside the norms of their subculture. They may feel that they have special powers to sense events before they happen or to read others' thoughts. They may believe that they have magical control over others, which can be implemented directly (e.g., believing that their spouse taking the dog out for a walk is the direct result of thinking it should be done an hour earlier) or indirectly through compliance with magical rituals (e.g., walking past a specific object three times to avoid a certain harmful outcome). Perceptual alterations may be present (e.g., sensing that another person is present or hearing a voice murmuring his or her name). Their speech may include unusual or idiosyncratic phrasing and construction. It is often loose, digressive, or vague, but without actual derailment or incoherence. Responses can be either overly concrete or overly abstract, and words or concepts are sometimes applied in unusual ways (e.g., the person may state that he or she was not "talkable" at work).

Individuals with this disorder are often suspicious and may have paranoid ideation (e.g., believing their colleagues at work are intent on undermining their reputation with the boss). They are usually not able to negotiate the full range of affects and interpersonal cuing required for successful relationships and thus often appear to interact with others in an inappropriate, stiff, or constricted fashion. These individuals are often considered to be odd or eccentric because of unusual mannerisms, an often unkempt manner of dress that does not quite "fit together," and inattention to the usual social conventions (e.g., the person may avoid eye contact, wear clothes that are ink stained and ill-fitting, and be unable to join in the give-and-take banter of co-workers).

Individuals with Schizotypal Personality Disorder experience interpersonal relatedness as problematic and are uncomfortable relating to other people. Although they may express unhappiness about their lack of relationships, their behavior suggests a decreased desire for intimate contacts. As a result, they usually have no or few close friends or confidants other than a first-degree relative. They are anxious in social situations, particularly those involving unfamiliar people. They will interact with other people when they have to, but prefer to keep to themselves because they feel that they are different and just do not "fit in." Their social anxiety does not easily abate, even when they spend more time in the setting or become more familiar with the other people, because their anxiety tends to be associated with suspiciousness regarding others' motivations. For example, when attending a dinner party, the individual with Schizotypal Personality Disorder will not become more relaxed as time goes on, but rather may become increasingly tense and suspicious.

2)   Associated Features

Individuals with Schizotypal Personality Disorder often seek treatment for the associated symptoms of anxiety, depression, or other dysphoric affects rather than for the personality disorder features per se.

2.   Cluster B (Dramatic, Emotional or Erratic)

a.   Antisocial

1)   Diagnostic Features

The essential feature of Antisocial Personality Disorder is a pervasive pattern of disregard for, and violation of, the rights of others that begins in childhood or early adolescence and continues into adulthood.

This pattern has also been referred to as psychopathy, sociopathy, or dyssocial personality disorder. Because deceit and manipulation are central features of Antisocial Personality Disorder, it may be especially helpful to integrate information acquired from systematic clinical assessment with information collected from collateral sources.

For this diagnosis to be given, the individual must be at least age 18 years and must have had a history of some symptoms of Conduct Disorder before age 15 years. Conduct Disorder involves a repetitive and persistent pattern of behavior in which the basic rights of others or major age-appropriate societal norms or rules are violated. The specific behaviors characteristic of Conduct Disorder fall into one of four categories: aggression to people and animals, destruction of property, deceitfulness or theft, or serious violation of rules.

The pattern of antisocial behavior continues into adulthood. Individuals with Antisocial Personality Disorder fail to conform to social norms with respect to lawful behavior. They may repeatedly perform acts that are grounds for arrest (whether they are arrested or not), such as destroying property, harassing others, stealing, or pursuing illegal occupations. Persons with this disorder disregard the wishes, rights, or feelings of others. They are frequently deceitful and manipulative in order to gain personal profit or pleasure (e.g., to obtain money, sex, or power). They may repeatedly lie, use an alias, con others, or malinger. A pattern of impulsivity may be manifested by a failure to plan ahead. Decisions are made on the spur of the moment, without forethought, and without consideration for the consequences to self or others; this may lead to sudden changes of jobs, residences, or relationships. Individuals with Antisocial Personality Disorder tend to be irritable and aggressive and may repeatedly get into physical fights or commit acts of physical assault (including spouse beating or child beating). Aggressive acts that are required to defend oneself or someone else are not considered to be evidence for this item. These individuals also display a reckless disregard for the safety of themselves or others. This may be evidenced in their driving behavior (recurrent speeding, driving while intoxicated, multiple accidents). They may engage in sexual behavior or substance use that has a high risk for harmful consequences. They may neglect or fail to care for a child in a way that puts the child in danger.

Individuals with Antisocial Personality Disorder also tend to be consistently and extremely irresponsible. Irresponsible work behavior may be indicated by significant periods of unemployment despite available job opportunities, or by abandonment of several jobs without a realistic plan for getting another job. There may also be a pattern of repeated absences from work that are not explained by illness either in themselves or in their family. Financial irresponsibility is indicated by acts such as defaulting on debts, failing to provide child support, or failing to support other dependents on a regular basis. Individuals with Antisocial Personality Disorder show little remorse for the consequences of their acts. They may be indifferent to, or provide a superficial rationalization for, having hurt, mistreated, or stolen from someone (e.g., "life's unfair," "losers deserve to lose," or "he had it coming anyway"). These individuals may blame the victims for being foolish, helpless, or deserving their fate; they may minimize the harmful consequences of their actions; or they may simply indicate complete indifference. They generally fail to compensate or make amends for their behavior. They may believe that everyone is out to "help number one" and that one should stop at nothing to avoid being pushed around.

2) Associated Features

Individuals with Antisocial Personality Disorder frequently lack empathy and tend to be callous, cynical, and contemptuous of the feelings, rights, and sufferings of others. They may have an inflated and arrogant self-appraisal (e.g., feel that ordinary work is beneath them or lack a realistic concern about their current problems or their future) and may be excessively opinionated, self-assured, or cocky. They may display a glib, superficial charm and can be quite voluble and verbally facile (e.g., using technical terms or jargon that might impress someone who is unfamiliar with the topic). Lack of empathy, inflated self-appraisal, and superficial charm are features that have been commonly included in traditional conceptions of psychopathy and may be particularly distinguishing of Antisocial Personality Disorder in prison or forensic settings where criminal delinquent or aggressive acts are likely to be nonspecific. These individuals may also be irresponsible and exploitative in their sexual relationships. They may have a history of many sexual partners and may never have sustained a monogamous relationship. They may be irresponsible as parents, as evidenced by malnutrition of a child, an illness in the child resulting from a lack of minimal hygiene, a child's dependence on neighbors or nonresident relatives for food or shelter, a failure to arrange for a caretaker for a young child when the individual is away from home, or repeated squandering of money required for household necessities. These individuals may receive dishonorable discharges from the armed services, may fail to be self-supporting, may become impoverished or even homeless, or may spend many years in penal institutions. Individuals with Antisocial Personality Disorder are more likely than people in the general population to die prematurely by violent means (e.g., suicide, accidents, and homicides).

b. Borderline

1) Diagnostic Features

The essential feature of Borderline Personality Disorder is a pervasive pattern of instability of interpersonal relationships, self-image, and affects, and marked impulsivity that begins by early adulthood and is present in a variety of contexts.

Individuals with Borderline Personality Disorder make frantic efforts to avoid real or imagined abandonment. The perception of impending separation or rejection, or the loss of external structure, can lead to profound changes in self-image, affect, cognition, and behavior. These individuals are very sensitive to environmental circumstances. They experience intense abandonment fears and inappropriate anger even when faced with a realistic time-limited separation or when there are unavoidable changes in plans (e.g., sudden despair in reaction to a clinician's announcing the end of the hour; panic or fury when someone important to them is just a few minutes late or must cancel an appointment). They may believe that this "abandonment" implies they are "bad." These abandonment fears are related to an intolerance of being alone and a need to have other people with them. Their frantic efforts to avoid abandonment may include impulsive actions such as self-mutilating or suicidal behaviors.

Individuals with Borderline Personality Disorder have a pattern of unstable and intense relationships. They may idealize potential caregivers or lovers at the first or second meeting, demand to spend a lot of time together and share the most intimate details early in a relationship. However, they may switch quickly from idealizing other people to devaluing them, feeling that the other person does not care enough, does not give enough, is not "there" enough. These individuals can empathize with and nurture other people, but only with the expectation that the other person will "be there" in return to meet their own needs on demand. These individuals are prone to sudden and dramatic shifts in their view of others, who may alternately be seen as beneficent supports or as cruelly punitive. Such shifts often reflect disillusionment with a caregiver whose nurturing qualities had been idealized or whose rejection or abandonment is expected.

There may be an identity disturbance characterized by markedly and persistently unstable self-image or sense of self. There are sudden and dramatic shifts in self-image, characterized by shifting goals, values, and vocational aspirations. There may be sudden changes in opinions and plans about career, sexual identity, values and types of friends. These individuals may suddenly change from the role of a needy supplicant for help to a righteous avenger of past mistreatment. Although they usually have a self-image that is based on being bad or evil, individuals with this disorder may at times have feelings that they do not exist at all. Such experiences usually occur in situations in which the individual feels a lack of a meaningful relationship, nurturing, and support. These individuals may show worse performance in unstructured work or school situations.

Individuals with this disorder display impulsivity in at least two areas that are potentially self-damaging. They may gamble, spend money irresponsibly, binge eat, abuse substances, engage in unsafe sex, or drive recklessly. Individuals with Borderline Personality Disorder display recurrent suicidal behavior, gestures, or threats, or self-mutilating behavior. Completed suicide occurs in 8%-10% of such individuals, and self-mutilative acts (e.g., cutting or burning) and suicide threats and attempts are very common. Recurrent suicidality is often the reason that these individuals present for help. These self-destructive acts are usually precipitated by threats of separation or rejection or by expectations that they assume increased responsibility. Self-mutilation may occur during dissociative experiences and often brings relief by reaffirming the ability to feel or by expiating the individual's sense of being evil.

Individuals with Borderline Personality Disorder may display affective instability that is due to a marked reactivity of mood (e.g., intense episodic dysphoria, irritability, or anxiety usually lasting a few hours and only rarely more than a few days). The basic dysphoric mood of those with Borderline Personality Disorder is often disrupted by periods of anger, panic, or despair and is rarely relieved by periods of well-being or satisfaction. These episodes may reflect the individual's extreme reactivity to interpersonal stresses. Individuals with Borderline Personality Disorder may be troubled by chronic feelings of emptiness. Easily bored, they may constantly seek something to do. Individuals with Borderline Personality Disorder frequently express inappropriate, intense anger or have difficulty controlling their anger. They may display extreme sarcasm, enduring bitterness, or verbal outbursts. The anger is often elicited when a caregiver or lover is seen as neglectful, withholding, uncaring, or abandoning. Such expressions of anger are often followed by shame and guilt and contribute to the feeling they have of being evil. During periods of extreme stress, transient paranoid ideation or dissociative symptoms (e.g., depersonalization) may occur, but these are generally of insufficient severity or duration to warrant an additional diagnosis. These episodes occur most frequently in response to a real or imagined abandonment. Symptoms tend to be transient, lasting minutes or hours. The real or perceived return of the caregiver's nurturance may result in a remission of symptoms.

2) Associated Features

Individuals with Borderline Disorder may have a pattern of undermining themselves at the moment a goal is about to be realized (e.g., dropping out of school just before graduation; regressing severely after a discussion of how well therapy is going; destroying a good relationship just when it is clear that the relationship could last).

c. Histrionic

1) Diagnostic Features

The essential feature of Histrionic Personality Disorder is pervasive and excessive emotionality and attention-seeking behavior. This pattern begins by early adulthood and is present in a variety of contexts.

Individuals with Histrionic Personality Disorder are uncomfortable or feel unappreciated when they are not the center of attention. Often lively and dramatic, they tend to draw attention to themselves and may initially charm new acquaintances by their enthusiasm, apparent openness, or flirtatiousness. These qualities wear thin, however, as these individuals continually demand to be the center of attention. They commandeer the role of "the life of the party." If they are not the center of attention, they may do something dramatic (e.g., make up stories, create a scene) to draw the focus of attention to themselves. This need is often apparent in their behavior with a clinician (e.g., flattery, bringing gifts, providing dramatic descriptions of physical and psychological symptoms that are replaced by new symptoms each visit).

The appearance and behavior of individuals with this disorder are often inappropriately sexually provocative or seductive. This behavior is directed not only toward persons in whom the individual has a sexual or romantic interest, but occurs in a wide variety of social, occupational, and professional relationships beyond what is appropriate for the social context. Emotional expression may be shallow and rapidly shifting. Individuals with this disorder consistently use physical appearance to draw attention to themselves. They are overly concerned with impressing others by their appearance and expend an excessive amount of time, energy, and money on clothes and grooming. They may "fish for compliments" regarding appearance and be easily and excessively upset by a critical comment about how they look or by a photograph that they regard as unflattering.

These individuals have a style of speech that is excessively impressionistic and lacking in detail. Strong opinions are expressed with dramatic flair, but underlying reasons are usually vague and diffuse, without supporting facts and details. For example, an individual with Histrionic Personality Disorder may comment that a certain individual is a wonderful human being, yet be unable to provide any specific examples of good qualities to support this opinion. Individuals with this disorder are characterized by self-dramatization, theatricality, and an exaggerated expression of emotion. They may embarrass friends and acquaintances by an excessive public display of emotions (e.g., embracing casual acquaintances with excessive ardor, sobbing uncontrollably on minor sentimental occasions, or having temper tantrums). However, their emotions often seem to be turned on and off too quickly to be deeply felt, which may lead others to accuse the individual of faking these feelings.

Individuals with Histrionic Personality Disorder have a high degree of suggestibility. Their opinions and feelings are easily influenced by others and by current fads. They may be overly trusting, especially of strong authority figures whom they see as magically solving their problems. They have a tendency to play hunches and to adopt convictions quickly. Individuals with this disorder often consider relationships more intimate than they actually are, describing almost every acquaintance as "my dear, dear friend" or referring to physicians met only once or twice under professional circumstances by their first names. Flights into romantic fantasy are common.

2) Associated Features

Individuals with Histrionic Personality Disorder may have difficulty achieving emotional intimacy in romantic or sexual relationships. Without being aware of it, they often act out a role (e.g., "victim" or "princess") in their relationships to others. They may seek to control their partner through emotional manipulation or seductiveness on one level, whereas displaying a marked dependency on them at another level. Individuals with this disorder often have impaired relationships with same-sex friends because their sexually provocative interpersonal style may seem a threat to their friends' relationships. These individuals may also alienate friends with demand for constant attention. They often become depressed and upset when they are not the center of attention. They may crave novelty, stimulation, and excitement and have a tendency to become bored with their usual routine. These individuals are often intolerant of, or frustrated by, situations that involve delayed gratification, and their actions are often directed at obtaining immediate satisfaction. Although they often initiate a job or project with great enthusiasm, their interest may lag quickly. Longer-term relationships may be neglected to make way for the excitement of new relationships.

d. Narcissistic

1) Diagnostic Features

The essential feature of Narcissistic Personality Disorder is a pervasive pattern of grandiosity, need for admiration, and lack of empathy that begins by early adulthood and is present in a variety of contexts.

Individuals with this disorder have a grandiose sense of self-importance. They routinely overestimate their abilities and inflate their accomplishments, often appearing boastful and pretentious. They may blithely assume that others attribute the same value to their efforts and may be surprised when the praise they expect and feel they deserve is not forthcoming. Often implicit in the inflated judgments of their own accomplishments is an underestimation (devaluation) of the contributions of others. They are often preoccupied with fantasies of unlimited success, power, brilliance, beauty, or ideal love. They may ruminate about "long overdue" admiration and privilege and compare themselves favorably with famous or privileged people.

Individuals with Narcissistic Personality Disorder believe that they are superior, special, or unique and expect others to recognize them as such. They may feel that they can only be understood by, and should only associate with, other people who are special or of high status and may attribute "unique," "perfect," or "gifted" qualities to those with whom they associate. Individuals with this disorder believe that their needs are special and beyond the ken of ordinary people. Their own self-esteem is enhanced (i.e., "mirrored") by the idealized value that they assign to those with whom they associate. They are likely to insist on having only the "top" person (doctor, lawyer, hairdresser, instructor) or being affiliated with the "best" institutions, but may devalue the creden-tials of those who disappoint them.

Individuals with this disorder generally require excessive admiration. Their self-esteem is almost invariably very fragile. They may be preoccupied with how well they are doing and how favorably they are regarded by others. This often takes the form of a need for constant attention and admiration. They may expect their arrival to be greeted with great fanfare and are astonished if others do not covet their possessions. They may constantly fish for compliments, often with great charm. A sense of entitlement is evident in these individuals' unreasonable expectation of especially favorable treatment. They expect to be catered to and are puzzled or furious when this does not happen. For example, they may assume that they do not have to wait in line and that their priorities are so important that others should defer to them, and then get irritated when others fail to assist "in their very important work." This sense of entitlement combined with a lack of sensitivity to the wants and needs of others may result in the conscious or unwitting exploitation of others. They expect to be given whatever they want or feel they need, no matter what it might mean to others. For example, these individuals may expect great dedication from others and may overwork them without regard for the impact on their lives. They tend to form friendships or romantic relationships only if the other person seems likely to advance their purposes or otherwise enhance their self-esteem. They often usurp special privileges and extra resources that they believe they deserve because they are so special.

Individuals with Narcissistic Personality Disorder generally have a lack of empathy and have difficulty recognizing the desires, subjective experiences, and feelings of others. They may assume that others are totally concerned about their welfare. They tend to discuss their own concerns in inappropriate and lengthy detail, while failing to recognize that others also have feelings and needs. They are often contemptuous and impatient with others who talk about their own problems and concerns. These individuals may be oblivious to the hurt their remarks may inflict (e.g., exuberantly telling a former lover that "I am now in the relationship of a lifetime"; boasting of health in front of someone who is sick). When recognized, the needs, desires, or feelings of others are likely to be viewed disparagingly as signs of weakness or vulnerability. Those who relate to individuals with Narcissistic Personality Disorder typically find an emotional coldness and lack of reciprocal interest.

These individuals are often envious of others or believe that others are envious of them. They may begrudge others their successes or possessions, feeling that they better deserve those achievements, admiration, or privileges. They may harshly devalue the contributions of others, particularly when those individuals have received acknowledgement or praise for their accomplishments. Arrogant, haughty behaviors characterize these individuals. They often display snobbish, disdainful, or patronizing attitudes. For example, an individual with this disorder may complain about a clumsy waiter's "rudeness" or "stupidity" or conclude a medical evaluation with a condescending evaluation of the physician.

2) Associated Features

Vulnerability in self-esteem makes individuals with Narcissistic Personality Disorder very sensitive to "injury" from criticism or defeat. Although they may not show it outwardly, criticism may haunt these individuals and may leave them feeling humiliated, degraded, hollow, and empty. They may react with disdain, rage, or defiant counterattack. Such experiences often lead to social withdrawal or an appearance of humility that may mask and protect the grandiosity. Interpersonal relations are typically impaired due to problems derived from entitlement, the need for admiration, and the relative disregard for the sensitivities of others. Though overweening ambition and confidence may lead to high achievement, performance may be disrupted due to intolerance of criticism or defeat. Sometimes vocational functioning can be very low, reflecting an unwillingness to take a risk in competitive or other situations in which defeat is possible.

3. Cluster C (Anxious or Fearful)

   a. Avoidant

      1) Diagnostic Features

      The essential feature of Avoidant Personality Disorder is a pervasive pattern of social inhibition, feelings of inadequacy, and hypersensitivity to negative evaluation that begins by early adulthood and is present in a variety of contexts.

Individuals with Avoidant Personality Disorder avoid work or school activities that involve significant interpersonal contact because of fears of criticism, disapproval, or rejection. Offers of job promotions may be declined because the new responsibilities might result in criticism from co-workers. These individuals avoid making new friends unless they are certain they will be liked and accepted without criticism. Until they pass stringent tests proving the contrary, other people are assumed to be critical and disapproving. Individuals with this disorder will not join in group activities unless there are repeated and generous offers of support and nurturance. Interpersonal intimacy is often difficult for these individuals, although they are able to establish intimate relationships when there is assurance of uncritical acceptance. They may act with restraint, have difficulty talking about themselves, and withhold intimate feelings for fear of being exposed, ridiculed, or shamed.

Because individuals with this disorder are preoccupied with being criticized or rejected in social situations, they may have a markedly low threshold for detecting such reactions. If someone is even slightly disapproving or critical, they may feel extremely hurt. They tend to be shy, quiet, inhibited, and "invisible" because of the fear that any attention would be degrading or rejecting. They expect that no matter what they say, others will see it as "wrong," and so they may say nothing at all. They react strongly to subtle cues that are suggestive of mockery or derision. Despite their longing to be active participants in social life, they fear placing their welfare in the hands of others. Individuals with Avoidant Personality Disorder are inhibited in new interpersonal situations because they feel inadequate and have low self-esteem. Doubts concerning social competence and personal appeal become especially manifest in settings involving interactions with strangers. These individuals believe themselves to be socially inept, personally unappealing, or inferior to others. They are unusually reluctant to take personal risks or to engage in any new activities because these may prove embarrassing. They are prone to exaggerate the potential dangers of ordinary situations, and a restricted lifestyle may result from their need for certainty and security. Someone with this disorder may cancel a job interview for fear of being embarrassed by not dressing appropriately. Marginal somatic symptoms or other problems may become the reason for avoiding new activities.

2) Associated Features

Individuals with Avoidant Personality Disorder often vigilantly appraise the movements and expressions of those with whom they come into contact. Their fearful and tense demeanor may elicit ridicule and derision from others, which in turn confirms their self-doubts. They are very anxious about the possibility that they will react to criticism with blushing or crying. They are described by others as being "shy", "timid," "lonely," and "isolated." The major problems associated with this disorder occur in social and occupational functioning. The low self-esteem and hypersensitivity to rejection are associated with restricted interpersonal contacts. These individuals may become relatively isolated and usually do not have a large social support network that can help them weather crises. They desire affection and acceptance and may fantasize about idealized relationships with others. The avoidant behaviors can also adversely affect occupational functioning because these individuals try to avoid the types of social situations that may be important for meeting the basic demands of the job or for advancement.

b. Dependent

1) Diagnostic Features

The essential feature of Dependent Personality Disorder is a pervasive and excessive need to be taken care of that leads to submissive and clinging behavior and fears of separation. This pattern begins by early adulthood and is present in a variety of contexts. The dependent and submissive behaviors are designed to elicit caregiving and arise from a self-perception of being unable to function adequately without the help of others.

Individuals with Dependent Personality Disorder have great difficulty making everyday decisions (e.g., what color shirt to wear to work or whether to carry an umbrella) without an exccessive amount of advice and reassurance from others. These individuals tend to be passive and to allow other people (often a single other person) to take the initiative and assume responsibility for most major areas of their lives. Adults with this disorder typically depend on a parent or spouse to decide where they should live, what kind of job they should have, and which neighbors to befriend. Adolescents with this disorder may allow their parent(s) to decide what they should wear, with whom they should associate, how they should spend their free time, and what school or college they should attend. This need for others to assume responsibility goes beyond age-appropriate and situation-appropriate requests for assistance from others (e.g., the specific needs of children, elderly persons, and handicapped persons). Dependent Personality Disorder may occur in an individual who has a serious general medical condition or disability, but in such cases the difficulty in taking responsibility must go beyond what would normally be

68

associated with that condition or disability.

Because they fear losing support or approval, individuals with Dependent Personality Disorder often have difficulty expressing disagreement with other people, especially those on whom they are dependent. These individuals feel so unable to function alone that they will agree with things that they feel are wrong rather than risk losing the help of those to whom they look for guidance. They do not get appropriately angry at others whose support and nurturance they need for fear of alienating them. If the individual's concerns regarding the consequences of expressing disagreement are realistic (e.g., realistic fears of retribution from an abusive spouse), the behavior should not be considered to be evidence of Dependent Personality Disorder.

Individuals with this disorder have difficulty initiating projects or doing things independently. They lack self-confidence and believe that they need help to begin and carry through tasks. They will wait for others to start things because they believe that as a rule others can do them better. These individuals are convinced that they are incapable of functioning independently and present themselves as inept and requiring constant assistance. They are, however, likely to function adequately if given the assurance that someone else is supervising and approving. There may be a fear of becoming or appearing to be more competent, because they may believe that this will lead to abandonment. Because they rely on others to handle their problems, they often do not learn the skills of independent living, thus perpetuating dependency.

Individuals with Dependent Personality Disorder may go to excessive lengths to obtain nurturance and support from others, even to the point of volunteering for unpleasant tasks if such behavior will bring the care they need. They are willing to submit to what others want, even if the demands are unreasonable. Their need to maintain an important bond will often result in imbalanced or distorted relationships. They may make extraordinary self-sacrifices or tolerate verbal, physical, or sexual abuse. (It should be noted that this behavior should be considered evidence of Dependent Personality Disorder only when it can clearly be established that other options are available to the individual). Individuals with this disorder feel uncomfortable or helpless when alone, because of their exaggerated fears of being unable to care for themselves. They will "tag along" with important others just to avoid being alone, even if they are not interested or involved in what is happening.

When a close relationship ends (e.g., a breakup with a lover; the death of a caregiver), individuals with Dependent Personality Disorder may urgently seek another relationship to provide the care and support they need. Their belief that they are unable to function in the absence of a close relationship motivates these individuals to become quickly and indiscriminately attached to another person. Individuals with this disorder are often preoccu-pied with fears of being left to care for themselves. They see them-selves as so totally dependent on the advice and help of an impor-tant other person that they worry about being abandoned by that person when there are no grounds to justify such fears. To be considered as evidence of this criterion, the fears must be exces-sive and unrealistic. For example, an elderly man with cancer who moves into his son's household for care is exhibiting dependent behavior that is appropriate given this person's life circumstances.

2) Associated Features

Individuals with Dependent Personality Disorder are often char-acterized by pessimism and self-doubt, tend to belittle their abili-ties and assets, and may constantly refer to themselves as "stu-pid." They take criticism and disapproval as proof of their worth-lessness and lose faith in themselves. They may seek overprotec-tion and dominance from others. Occupational functioning may be impaired if independent initiative is required. They may avoid positions of responsibility and become anxious when faced with decisions. Social relations tend to be limited to those few people on whom the individual is dependent.

c. Obsessive - Compulsive

1) Diagnostic Features

The essential feature of Obsessive-Compulsive Personality Disor-der is a preoccupation with orderliness, perfectionism, and men-tal and interpersonal control, at the expense of flexibility, open-ness, and efficiency. This pattern begins by early adulthood and is present in a variety of contexts.
   Individuals with Obsessive-Compulsive Personality Disorder at-tempt to maintain a sense of control through painstaking attention to rules, trivial details, procedures, lists, schedules, or form to the extent that the major point of the activity is lost. They are exces-sively careful and prone to repetition, paying extraordinary atten-tion to detail and repeatedly checking for possible mistakes. They are oblivious to the fact that other people tend to become very annoyed at the delays and inconveniences that result from this behavior. For example, when such individuals misplace a list of things to be done, they will spend an inordinate amount of time looking for the list rather than spending a few moments re-creat-ing it from memory and proceeding to accomplish the tasks. Time is poorly allocated, the most important tasks being left to the last moment. The perfectionism and self-imposed high standards of performance cause significant dysfunction and distress in these

70

individuals. They may become so involved in making every detail of a project absolutely perfect that the project is never finished. For example, the completion of a written report is delayed by numerous time-consuming rewrites that all come up short of "perfection." Deadlines are missed, and aspects of the individual's life that are not the current focus of acitivity may fall into disarray.

Individuals with Obsessive-Compulsive Personality Disorder display excessive devotion to work and productivity to the exclusion of leisure activities and friendships. This behavior is not accounted for by economic necessity. They often feel that they do not have time to take an evening or a weekend day off to go on an outing or to just relax. They may keep postponing a pleasurable activity, such as a vacation, so that it may never occur. When they do take time for leisure activities or vacations, they are very uncomfortable unless they have taken along something to work on so they do not "waste time." There may be a great concentration on household chores (e.g., repeated excessive cleaning so that "one could eat off the floor"). If they spend time with friends, it is likely to be in some kind of formally organized activity (e.g., sports). Hobbies or recreational activities are approached as serious tasks requiring careful organization and hard work to master. The emphasis is on perfect performance. These individuals turn play into a structured task (e.g., correcting an infant for not putting rings on the post in the right order; telling a toddler to ride his or her tricycle in a straight line; turning a baseball game into a harsh "lesson").

Individuals with Obsessive-Compulsive Personality Disorder may be excessively conscientious, scrupulous, and inflexible about matters of morality, ethics, or values. They may force themselves and others to follow rigid moral principles and very strict standards of performance. They may also be mercilessly self-critical about their own mistakes. Individuals with this disorder are rigidly deferential to authority and rules and insist on quite literal compliance, with no rule bending for extenuating circumstances. For example, the individual will not lend a quarter to a friend who needs one to make a telephone call, because "neither a borrower or lender be" or because it would be "bad" for the person's character. These qualities should not be accounted for by the individual's cultural or religious identification.

Individuals with this disorder may be unable to discard worn-out or worthless objects, even when they have no sentimental value. Often these individuals will admit to being "pack rats." They regard discarding objects as wasteful because "you never know when you might need something" and will become upset if someone tries to get rid of the things they have saved. Their spouses or roommates may complain about the amount of space taken up by old parts, magazines, broken appliances, and so on.

Individuals with Obsessive-Compulsive Personality Disorder are reluctant to delegate tasks or to work with others. They stubbornly and unreasonably insist that everything be done their way and that people conform to their way of doing things.They often give very detailed instructions about how things should be done (e.g., there is one and only one way to mow the lawn, wash the dishes, build a doghouse) and are surprised and irritated if others suggest creative alternatives. At other times they may reject offers of help even when behind schedule because they believe no one else can do it right.

Individuals with this disorder may be miserly and stingy and maintain a standard of living far below what they can afford, believing that spending must be tightly controlled to provide for future catastrophes. Individuals with Obsessive-Compulsive Personality Disorder are characterized by rigidity and stubbornness. They are so concerned about having things done the one "correct" way that they have trouble going along with anyone else's ideas. These individuals plan ahead in meticulous detail and are unwilling to consider changes. Totally wrapped up in their own perspective, they have difficulty acknowledging the viewpoints of others. Friends and colleagues may become frustrated by this constant rigidity. Even when individuals with Obsessive-Compulsive Personality Disorder recognize that it may be in their interest to compromise, they may stubbornly refuse to do so, arguing that it is "the principle of the thing."

2)   Associated Features

When rules and established procedures do not dictate the correct answer, decision making may become a time-consuming, often painful process. Individuals with Obsessive-Compulsive Personality Disorder may have such difficulty deciding which tasks take priority or what is the best way of doing some particular task that they may never get started on anything. They are prone to become upset or angry in situations in which they are not able to maintain control of their physical or interpersonal environment, although the anger is typically not expressed directly. For example, a person may be angry when service in a restaurant is poor, but instead of complaining to the management, the individual ruminates about how much to leave as a tip. On other occasions, anger may be expressed with righteous indignation over a seemingly minor matter. People with this disorder may be especially attentive to their relative status in dominance-submission relationships and may display excessive deference to an authority they respect and excessive resistance to authority that they do not respect.

Individuals with this disorder usually express affection in a highly controlled or stilted fashion and may be very uncomfortable in the presence of others who are emotionally expressive. Their everyday relationships have a formal and serious quality, and they may be stiff in situations in which others would smile and be happy (e.g., greeting a lover at the airport). They carefully hold themselves back until they are sure that whatever they say will be perfect. They may be preoccupied with logic and intellect, and intolerant of affective behavior in others. They often have difficulty expressing tender feelings, rarely paying compliments. Individuals with this disorder may experience occupational difficulties and distress, particularly when confronted with new situations that demand flexibility and compromise.

It should be noted, finally, that sometimes a diagnosis of *Personality Disorder Not Otherwise Specified* is made. This category is for disorders of personality functioning that do not meet criteria for any specific Personality Disorder. An example is the presence of features of more than one specific Personality Disorder that do not meet the full criteria for any one Personality Disorder ("mixed personality"), but that together cause clinically significant distress or impairment in one or more important areas of functioning (e.g., social or occupational). This category can also be used when the clinician judges that a specific Personality Disorder that is not included in the Classification is appropriate. Examples include depressive personality disorder and passive-aggressive personality disorder.

C. A Jurisprudence

As for the effect a Personality Disorder might have on the validity of a marriage, the following remarks, grouped according to the four standard areas of investigation in cases of incompetence, would seem in order.

1. *Severity*

The nature and degree of impairment resulting from Personality Disorders depends on the type and severity of the Disorder in question. In every case, therefore, the judge must determine whether or not the disorder has, in fact, rendered the person incompetent, i.e. disabled from assuming the essential obligations of marriage.

2. *Antecedence*

Whenever a Personality Disorder has been diagnosed, it may be presumed to have antedated the marriage, since Personality Disorders are, usually from adolescence, part of the warp and woof of the personality.

3. *Perpetuity*

Usually a severe Personality Disorder will result in disruptive behavior early on in a marriage, making it clear that the person lacked the ability at the time of marriage to assume the essential obligations. In those cases, however, where the couple truly relate well for the first several years of marriage, the judge must consider the possibility that the disorder was moderate and controllable at the time of marriage and was not therefore invalidating. In order to arrive at a decision in a case of this sort it will be particularly helpful to have a complete anamnesis of the person, describing the person's premarital (including pre-adolescent and adolescent) as well as postmarital behavior.

4. *Relativity*

It is also possible in a given marriage that the two people both suffer from moderate disorders not sufficiently severe to render them absolutely incompetent as indviduals but so conflicting that the two people are incompetent relative to each other. For example, two people who suffer from moderate Dependent Personality Disorders marry each other. They are both in need of a supportive, nurturant person as a spouse but are unable to meet each other's needs and the marriage flounders from the beginning. A judge may justifiably conclude that the couple, as a couple, was incompetent for marriage, or, perhaps, more accurately (from a jurisprudential point of view), that one party was incompetent for marriage with the other.

ANXIETY DISORDERS

A. Description

Anxiety Disorders are a group of disorders involving symptoms of anxiety and avoidance behavior.

In terms of their being potentially disruptive of a marital relationship, the most notable Anxiety Disorders are Agoraphobia, Obsessive-Compulsive Disorder and Posttraumatic Stress Disorder. These are described in DSM IV as follows:

B. Agoraphobia

The essential feature of Agoraphobia is anxiety about being in places or situations from which escape might be difficult (or embarrassing) or in which help may not be available in the event of having a Panic Attack or panic-like symptoms (e.g., fear of having a sudden attack of dizziness or a sudden attack of diarrhea). The anxiety typically leads to a pervasive avoidance of a variety of situations that may include being alone outside the home or being home alone; being in a crowd of people; traveling in an automobile, bus, or airplane; or being on a bridge or in an elevator. Some individuals are able to expose themselves to the feared situations but endure these experiences with considerable dread. Often an individual is better able to confront a feared situation when accompanied by a companion. Individuals' avoidance of situations may impair their ability to travel to work or to carry out homemaking responsibilities (e.g., grocery shopping, taking children to the doctor).

C. Obsessive-Compulsive Disorder

1. Diagnostic Features

The essential features of Obsessive-Compulsive Disorder are recurrent obsessions or compulsions that are severe enough to be time consuming (i.e., they take more than 1 hour a day) or cause marked distress or significant impairment. At some point during the course of the disorder, the person has recognized that the obsessions or compulsions are excessive or unreasonable.

Obsessions are persistent ideas, thoughts, impulses, or images that are experienced as intrusive and inappropriate and that cause marked anxiety or distress. The intrusive and inappropriate quality of the obsessions has been referred to as "ego-dystonic." This refers to the individual's sense that the content of the obsession is alien, not within his or her own control, and not the kind of thought that he or she would expect to have. However, the individual is able to recognize that the obsessions are the product of his or her own mind and are not imposed from without (as in thought insertion).

The most common obsessions are repeated thoughts about contamination (e.g., becoming contaminated by shaking hands), repeated doubts (e.g., wondering whether one has performed some act such as having hurt someone in a traffic accident or having left a door unlocked), a need to have things in a particular order (e.g., intense distress when objects are disordered or asymmetrical), aggressive or horrific impulses (e.g., to hurt one's child or to shout an obscenity in church), and sexual imagery (e.g., a recurrent pornographic image). The thoughts, impulses, or images are not simply excessive worries about real-life problems (e.g., concerns about current ongoing difficulties in life, such as financial, work, or school problems) and are unlikely to be related to a real-life problem.

The individual with obsessions usually attempts to ignore or suppress such thoughts or impulses or to neutralize them with some other thought or action (i.e., a compulsion). For example, an individual plagued by doubts about having turned off the stove attempts to neutralize them by repeatedly checking to ensure that it is off.

Compulsions are repetitive behaviors (e.g., hand washing, ordering, checking) or mental acts (e.g., praying, counting, repeating words silently) the goal of which is to prevent or reduce anxiety or distress, not to provide pleasure or gratification. In most cases, the person feels driven to perform the compulsion to reduce the distress that accompanies an obsession or to prevent some dreaded event or situation. For example, individuals with obsessions about being contaminated may reduce their mental distress by washing their hands until their skin is raw; individuals distressed by obsessions about having left a door unlocked may be driven to check the lock every few minutes; individuals distressed by unwanted blasphemous thoughts may find relief in counting to 10 backward and forward 100 times for each thought. In some cases, individuals perform rigid or stereotyped acts according to idiosyncratically elaborated rules without being able to indicate why they are doing them. By definition, compulsions are either clearly excessive or are not connected in a realistic way with what they are designed to neutralize or prevent. The most common compulsions involve washing and cleaning, counting, checking, requesting or demanding assurances, repeating actions, and ordering.

By definition, adults with Obsessive-Compulsive Disorder have at some point recognized that the obsessions or compulsions are excessive or unreasonable. This requirement does not apply to children because they may lack sufficient cognitive awareness to make this judgment. However, even in adults there is a broad range of insight into the reasonableness of the obsessions or compulsions. Some individuals are uncertain about the reasonableness of their obsessions or compulsions, and any given individual's insight may vary across times and situations. For example, the person may recognize a contamination compulsion as unreasonable when discussing it in a "safe situation" (e.g., in the therapist's office), but not when forced to handle money. At those times when the individual recognizes that the obsessions and compulsions are unreasonable, he or she may desire or attempt to resist them. When attempting to resist a compulsion, the individual may have a sense of mounting anxiety or tension that is often relieved by yielding to the compulsion. In the course of the disorder, after repeated failure to resist the obsessions or compulsions, the individual may give in to them, no longer experience a desire to resist them, and may incorporate the compulsions into his or her daily routines.

The obsessions or compulsions must cause marked distress, be time consuming (take more than 1 hour per day), or significantly interfere with the individual's normal routine, occupational functioning, or usual social activities or relationships with others. Obsessions or compulsions can displace useful and satisfying behavior and can be highly disruptive to overall functioning. Because obsessive intrusions can be distracting, they frequently result in inefficient performance of cognitive tasks that require concentration, such as reading or computation. In addition, many individuals avoid objects or situations that provoke obsessions or compulsions. Such avoidance can become extensive and can severely restrict general functioning.

2. Associated Features

Frequently there is avoidance of situations that involve the content of the obsessions, such as dirt or contamination. For example, a person with obsessions about dirt may avoid public restrooms or shaking hands with strangers. Hypochondriacal concerns are common, with repeated visits to physicians to seek reassurance. Guilt, a pathological sense of responsibility, and sleep disturbances may be present. There may be excessive use of alcohol or of sedative, hypnotic, or anxiolytic medications. Performing compulsions may become a major life activity, leading to serious marital, occupational, or social disability. Pervasive avoidance may leave an individual housebound.

D. Posttraumatic Stress Disorder

1. Diagnostic Features

The essential feature of Posttraumatic Stress Disorder is the development of characteristic symptoms following exposure to an extreme traumatic stressor involving direct personal experience of an event that involves actual or threatened death or serious injury, or other threat to one's physical integrity; or witnessing an event that involves death, injury, or a threat to the physical integrity of another person; or learning about unexpected or violent death, serious harm, or threat of death or injury experienced by a family member or other close associate. The person's response to the event must involve intense fear, helplessness, or horror (or in children, the response must involve disorganized or agitated behavior). The characteristic symptoms resulting from the exposure to the extreme trauma include persistent reexperiencing of the traumatic event, persistent avoidance of stimuli associated with the trauma and numbing of general responsiveness, and persistent symptoms of increased arousal. The full symptom picture must be present for more than 1 month, and the disturbance must cause clinically significant distress or impairment in social, occupational, or other important areas of functioning.

Traumatic events that are experienced directly include, but are not limited to, military combat, violent personal assault (sexual assault, physical attack, robbery, mugging), being kidnapped, being taken hostage, terrorist attack, torture, incarceration as a prisoner of war or in a concentration camp, natural or manmade disasters, severe automobile accidents, or being diagnosed with life-threatening illness. For children, sexually traumatic events may include developmentally inappropriate sexual experiences without threatened or actual violence or injury. Witnessed events include, but are not limited to, observing the serious injury or unnatural death of another person due to violent assault, accident, war, or disaster or unexpectedly witnessing a dead body or body parts. Events experienced by others that are learned about include, but are not limited to, violent personal assault, serious accident, or serious injury experienced by a family member or a close friend; learning about the sudden, unexpected death of a family member or a close friend; or learning that one's child has a life-threatening disease. The disorder may be especially severe or long lasting when the stressor is of human design (e.g., torture, rape). The likelihood of developing this disorder may increase as the intensity of and physical proximity to the stressor increase.

The traumatic event can be reexperienced in various ways. Commonly the person has recurrent and intrusive recollections of the event or recurrent distressing dreams during which the event is replayed. In rare instances, the person experiences dissociative states that last from a few seconds to several hours, or even days, during which components of the event are relived and the person behaves as though experiencing the event at that moment. Intense psychological distress or physiological reactivity often occurs when the person is exposed to triggering events that resemble or symbolize an aspect of the traumatic event (e.g., anniversaries of the traumatic event; cold, snowy weather or uniformed guards for survivors of death camps in cold climates; hot, humid weather for combat veterans of the South Pacific; entering any elevator for a woman who was raped in an elevator).

Stimuli associated with the trauma are persistently avoided. The person commonly makes deliberate efforts to avoid thoughts, feelings, or conversations about the traumatic event and to avoid activities, situations, or people who arouse recollections of it. This avoidance of reminders may include amnesia for an important aspect of the traumatic event. Diminished responsiveness to the external world, referred to as "psychic numbing" or "emotional anesthesia," usually begins soon after the traumatic event. The individual may complain of having markedly diminished interest or participation in previously enjoyed activities, of feeling detached or estranged from other people, or of having markedly reduced ability to feel emotions (especially those associated with intimacy, tenderness, and sexuality). The individual may have a sense of a foreshortened future (e.g., not expecting to have a career, marriage, children, or a normal life span).

The individual has persistent symptoms of anxiety or increased arousal that were not present before the trauma. These symptoms may include difficulty falling or staying asleep that may be due to recurrent nightmares during which the traumatic event is relived, hypervigilance, and exaggerated startle response. Some individuals report irritability or outbursts of anger or difficulty concentrating or completing tasks.

2. Associated Features

Individuals with Posttraumatic Stress Disorder may describe painful guilt feelings about surviving when others did not survive or about the things they had to do to survive. Phobic avoidance of situations or activities that resemble or symbolize the original trauma may interfere with interpersonal relationships and lead to marital conflict, divorce, or loss of job. The following associated constellation of symptoms may occur and are more commonly seen in association with an interpersonal stressor (e.g., childhood sexual or physical abuse, domestic battering, being taken hostage, incarceration as a prisoner of war or in a concentration camp, torture): impaired affect modulation; self-destructive and impulsive behavior; dissociative symptoms; somatic complaints; feelings of ineffectiveness, shame, despair, or hopelessness; feeling permanently damaged; a loss of previously sustained beliefs; hostility; social withdrawal; feeling constantly threatened; impaired relationships with others; or a change from the individual's previous personality characteristics.

E. A Jurisprudence

When the four usual areas of investigation are applied to the Anxiety Disorders, the following observations might be useful.

1. *Severity*

It is clear from DSM IV that these Anxiety Disorders can cause significant impairment in general functioning, can markedly reduce one's ability to relate to others and sometimes incapacitate a person for basic responsibilities. When sufficiently severe, at any rate, these disorders clearly have the potential for depriving the person of the capacity for self revelation, understanding and loving.

2 *Antecedence*

In order to determine whether the disorder was present at the time of the exchange of consent the court must examine the behavior of the person prior to and immediately following the wedding.

3. *Perpetuity*

If the disorder was present at the time of the wedding and if it eventually destroyed the marriage because the affected person was unable to fulfill the essential obligations of marriage, especially self revelation, understanding and loving, then the person must be considered to have lacked due competence for the marriage since he or she was not, at the time of the wedding, able to assume the perpetual obligations of marriage.

4. *Relativity*

The low threshold of the other spouse to relate to even a moderately impaired partner could, in practice, result in relative incompetence.

SCHIZOPHRENIA

A. Description

Schizophrenia is a psychotic disturbance that lasts for at least six months and includes at least one month of active-phase symptoms, i.e. two or more of the following five symptoms: delusions, hallucinations, disorganized speech, grossly disorganized or catatonic behavior, and the negative symptoms.

B. Characteristic Symptoms

1. Positive

   a. Delusions

   Delusions are erroneous beliefs that usually involve a misinterpretation of perceptions or experiences. Their content may include a variety of themes (e.g., persecutory, referential, somatic, religious, or grandiose). Persecutory delusions are most common; the person believes he or she is being tormented, followed, tricked, spied on, or subjected to ridicule. Referential delusions are also common; the person believes that certain gestures, comments, passages from books, newspapers, song lyrics, or other environmental cues are specifically directed at him or her. The distinction between a delusion and a strongly held idea is sometimes difficult to make and depends on the degree of conviction with which the belief is held despite clear contradictory evidence.

   Although bizarre delusions are considered to be especially characteristic of Schizophrenia, "bizarreness" may be difficult to judge, especially across different cultures. Delusions are deemed bizarre if they are clearly implausible and not understandable and do not derive from ordinary life experiences. An example of a bizarre delusion is a person's belief that a stranger has removed his or her internal organs and has replaced them with someone else's organs without leaving any wounds or scars. An example of a nonbizarre delusion is a person's false belief that he or she is under surveillance by the police. Delusions that express a loss of control over mind or body (i.e., those included among Schneider's list of "first-rank symptoms") are generally considered to be bizarre; these include a person's belief that his or her thoughts have been taken away by some outside force ("thought withdrawal"), that alien thoughts have been put into his or her mind ("thought insertion"), or that his or her body or actions are being acted on or manipulated by some outside force ("delusions of control"). If the delusions are judged to be bizarre, only this single symptom is needed for a diagnosis of Schizophrenia.

b. Hallucinations

Hallucinations may occur in any sensory modality (e.g., auditory, visual, olfactory, gustatory, and tactile), but auditory hallucinations are by far the most common and characteristic of Schizophrenia. Auditory hallucinations are usually experienced as voices, whether familiar or unfamiliar, that are perceived as distinct from the person's own thoughts. The content may be quite variable, although pejorative or threatening voices are especially common. Certain types of auditory hallucinations (i.e., two or more voices conversing with one another or voices maintaining a running commentary on the person's thoughts or behavior) have been considered to be particularly characteristic of Schizophrenia and were included among Schneider's list of first-rank symptoms. If these types of hallucinations are present, then only this single symptom is needed to diagnose Schizophrenia. The hallucinations must occur in the context of a clear sensorium; those that occur while falling asleep (hypnagogic) or waking up (hypnopompic) are considered to be within the range of normal experience. Isolated experiences of hearing one's name called or experiences that lack the quality of an external percept (e.g., a humming in one's head) are also not considered to be hallucinations characteristic of Schizophrenia. Hallucinations may also be a normal part of religious experience in certain cultural contexts.

c. Disorganized Speech

The speech of individuals with Schizophrenia may be disorganized in a variety of ways. The person may "slip off the track" from one topic to another ("derailment" or "loose associations"); answers to questions may be obliquely related or completely unrelated ("tangentiality"); and, rarely, speech may be so severely disorganized that it is nearly incomprehensible and resembles receptive aphasia in its linguistic disorganization ("incoherence" or "word salad"). Because mildly disorganized speech is common and nonspecific, the symptom must be severe enough to substantially impair effective communication. Less severe disorganized thinking or speech may occur during the prodromal and residual periods of Schizophrenia.

d. Grossly Disorganized or Catatonic Behavior

Grossly disorganized behavior may manifest itself in a variety of ways, ranging from childlike silliness to unpredictable agitation. Problems may be noted in any form of goal-directed behavior, leading to difficulties in performing activities of daily living such as organizing meals or maintaining hygiene. The person may appear markedly disheveled, may dress in an unusual manner (e.g., wearing multiple overcoats, scarves, and gloves on a hot day), or may display clearly inappropriate sexual behavior (e.g., public masturbation) or unpredictable and untriggered agitation (e.g., shouting or swearing). Care should be taken not to apply this criterion too broadly. Grossly disorganized behavior must be distinguished from behavior that is merely aimless or generally unpurposeful and from organized behavior that is motivated by delusional beliefs. Similarly, a few instances of restless, angry, or agitated behavior should not be considered to be evidence of Schizophrenia, especially if the motivation is understandable.

Catatonic motor behaviors include a marked decrease in reactivity to the environment, sometimes reaching an extreme degree of complete unawareness (catatonic stupor), maintaining a rigid posture and resisting efforts to be moved (catatonic rigidity), active resistance to instructions or attempts to be moved (catatonic negativism), the assumption of inappropriate or bizarre postures (catatonic posturing), or purposeless and unstimulated excessive motor activity (catatonic excitement).

2. Negative

The negative symptoms of Schizophrenia account for a substantial degree of the morbidity associated with the disorder. Three negative symptoms - affective flattening, alogia, and avolition - are included in the defintion of Schizophrenia. Affective flattening is especially common and is characterized by the person's face appearing immobile and unresponsive, with poor eye contact and reduced body language. Although a person with affective flattening may smile and warm up occasionally, his or her range of emotional expressiveness is clearly diminished most of the time. It may be useful to observe the person interacting with peers to determine whether affective flattening is sufficiently persistent to meet the criterion. Alogia (poverty of speech) is manifested by brief, laconic, empty replies. The individual with alogia appears to have a diminution of thoughts that is reflected in decreased fluency and productivity of speech. This must be differentiated from an unwillingness to speak, a clinical judgment that may require observation over time and in a variety of situations. Avolition is characterized by an inability to initiate and persist in goal-directed activities. The person may sit for long periods of time and show little interest in participating in work or social activities.

C. A Jurisprudence

1. The typical scenario involving a schizophrenic that comes to the attention of a tribunal includes a fairly youthful marriage prior to the first psychotic episode; then one or more, often extended, hospitalizations; the deterioration of the schizophrenic spouse; and the termination of any genuine relationship between husband and wife.

2. As in all cases involving lack of due competence, it is important for the court to examine the four usual areas. As applied to the Schizophrenic Disorders, the following observations may be made:

    a. *Severity*

        Schizophrenia is grossly disabling and is characterized generally as a loss of contact with the real world.

    b. *Antecedence*

        Whenever the schizophrenia of one of the spouses destroys the marriage, the antecedence of the incompetence can usually be demonstrated. Generally the prepsychotic personality of the person who later develops a schizophrenic disorder is itself pathological. Often the person is shy, withdrawn and schizoid, without close friends and sometimes antisocial early on in life. Also, the onset of these disorders is usually insidious and subtle, with a prodromal or precursive period during which social withdrawal, diminished effectiveness at school or work, depression and anxiety are in evidence. The court should investigate the psychological state of the person at the time of marriage, but once there is evidence that the proximate disposition for what later became a full blown disorder was indeed present at the time of marriage, it may be fairly concluded that the incompetence was at least virtually and causally antecedent to the marriage.

    c. *Perpetuity*

        If a schizophrenic disorder does, in fact, eventually render a spouse incapable of *fulfilling* the essential obligations of marriage then, since marital obligations are, by their nature, perpetual, a tribunal is justified, assuming that a proximate disposition for the disorder can be shown to have existed at the time of the wedding, in concluding that, at the time of the marriage, the person was incapable of *assuming* those obligations.

    d. *Relativity*

        Given the pervasiveness of this disorder, the relativity of the incompetence is not really a factor.

DYSTHYMIC DISORDER

A. Features

1. Diagnostic Features

   The essential feature of Dysthymic Disorder is a chronically depressed mood that occurs for most of the day more days than not for at least 2 years. Individuals with Dysthymic Disorder describe their mood as sad or "down in the dumps." In children, the mood may be irritable rather than depressed, and the required minimum duration is only 1 year. During periods of depressed mood, at least two of the following additional symptoms are present: poor appetite or overeating, insomnia or hypersomnia, low energy or fatigue, low self-esteem, poor concentration or difficulty making decisions, and feeling of hopelessness. Individuals may note the prominent presence of low interest and self-criticism, often seeing themselves as uninteresting or incapable. Because these symptoms have become so much a part of the individual's day-to-day experience (e.g., "I've always been this way," "That's just how I am"), they are often not reported unless directly asked about by the interviewer.

2. Associated Features

   The associated features of Dysthymic Disorder are similar to those of a Major Depressive Episode. Regarding these, DSM IV notes that individuals with a Major Depressive Episode frequently present with tearfulness, irritability, brooding, obsessive rumination, anxiety, phobias, excessive worry over physical health, and complaints of pain (e.g., headaches or joint, abdominal, or other pains). During a Major Depressive Episode, some individuals have Panic Attacks that occur in a pattern that meets criteria for Panic Disorder. In children, separation anxiety may occur. Some individuals note difficulty in intimate relationships, less satisfying social interactions, or difficulties in sexual functioning (e.g., anorgasmia in women or erectile dysfunction in men). There may be marital problems (e.g., divorce), occupational problems (e.g., loss of job), academic problems (e.g., truancy, school failure), Alcohol or Other Substance Abuse, or increased utilization of medical services. The most serious consequence of a Major Depressive Episode is attempted or completed suicide.

   Several studies suggest that the most commonly encountered symptoms in Dysthymic Disorder may be feelings of inadequacy; generalized loss of interest or pleasure; social withdrawal; feelings of guilt or brooding about the past; subjective feelings of irritability or excessive anger; and decreased activity, effectiveness, or productivity.

B. A Jurisprudence

In making a judgment on the validity of a marriage involving a person with a Dysthymic Disorder, the four standard areas of investigation regarding lack of due competence must be considered.

a. *Severity*

While the symptoms of Dysthymic Disorder tend to be less severe than those of a Major Depressive Disorder, it is nevertheless true that a Dysthymic Disorder, in its more severe manifestations, can truly disable a person for the essential obligations of marriage. Individuals with this disorder, can, in other words, be so pervasively and chronically depressed that they lack the capacity for those obligations that stem from the bonum prolis, bonum fidei, bonum sacramenti and bonum coniugum.

b. *Antecedence*

Dysthymic Disorder often has an early and insidious onset, i.e. in childhood, adolescence or early adult life. It is important, therefore, for the judge to develop during the trial the kind of evidence that will allow the expert to determine whether or not, in a given case, the disorder was present at the time of the marriage.

c. *Perpetuity*

Oftentimes a Dysthymic Disorder can be controlled by the use of chemotherapy. Though the chemotherapy may have to be continued indefinitely, when successful, a relatively normal life is possible. Relative to the marriage, however, it is still possible that such a disorder would destroy the marriage before it could be controlled. In such a case the person lacked due competence for marriage since, at the time of the wedding, he or she was not capable of assuming the *perpetual* obligations of marriage.

d. *Relativity*

It would appear that an individual with Dysthymic Disorder might be capable of marriage with one person but not with another. A woman with Dysthymic Disorder, for example, might be capable of marriage with a very supportive, understanding, patient husband but not with an intolerant, abusive, demeaning man. With the former she might be a loving wife, while the latter would only exacerbate her condition and make it truly impossible for her to fulfill the essential obligations of marriage.

ALCOHOL DEPENDENCE

A. **Essential Feature**

The essential feature of Alcohol Dependence is a cluster of cognitive, behavioral, and physiological symptoms indicating that the individual continues use of the substance despite significant alcohol-related problems.

B. **Symptoms of Alcohol Dependence**

DSM IV defines Alcohol Dependence as a cluster of three or more of the following symptoms occurring at any time in the same twelve month period.

1. *Tolerance* - as defined by either:
    a. a need for markedly increased amounts of alcohol to achieve intoxication or the desired effect.
    b. a markedly diminished effect with continued use of the same amount.

2. *Withdrawal* - as manifested by either:
    a. the characteristic withdrawal syndrome for alcohol, namely two or more of the following, developing within several hours to a few days after cessation of or reduction in alcohol use that has been heavy and prolonged:
        1) autonomic hyperactivity (e.g., sweating or pulse rate greater than 100)
        2) increased hand tremor
        3) insomnia
        4) nausea or vomiting
        5) transient visual, tactile or auditory hallucinations or illusions
        6) psychomotor agitation
        7) anxiety
        8) grand mal seizures

    b. the use of alcohol to relieve or avoid withdrawal symptoms.

3. *Increased Amount* - alcohol is taken in larger amounts or over a longer period of time than was intended.

4. *Desire to Control* - there is a persistent desire or unsuccessful efforts to cut down or control alcohol abuse.

5. *Time Expended* - a great deal of time is spent in activities necessary to obtain, use, or recover from the effects of alcohol.

6. *Activities Curtailed* - important social, occupational or recreational activities are given up or reduced because of alcohol abuse.

7. *Continued Drinking Despite Problems* - the alcohol abuse is continued de-spite knowledge of having a persistent or recurrent physical or psychologi-cal problem that is likely to have been caused or exacerbated by the use of alcohol.

C. A Jurisprudence

1. Marriage cases in which Alcohol Dependence is the only diagnosis are rare. Generally the psychiatric expert sees the alcoholism as one aspect of a larger syndrome. Occasionally, however, the drinking is so heavy and fre-quent that there is no clear picture of how the person functions when so-ber, so that a broader diagnosis would not be justified by the evidence.

2. In determining whether Alcohol Dependence is invalidating of a marriage, the usual four areas must be investigated.

   a. *Severity*

   Alcohol Dependence is profoundly disruptive of marriage life. Mem-bers of an alcoholic's family often live in fear, embarrassment and dep-rivation. And, almost by definition, the alcoholic lacks the capacity for those specifically marital acts of self revelation, understanding and lov-ing.

   b. *Antecedence*

   Generally, in cases that come before a tribunal, the alcoholic party was either already drinking excessively during the courtship but the other party did not consider it a serious problem, or the alcoholic had a drinking problem earlier in life but had managed to bring it under con-trol prior to the marriage only to have it flare up again afterwards. In such cases it may be presumed that the incompetence resulting from the alcoholism was at least causally antecedent.

   Occasionally the person whose Alcohol Dependence eventually de-stroys the marriage never drank at all before marriage. In such cases a rule of thumb might be that if alcohol abuse began in the first few years of marriage then the incompetence may be presumed to have been virtually antecedent, i.e. the proximate disposition to alcoholism and the proximate causes of its onset were present at the time of marriage (78, 759). If, however, alcohol abuse began only after several years of marriage, then the legal presumption would be against antecedence.

   c. *Perpetuity*

   Since the essential obligations of marriage are perpetual obligations, a person must, in order to enter a valid marriage, have the capacity, at the time of the exchange of consent, to assume those perpetual obligations. If therefore it is shown 1) that a person suffered at least virtually or causally from Alcohol Dependence at the time of marriage and 2) that the cumulative effect of the drinking eventually deprived the person of the ability to fulfill the essential marital obligations, then the person is considered to have lacked due competence.

    d.   *Relativity*

The alcoholic's choice of partner could conceivably be critical. It could happen, for example, that a man who was abusing alcohol at the time of marriage but was not dependent on it, married a woman whose own problems would certainly exacerbate the man's attachment to alcohol. In such a case it could be argued that the alcohol abuse plus the exacerbating spouse would constitute marital incompetence, i.e. the incapacity of the man to function in marriage (that is, to fulfill perpetually the essential obligations of marriage) with this particular woman.

D. Similar Disorders

Other Psychoactive Substance Use Disorders, like Cannabis Dependence, Cocaine Dependence and Opioid Dependence, as well as certain Impulse Control Disorders like Kleptomania and Pathological Gambling would follow the same general jurisprudence outlined here.

HOMOSEXUALITY

A. Description

Homosexuality is a strong preferential erotic attraction to members of one's own sex.

DSM IV (p. 538 under 302.9, n. 3) does not regard homosexuality in itself as a disorder. It is considered a disorder only when it is ego-dystonic, that is to say, in the case of a person who experiences persistent and marked distress about his or her sexual orientation.

Within the context of marital jurisprudence, however, the issue is not whether homosexuality is a disorder; the only issue is whether a particular *homosexual* was capable of sustaining a *heterosexual* relationship like marriage.

B. Degrees Of Homosexuality

Kinsey and his associates in 1948 suggested the following scale that would describe points on a heterosexual-homosexual continuum:

0   exclusively heterosexual
1   predominantly heterosexual, only incidentally homosexual
2   predominantly heterosexual but more than incidentally homosexual
3   equally heterosexual and homosexual
4   predominantly homosexual but more than incidentally heterosexual
5   predominantly homosexual, only incidentally heterosexual
6   exclusively homosexual

Those people who are 1 and 2 on the scale are sometimes referred to as *facultative homosexuals;* those who rate 3 and 4 are *bisexual;* and those who are 5 and 6 on the scale are *obligatory homosexuals.*

C. A Jurisprudence

1. *Severity*

In speaking of the severity of homosexuality several points must be clarified. First of all we are speaking always of genuine homosexuals and not pseudo homosexuals (heterosexuals who, in circumstances where opposite sex partners are not available, turn to persons of the same sex for gratification). Secondly, whereas Alcohol Dependence is defined as including overt acts of drinking, homosexuality is defined apart from any overt acts, simply as "a strong preferential erotic attraction." This obviously involved the jurisprudential judgment that the erotic homosexual attraction, even without there being any overt acts, is likely to interfere substantially with functioning in an intimate heterosexual relationship, whereas totally controlled alcoholism is not. Thirdly, it can be said, as a rule of thumb, that obligatory homosexuals and bisexuals would probably be incapable of marriage, whereas facultative homosexuals would probably be capable. Here again, though, an attempt must be made in every individual case to determine the competence of the homosexual to function in a heterosexual relationship.

2.   *Antecedence*

When a person is known to be homosexual, the homosexuality may always be presumed antecedent to marriage since a person's psychosexual preference is always fixed at least by early adolescence.

3.   *Perpetuity*

Whenever homosexuality does, in fact, destroy a marriage, even if it be some years into the marriage, then the person may be regarded as having been incompetent for marriage at the time of the exchange of consent since he or she was, at that time, incapable of assuming the perpetual obligations.

4.   *Relativity*

The choice of marriage partner by a homosexual can sometimes be significant. A female homosexual, for example, might function less well with an aggressive husband than with a gentle, passive man. It is always possible, therefore, that a homosexual condition not invalidating in itself could, given the wrong partner, result in an inability of the two parties to relate.

IGNORANCE (ERROR OF SUBSTANCE)

A. The Pertinent Canons

C. 1096 - CCEO, c. 819 - §1. For matrimonial consent to be valid it is necessary that the contracting parties at least not be ignorant that marriage is a permanent consortium between a man and a woman which is ordered toward the procreation of offspring by means of some sexual cooperation.
§2. Such ignorance is not presumed after puberty.

C. 126-CCEO, c. 933 - An act placed because of ignorance or error concerning an element which constitutes its substance or which amounts to a condition *sine qua non* is invalid; otherwise it is valid, unless the law makes some other provision. However, an act placed out of ignorance or error can be the occasion for a recissory action in accord with the norm of law.

B. Ignorance or Error?

Ignorance is lack of knowledge. Error is false judgment. Ignorance, therefore, is negative and static whereas error is positive and dynamic.

In a decision of March 22, 1963 (55, 197-211), Aurelio Sabattani argued that the ground being considered here (for Sabattani c. 1082 of the 1917 Code) would be better viewed as error than as ignorance, since error is the direct and immediate cause of the invalidity, and since the notion of error, because of its greater specificity and concreteness, tends to put the matter in clearer focus than does ignorance. See also Coronata, *De Sac.* III, n. 447, including note 9.

Nevertheless c. 1096 of the 1983 Code (the revised version of the old c. 1082) continues to speak of ignorance rather than of error; and c. 126 speaks of both ignorance and error, whereas the corresponding canon in the 1917 Code (c. 104) spoke only of error.

It is clear, therefore, that the present code views this ground as primarily involving ignorance.

C. Canons 1096 and 126

Leaving aside the matter of a condition sine qua non, which is a separate case, c. 126 states a general rule which is made specific in c. 1096 as it applies to marriage.

The general rule of c. 126 is that an act placed out of ignorance or error is invalid *only when the error or ignorance concerns an element that constitutes the substance of the act.*

When, therefore, c. 1096 indicates that a marriage is invalid when a party is in ignorance about certain elements, the canon is saying, in effect, that the elements mentioned in the canon and only those elements (except for the one treated separately in c. 1097 §1) constitute the substance of the act of marriage.

The "substance of the act" is a technical term which refers not to all the constitutive elements of something but only to those constitutive elements that must be explicitly intended by a human agent, and therefore only to those constitutive elements of which the agent is knowledgable, since one cannot explicitly intend an element of which one is ignorant (Michiels, *De Personis*, p. 657).

Permanence (i.e. stability) and perpetuity (i.e. indissolubility), for example, are both constitutive elements of marriage (regarding permanence see c. 1096; regarding perpetuity, see c. 1056). Since, however, c. 1096 mentions permanence but not perpetuity, it is clear (when c. 1096 is read in conjunction with c. 126) that permanence belongs to the substance of marriage whereas perpetuity does not.

It follows that a person ignorant of the fact that marriage, by its nature, enjoys a certain *permanence cannot* enter a valid marriage, whereas a person who is in error about or who does not believe in the *perpetuity* of marriage *can* enter a valid marriage (provided, as c. 1099 notes, that the ignorance or error "does not determine the will"). See 31, 392 and 60, 345.

D. The Elements That Constitute The Substance Of The Act Of Marriage

C. 1096 notes that for matrimonial consent to be valid it is necessary that the contracting parties at least not be ignorant that marriage is a (1) permanent (2) consortium (3) between a man and a woman (4) which is ordered toward the procreation of offspring (5) by means of some sexual cooperation.

> 1. *Permanence* - as noted above, ignorance or error about perpetuity is not invalidating unless it determines the will, whereas ignorance or error about permanence (because it is so absolutely fundamental and part of the identity (60, 345) or substance of marriage) ipso facto invalidates.

> 2. *Consortium* - marriage must be understood as, in some sense, a partnership. If, therefore, a man, for example, were to view marriage simply as a contract by which he hired a housekeeper or social secretary and not as a true partnership involving fundamental equality, the marriage would be invalid on the ground of ignorance.

> 3. *Heterosexuality* - although ignorance or error about the unity of marriage (marriage between one man and one woman) is *not* necessarily invalidating, ignorance or error about the heterosexual nature of marriage (i.e. that a marriage takes place not between two women or two men but between a man and a woman) *is* automatically invalidating.

4. *Procreative Ordering* - if a person enters marriage totally unaware that marriage is, in some way, ordered towards children, the marriage is invalid.

5. *Sexual Cooperation* (55, 205-210)

    a. *Invalidating Ignorance* - there are two categories of ignorance about sexual cooperation that render a marriage invalid:

        1). *When it is judged that marriage entails no right to the body whatsoever.* And in this case other accidental knowledge can never render the marriage valid. A girl for example might understand that she becomes pregnant and gives birth. She might even understand that boys are different from girls, perhaps like roses are different from tulips. But if, in spite of all this, she judges that marriage does not mean that she must give to her husband the right to her body (if for example she thinks generation is spontaneous or God implants the seed or the stork brings the baby) the marriage is invalid.

        2). *When it is judged that some right to the body is transferred but one that is substantially different from the real one.* If, for example, a girl thinks that she has given her husband only the right to give her a fertility pill or an injection or to breathe on her in some mysterious way or to employ some magnetic power or if she thinks that the marriage right consists in a warm embrace, then the marriage is invalid because although she has given him some right to her body it is substantially different from the substance of the matrimonial action.

    b. *Non Invalidating Ignorance* - The marriage, on the other hand, is valid if the person knows that the physical coming together is placed by certain specific organs which are apt for and proper to generation, even though the identity of these organs is not clearly understood. If the woman knows this much she is not erring about the substance of the action and at the same time the marriage right for her is sufficiently unique. She understands that she is giving to her husband a very special right, something more, for example, than the warm embrace she might give her brother.

    c. *Practical Criteria* - the following criteria may be of some use in determining the presence of invalidating ignorance regarding sexual cooperation.

        1). *The Psycho-Physical Criterion* - ignorance is more likely present in the person who matures late and who has subnormal sexual drives than it is in the average person.

2). *The Educational Criterion* - ignorance is more likely present in people whose parents were extremely severe and strict disciplinarians and in people who tend to be asocial than it is in the average person.

3). *The Prenuptial Criterion* - ignorance is more likely present in people who were pushed into marriage or who were silly and immature during their courtship than it is in others.

4). *The Postnuptial Criterion* - shyness or even shame on the occasion of the first attempt at intercourse is not considered particularly indicative of anything. If, however, there was an easy adjustment to the initial surprise at discovering the nature of intercourse, then the presumption is that there was no ignorance about the giving of the matrimonial right, whereas, if there was a horror or repugnance or if the woman could not be persuaded to have intercourse even after being patiently and gently instructed by her husband, then the presumption is that she was truly ignorant, that she didn't think that she had given her husband that right, and the presumption therefore favors invalidity.

E. Proof Of Ignorance

The usual proofs: declarations of the parties, affidavits, testimony of witnesses (see the pertinent canons in the simulation chapters) and circumstantial evidence (especially the person's family environment) should be utilized in a case of ignorance.

ERROR OF QUALITY (ERROR OF FACT)

A. The Pertinent Canons

C. 1097 - CCEO, c. 820 - §1. Error concerning the person renders marriage invalid.

§2. Error concerning a quality of a person, even if such error is the cause of the contract, does not invalidate matrimony unless this quality was directly and principally intended.

C. 126 - CCEO, c. 933 - An act placed because of ignorance or error concerning an element which constitutes its substance or which amounts to a condition *sine qua non* is invalid; otherwise it is valid, unless the law makes some other provision. However, an act placed out of ignorance or error can be the occasion for a recissory action in accord with the norm of law.

B. Basic Concepts

1. *Error.* Error is a false judgment. Error is different from ignorance, which is lack of knowledge. In terms of juridic effects regarding error of quality, however, the two need not be distinguished (Thomas Aquinas, ST, Suppl. Q 51, a. 1, ad 1; L. Bender, *Normae Generales de Personis*, pp. 178-179; and canon 126). When, for example, a woman unwittingly marries a drug addict, it does not really make any difference whether she is simply unaware of his addiction (ignorance) or whether she had judged him to be non-addicted (error).

2. *Error of person.* Error of person is the mistaking of one physical person for another. The classic example of a marriage involving error of person is the marriage of Jacob where Leah was substituted for Rachel (Gn. 29: 6 - 31). The likelihood of such an error occurring in a marriage in our society is negligible.

3. *Error of quality.* Error of quality is an error regarding some characteristic in the other person, such as wealth, social status, mental acuity or health. A woman, for example, marries a man thinking he is rich when in fact he is poor. She is in error about the quality of wealth.

4. *Error of quality redounding to error of person.* This is a phrase that was coined by St. Thomas Aquinas (ST, Suppl. Q 51, a. 2, ad 5) and used in the 1917 Code (c. 1083 §2, 1°) but dropped from the 1983 Code. For St. Thomas the phrase referred to a quality which *circumscribed* a person within a category directly intended by the other person. If, for example, a woman directly intended to marry a prince while the man she thought to be a prince was, in fact, a commoner, that error would redound or amount to an error of person. Later authors, beginning with Sanchez, used Aquinas' phrase but restricted it to a quality that absolutely *individuated* a single, definite per -

son. A woman, for example, directly intended to marry Prince John, whom she had never seen. Prince Harold came to her claiming to be Prince John, and she married him. According to this more restrictive opinion, this and only this type of error would truly amount to an error of person.

It was generally understood by the commentators on the 1917 Code that the phrase "error of quality amounting to an error of person", as used in c. 1083 §2, 1°, referred only to this narrower interpretation and not to the broader understanding of the term as given by St. Thomas.

5. *Error of quality directly and principally intended.* St. Thomas (d. 1274), as noted above, held that while the quality about which a person was in error did not have to be absolutely individuating in order to be invalidating, it did have to be *directly* intended. St. Alphonsus Liguori (d. 1787) agreed with Thomas but added the word *principally*. The quality, said Alphonsus, would have to be "directly and principally" intended in order to be invalidating (Theol. Mor., De mat., n. 1016). It is this phrase that has been incorporated into canon 1097 §2 of the 1983 Code.

    When a quality is *directly* intended, it is intended in and of itself; when it is *principally* intended, it is intended as the most important aspect of a transaction. In marriage a quality is *directly* intended when the quality rather than the person is intended in and of itself; it is *principally* intended when the quality is more important than the person. See the decision of October 24, 1991 coram Stankiewicz (83, 676).

6. *Error of quality that is the cause of the contract* - this phrase includes two notions, first that the person decides to marry precisely because the intended quality is thought to be present in the other person, and secondly that if the erring person had known that the quality was in fact not present in the other person, he or she would not have married. (see Cappello, de mat. n. 585, 5° and Navarrete, in *Periodica*, 1992, 3-4, pp. 488-489 and 1993, 4 pp. 665-667).

    From a jurisprudential point of view, what canon 1097 §2 seems to be saying when it adds this phrase is that, for a tribunal to declare a marriage invalid on this ground, *it is not enough to show,* 1) that the person had decided to marry precisely because the intended quality was thought to be present in the other person, and 2) that the person would not have married had he or she known that the intended quality was not, in fact, present; *but beyond that it must also be proved* that the person actually did directly and principally intend the desired quality. To prove the first two points would no doubt give rise to a strong presumption that the marriage was invalid on this ground; the canon seems to be saying, however, that moral certitude of invalidity is only arrived at by proving specifically that the erring person, by a positive act of the will, directly and principally intended the quality.

7. *Antecedent and Concomitant Error.* Antecedent error is a synonym for the phrase "error of quality that is the cause of the contract". In antecedent error, in other words, the error motivates the person to marry to the point where, if the person had become aware of the error, he or she would not have married. In concomitant error, if the person became aware that the desired quality was, in fact, not present, he or she would have married anyway.

8. *Error of fact and error of law.* Error of person or of quality (c. 1097) may be classified as an error of fact, while error about the unity, indissolubility or sacramental dignity of marriage (c. 1099) is an error of law.

C. An Overview Of Error Of Quality In The Twentieth Century

1. Throughout the first seven decades of the twentieth century, it was generally accepted by the authors and jurists that an error of quality could only amount to an error of person when that quality was absolutely individuating, that is to say, when the quality was the one and only factor that identified the person. If, for example, a woman intended to marry Prince John, whom she had never seen, but wound up marrying Prince Harold because he convinced her on the occasion of the wedding that he was indeed Prince John, then the error about the quality of Prince Johnness would amount to an error of person, and the marriage would be invalid, because the woman married the wrong person. If, however, the woman got to know Prince Harold before the wedding, even though she married him thinking he was Prince John, then the error of quality, that is, her conviction that he was Prince John, would not amount to an error of person because in fact the woman knew the man she was marrying, and the marriage would not therefore be invalid. During the first seven decades of the twentieth century, in other words, there was general agreement that a marriage could not be proved invalid on this ground unless the person in whom the desired quality resided was entirely unknown to the other party.

    In a Rotal decision of December 9, 1952, for example, Brennan wrote "Error of quality is said to amount to error of person if the quality is the only means of recognizing an otherwise unknown person. Then, if that quality is lacking, the binding force of the contract is also lacking. Two things therefore are required: a) that the person be unknown to the other party, and b) that the means of knowing, or determining, the unknown physical person be a quality so specific to that person that the physical person is known only by way of that quality or denomination" (44, 653).

2. By the late 1950s, however, and in some isolated instances, even before, the strictness of this interpretation was being questioned. Joseph Bank, in

his 1959 edition of *Connubia Canonica* (p. 357), noted, "There are some who say that an error of quality can also amount to an error of person if the party, in contracting with a person well known to him or her, nevertheless principally and directly intends not the person but a special quality of that person, which quality is in fact absent. For in this case the consent is directly and principally directed at the determined quality which is, as it were, identified with that person. Although this opinion is based on the authority of St. Alphonsus (Theol. mor. IV, n. 1013) and is strengthened by certain decisions of the Sacred Rota (the decision coram Mori of November 30, 1910 (2, 345) and the decision coram Heard of June 21, 1941 (33, 529-530)), it is nevertheless, not commonly accepted either in teaching or jurisprudence."

3.   On April 21, 1970, however, Salvador Canals issued a Rotal decision (62, 370-375) that disagreed with the then commonly accepted jurisprudence. Heard, as Bank noted, had done something similar in 1941 but in 1941 the world of jurisprudence was not ready to reverse itself on this issue. Even Heard himself, in two later decisions (47, 759 and 48, 49) reverted to the more conventional jurisprudence. But in 1970 the timing seemed perfect, and rather quickly the Rota came to reject the older jurisprudence, as articulated, for example, by Brennan (and as based on Sanchez) and came instead to endorse the Canals position (as based on Aquinas and Alphonsus).

Canals was a Spaniard from Valencia. He was appointed an Auditor on the Rota in 1960, at the age of thirty-nine, and died in 1975 at the age of fifty-four. His decision of April 21, 1970 was, hands down, his most influential decision. Of the thirty-five sentences published by the Rota on this ground over the next twenty years, almost three quarters of them refer to the Canals decision in one way or another, most of them by an explicit citation of that sentence.

In a 1988 decision (80, 144) Funghini wrote:

In 1970 the jurisprudence of the Tribunal took a step. The well known sentence coram Canals, dated April 21, 1970, which all subsequent decisions have followed, restored to its pristine dignity a stream of rotal jurisprudence which although founded in the teaching of St. Alphonsus Liguori, had never flowed into the river. The Canals decision embraced a less strict notion of error of quality, affirming that quality redounds to the person when, as Canals said (62, 371, 2) "the quality is intended ahead of the person" and "when a moral juridical social quality is so connected to the physical person that, when the quality is lacking, an entirely different physical person results".

And, in a 1991 decision (83, 77) Jarawan observed:

Since the year 1970 (see the sentence of Canals....) the determination of the person in rotal jurisprudence is no longer circumscribed by criteria and reasons that are almost exclusively physical, but also embrace moral, juridical and social qualities by which a person is determined and constituted.

Canals made several important points in his decision, among them being the following: a) that the more strict interpretation of error of quality goes back to pre-tridentine days when most marriages were arranged and when factors like whether or not a person was intelligent, educated, even tempered, virtuous etc. were far less important than they are today; b) that the more strict interpretation was based on the teaching of Sanchez who "does not seem to give a correct interpretation of the teaching of St. Thomas" and c) that "after so much progress in science, after the horrible wars, after the dignity and freedom of the human being have been so admirably revindicated, and especially after the Second Vatican Council, the world has changed too much for us to continue to apply the concept of the invalidating error of quality only to those qualities which single out a given physical person".

For a translation of the law section from the Canals decision, see *The Jurist,* 1972: 2, pgs. 296 - 298 and DI, pgs. 133 - 135.

4.   In the years following the Canals decision, to sum up, it became generally accepted, contrary to the position stated by Brennan and others, that *it is NOT required* a) that the other person be entirely unknown to the erring person, or b) that the quality be the sole means of identifying the other person and of distinguishing that person from all others; but *it IS required* a) that one person be ignorant of or in error about a quality in the other person, and b) that that quality be intended ahead of the person (qualitas prae persona), i.e. that the quality be directly and principally intended and the person less principally (minus principaliter persona).

5.   This position was, indeed, so firmly in possession by 1983 that it was incorporated into canon 1097 §2, as follows: "Error concerning a quality of a person, even if such error is the cause of the contract, does not invalidate matrimony unless this quality was directly and principally intended".

D.   Qualities Of The Intention

In order for error of quality to be invalidating, the quality must be directly and principally *intended.* The meaning of "directly" and "principally" has already been touched on. Since, however, an intention on the part of the erring person is essential for invalidity, the various general types of intention and their relevance deserve mention.

1. Intentions That Are *Not Sufficient*

   a. A *Presumed* Intention - which is an intention whose actual existence is not really known, but is rather based on a more or less probable conjecture. If, for example, one were to conclude that a woman intended to marry a Catholic simply on the basis that she herself was Catholic and tended to associate with other Catholics, that would be only a presumed intention (56, 756-757).

   b. An *Interpretive* Intention - which is an intention that would have been made had the person thought of it, as for example, "If I had known he was not a practicing Catholic, I would not have married him."

   c. A *Generic* Intention - which amounts really to a disposition of mind, as if one were to say "I'd prefer to marry a practicing Catholic."

   d. An *Habitual* Intention - which is one step beyond a generic intention but which still does not determine the act or enter the consent, as when a person decides, "When I marry, I intend to marry a practicing Catholic."

2. Intentions That Are *Not Required*

   a. An *Actual* Intention - which is made at the very moment of marriage, as for example, "As I stand here exchanging marital consent, I intend to marry only if John is really a practicing Catholic."

   b. An *Explicit* Intention - which expresses a condition in clear and definite terms. E.g. "I intend the validity of this marriage to hinge on the condition that John is a practicing Catholic."

3. Intentions That Are *Required and Sufficient*

   a. A *Positive* Intention - which is an intention that is more than a presumed, interpretive, generic or habitual intention.

   b. A *Virtual* Intention - which is an intention that is not constructed at the moment of the marriage but which nevertheless perdures and is part of the marital consent.

   c. An *Implicit* Intention - which is an express (as opposed to an unexpressed or tacit) intention but which is expressed only indirectly or obliquely. Etymologically an implicit intention is one which is contained "in plico", i.e. in the folds of something else. In practice it refers to two different situations. The *first* is where the intention is expressed in words but only indirectly, as when a part is expressed in the whole, an effect in its cause, a species in its genus. When a man, for example, explicitly

101

states that he will never cohabit with a woman, he implicitly simulates marriage. The *second* type of implicit intention is where the intention is expressed not in words but in actions, actions which can have no other meaning but that a certain intention was present motivating them. A man, for example, who says nothing but disappears immediately after the wedding ceremony never to be heard from again may be said to have excluded cohabitation implicitly (56, 929-931).

An example of a positive, virtual, implicit intention is the following "The man I marry must absolutely be, in every sense of the word, a good role model for our Catholic children".

It bears repeating, however, that for error of quality to be invalidating, not only must the quality be intended by a positive act of the will that is at least virtual and implicit, but also the quality must be intended directly and principally. In the example given, therefore, the woman must, at least implicitly, a) intend John's practical Catholicity in and of itself, and b) consider John's practical Catholicity as more important than John himself.

Finally it is important to note that, in practice, a tribunal will sometimes be called upon to distinguish carefully between an *implicit* intention on the one hand, and on the other, a *presumed* or *interpretive* intention. In order to find for invalidity, in other words, it is not enough to conclude that, based on certain circumstantial evidence, a person in all probability directly and principally intended a quality (a presumed intention) or that a person would have directly and principally intended the quality had he or she thought of it (an interpretive intention); rather it must be proved that the person actually did directly and principally intend the quality, and then express that intention, at least implicitly.

E. **Canons 1097 and 126**

1. Canon 126, found in Book I of the Code, states a general principle that may be applied to all other sections of the Code. Canon 126 states that error or ignorance invalidates an act either when a) it concerns an element that constitutes the substance of the act, or b) it amounts to a conditio sine qua non.

2. In effect, therefore, c. 126 says:

    a. that when the error or ignorance concerns an element that constitutes the substance of an act, the "contra element" need not be intended in order for the act to be invalid; rather the error or ignorance, by itself, invalidates the act.

    b. that when the error or ignorance concerns an element that does not constitute the substance of an act, then, in order to be invalidating, the error must amount to a conditio sine qua non, which, in terms of error of quality, means that the quality must be directly and principally intended.

3. The substance of an act is a technical term which means those constitutive elements of something which must be positively intended by a human agent in order for the thing to exist. It does not necessarily include all the constitutive elements of something but only those which must be positively intended by a human being. (Michiels, *De Personis,* p. 657).

4. The substance of the marriage act consists of the following elements:

    a.   a permanent consortium
    b.   between a man and a woman
    c.   which is ordered toward the procreation of offspring
    d.   by means of some sexual cooperation
    e.   with the man and the woman knowing each other's physical identity.

5. When, therefore, the general principle of c. 126 is applied to marriage the Code states in c. 1096 §1 (regarding elements a, b, c and d) and in c. 1097 §1 (regarding element e) that error or ignorance regarding these elements automatically invalidates a marriage because these elements constitute the substance of the marriage act. If, for example, a person enters marriage ignorant of or in error about the permanence of marriage (element a) then the marriage is automatically invalid. The person does not have to intend impermanence in order to render the marriage invalid (31, 392; 60, 345; 67, 467; 69, 506 and 70, 438).

When, however, c. 126 is applied to other aspects of marriage (i.e. those which do not constitute the substance of the act of marriage) even those aspects which, by the will of God, are essential to marriage, like unity and perpetuity (c. 1056), the Code states in c. 1097 §2 (regarding error of quality) and in c. 1099 and 1101 §2 (regarding the essential properties etc.) that error or ignorance, by themselves, do not cause invalidity but that beyond that there must be what amounts to a conditio sine qua non.

F. Error or Condition?

1. It has been noted that, in general, the authors and jurists of the past twenty-five years, have come to accept the Canals position that it is not required, in order to prove invalidity, either that the other person be entirely unknown to the erring person or that the quality be the sole means of identifying the other person. In another very important area, however, the total Canals position, as expressed in his decision of April 21, 1970, has *not* been generally accepted.

2. In that 1970 decision Canals noted that "redounding error", i.e. error of quality redounding to error of person (see B4 above) can be interpreted in three different ways:

a. The strictest interpretation "considers that case where a quality is the only possible means of establishing the identity of an otherwise unknown person".

b. A less strict interpretation applies to the case in which the quality is directly and principally intended, in accord with the teaching of Alphonsus Liguori.

c. "The third interpretation considers the case of a moral, social or juridical quality which is so intimately connected with the physical person that the person would be altogether different if that quality did not exist...The reason for this invalidity would not arise from any implicit condition, but rather be due to an error of quality amounting to an error concerning the person understood in a more complete and integral way" (D1, pp. 133-134).

It is clear that Canals himself favored this third interpretation which recognized that a merely circumscribing or common (i.e. non individuating) quality could redound to error of person "understood in a more complete and integral way" and that error, by itself, "sua vi", could invalidate a marriage, without it being required that the erring person directly and principally intend that quality. It was, indeed, on the basis of this jurisprudence, as is clear from the Argument section of that sentence, that the Canals court reached an affirmative decision in the April 21, 1970 case (62, 373-374).

This jurisprudence, however, never became generally accepted; partly, no doubt, because it was seen to be in conflict with the general and apparently sensible principle mentioned in c. 126 that error by itself invalidates only when it concerns an element that constitutes the substance of the act. Or to put it more bluntly, this third and entirely novel interpretation, which Canals endorsed, has, in general, been rejected by later authors and judges, and above all by c. 1097 of the 1983 Code of Canon Law (which, instead, endorsed Canals' second interpretation - the one based on Alphonsus Liguori).

3. Had Canals' third interpretation not been rejected but rather been accepted as having merit, then the proper ground on which to hear such cases would, even from a logical or theoretical point of view, be error. Since, however, c. 1097 §2 says that error of quality invalidates only when the quality is directly and principally intended, it seems clear that, *from a logical or theoretical point of view*, the proper ground on which to hear such cases is not error but condition (see the chapter on "Conditions", section D on p. 158).

Nevertheless, *from a systematic or structural point of view,* since the Code of Canon Law treats error of quality among the defects of the intellect (cc. 1095 - 1100) rather than among the defects of the will (cc. 1101 - 1103), such cases may be heard on the ground of error. See Navarrete, *Periodica,* 1993, p. 667.

For more on this question see *CLSAP,* 1973, pp 63-64 (Reinhardt); *The Jurist,* 1989 pp. 169-172 and 174 (Hennessey), and *Monitor Ecclesiasticus,* 1995, I-II, pp. 57-68 (Funghini).

G. Proof of Error of Quality

"The existence of error must be proved by solid arguments drawn either from the confession of the erring person or from the testimony of credible witnesses who learned of the matter at a nonsuspect time.

"The way the erring person acts both before and after marriage is extremely important in diagnosing what is truly in his or her mind.

"Error cannot be claimed if the contractant made no effort to investigate the matter even when, at the time of the engagement, he or she had, either directly or indirectly received some indications that the quality being demanded in the other party was, in fact, absent; nor can error be claimed if the first reaction of the erring person is complete passivity when he or she learns, after marriage, that the quality (which he or she now claims to have directly and principally intended) is, in fact, absent.

"Likewise that man is not to be trusted who says that he sought special qualities or virtues in his future wife, if, blinded by love after first meeting the woman, he engages in sexual intimacies with her and, convinced that he has found the ideal wife, rashly and quickly asks her to marry him.

"Finally, if from the acts and proofs, a prudent doubt remains about the quality being truly demanded and therefore about the existence of error, and if that doubt cannot be dispelled with moral certitude, then the validity of the marriage, which enjoys the favor of law, is to be upheld (see c. 1060). " (from the decision of December 18, 1991 coram Bruno - 83, 836-837).

H. Error of Person

Although this chapter deals primarily with error of *quality,* it seems appropriate to offer a few observations as well regarding error of *person.*

Canals, in his third interpretation, had spoken of the person "*understood in a more complete and integral way*". Accordingly, some canonists are of the opinon that the word "person" in c. 1097 §1 refers not just to the physical person but rather to the whole existential reality of the concrete human being, who is, of course, made up of a number of qualities; like, for example, wealth.

If, however, this were the correct meaning of the term "person" in c. 1097 §1, then it would follow that if John married Carla thinking that she were wealthy when, in fact, she was not, then the marriage would be invalid, because John had married the wrong person "understood in a more complete and integral way". John's error, all by itself, sua vi, would invalidate the marriage. It would not be necessary for John to *intend* Carla's wealth in order for the marriage to be invalid. Neither would it be necessary for John to be *deceived* into thinking that Carla was wealthy. Rather the invalidity would result from the mere error itself. Such an interpretation, in other words, would render completely meaningless both c. 1097 §2 (on error of quality) and c. 1098 (on error dolosus), and it must therefore be rejected on the ground that it attempts to interpret a law out of context, and that it is, furthemore, totally alien to the purpose and circumstances of the law and to the mind of the legislator.

For more on this point see *Periodica*, 1993, IV, pp. 659-665 (Navarrete) and the decision of July 22, 1993 coram Stankiewicz in *Monitor Ecclesiasticus*, 1995, I - II, pp. 172-175.

IMPOSED ERROR

A. The Pertinent Canon

C. 1098 - CCEO, c. 821 - A person contracts invalidly who enters marriage deceived by fraud, perpetrated to obtain consent, concerning some quality of the other party which of its very nature can seriously disturb the partnership of conjugal life.

B. Some Observations On The Canon

1. This is a canon on error, not on fraud or deceit. This is clear from the fact that, according to the canon, it is not the *deceiver* (the one who perpetrates the fraud) but the *deceived* (the one who is in error) who contracts invalidly.

2. Nevertheless, fraud or deceit is an essential element here. Indeed, in Latin the ground is usually referred to as "error dolosus." In English we might refer to it as "imposed error."

3. Although the deceiver will usually be the other party, the canon does not require that that be so. Conceivably the deceiver or defrauder could be a third party.

C. Criteria

Specific criteria that must be met in order for error to be invalidating are the following:

1. The quality must be a *true* quality, i.e. an inherent feature or property of the person, as opposed to some isolated past action. If, for example, a party had had intercourse with another person prior to marriage, that would not be considered a true quality. Whereas if one had had a criminal record or had been a prostitute or had been in a previous civil marriage, these would be considered true qualities.

2. The quality must be *present* at the time of marriage, as opposed to a hoped for, future quality. If, for example, a woman married a man because he said he hoped to be a doctor or a millionaire, even though in fact he had no such hopes, this would not be invalidating. Whereas, if the man passed himself off as *really being* a doctor or millionaire at the time of the marriage when in fact he was far from it, then this could be invalidating.

3. The quality must be *unknown*. If, therefore, the deceived party either learns of the quality independently or strongly suspects the existence of the quality, then error cannot be said to be present, and the marriage cannot be considered invalid on this ground. Because, in effect, the deceived party is no longer deceived. A practical test for determining whether the quality

was truly unknown at the time of the marriage would be whether the person reacts with surprise and bewilderment on discovery of the quality.

4. The quality must be one *which, by its very nature, has a potential for being seriously disruptive.* It bears noting that the canon does not require that the quality be, by its very nature, serious, but only that it have, by its very nature, a potential for being seriously disruptive. This could refer to any serious, i.e. grave quality, whether the gravity be objective or only subjective. See the decision of January 27, 1994 coram Stankiewicz, n. 25 in *Periodica*, 1995, 3, p. 539.

    A quality is considered to be *objectively* grave when society would regard its concealment or misrepresentation as a grave injustice to the other party. This would include such qualities as serious or contagious diseases, addictions to vice which would be seriously disruptive of marital harmony though perhaps not invalidating in themselves, a totally unacceptable reputation, etc. It would not include such qualities as being a heavy smoker or poor dancer, etc.

    A quality is *subjectively* grave when the deceived person has such an extraordinary, perhaps excessive, esteem for that attribute that although light in itself, it is nevertheless valued by the person as seriously desirable. It may happen, for example, that a woman is vigorously opposed to marrying a man addicted to heavy smoking. Perhaps because several of her friends and relatives have died from lung cancer. She tells her fiancé that she would never marry such a man and receives from him the assurance that in fact he doesn't smoke at all, only to discover later that he deceived her. In such a case the quality, although objectively light, *could* be considered grave.

5. The quality must be *fraudulently concealed in order to obtain consent.* Simple error about a quality, as c. 1097 §2 notes, is not ordinarily invalidating, but imposed error is. A couple may marry, for example, thinking they are in good health. Shortly after marriage, however, the man discovers that he has had multiple sclerosis for some time and will shortly be invalided. This quality is certainly extremely grave. It changes the whole marriage. The marriage, however, must be considered valid, since the couple presumably married unconditionally, in sickness and in health. If, however, the man knew all along that he had MS but fraudulently concealed it, the marriage would be invalid because the fraud constituted a grave injustice against the other person and deprived her of her freedom of choice.

D. Proof Of Imposed Error

In investigating imposed error a court looks to the usual sources: the declarations of the parties and testimony of witnesses (see canons in the chapters on simulation), circumstantial evidence (whether there is a history of deceit, whether special marriage arrangements were made to avoid detection), a motive (the basis for the deceiver's judgment that the other person would not marry were the quality revealed) and perhaps documents (a record of a previous civil marriage, a medical record showing prior awareness of debilitating or genetic disease).

E. Retroactivity Of The Canon

Since c. 1098 has no counterpart in the 1917 Code, the question arises "Does the canon apply only to those marriages which were entered after November 27, 1983 (the effective date of the Code) or is the canon a declaration of natural law and so retroactive?" Because the canon is very broad and even envisions the possibility that the fraud might be perpetrated by a third party without the knowledge of either of the spouses, the answer is not a simple one. It seems rather that the judge must examine each case on its merits. In some instances the judge may legitimately conclude that invalidity is based on the natural law itself (and so applies to marriages that predate the 1983 Code) while in other cases it will appear that invalidity is based solely on this positive law of c. 1098 (and so would not apply to marriages contracted before November 27, 1983). See Appendix Five on p. 229, and the Stankewicz decision cited under C. 4, nn. 15-20.

F. Applicability Of The Canon

A question allied to retroactivity is applicability: Does c. 1098 apply only to the marriages of Catholics (i.e. marriages in which at least one party is Catholic - c. 1059) or does it apply to all marriages? Once again the answer is not a simple one. If the deceit and error are so gross that it may legitimately be concluded that invalidity is based on the natural law itself, then, of course, it would apply to all marriages. If, however, the deceit and error are more subtle so that invalidity would come only from ecclesiastical law, then it would, according to c. 11, affect only the marriages of Catholics.

G. The Relationship Between Imposed Error And Condition

These two institutes are very closely allied (33, 529-530). When, for example, a man marries an alcoholic woman he may allege either that he was deceived or that he had placed a condition against marrying such a woman.

Circumstances, however, may suggest one or the other to be the preferable approach. For example, when deceit is high (the woman has completely concealed her problem) and awareness is low (he has no idea she has a problem) then ERROR is the likely ground. But where awareness is high (he has strong suspicions that she is alcoholic) and deceit is low (she has indicated to him that she drinks too much) then it would seem preferable to handle the case on the ground of a CONDITION.

DETERMINING ERROR (ERROR OF LAW)

A. The Pertinent Canons

C. 1099 - CCEO, c. 822 - Error concerning the unity, indissolubility or sacramental dignity of matrimony does not vitiate matrimonial consent so long as it does not determine the will.

C. 126 - CCEO, c. 933 - An act placed because of ignorance or error concerning an element which constitutes its substance or which amounts to a condition *sine qua non* is invalid; otherwise it is valid, unless the law makes some other provision. However, an act placed out of ignorance or error can be the occasion for a recissory action in accord with the norm of law.

B. The Term "Error Of Law"

The term "error of law" commonly refers to the error spoken of in c. 1099, i.e. error concerning the unity, indissolubility or sacramental dignity of matrimony; and is distinguished from "error of fact", which is the error spoken of in c. 1097, i.e. error concerning the person or concerning a quality of person.

C. The Term "Determining Error"

1. Although c. 1099 is phrased negatively (error concerning unity etc. does *not* vitiate consent so long as it is does *not* determine the will), it is quite clear that the canon has a positive meaning as well (namely that error about unity etc. *does* vitiate consent if it *does* determine the will). But there remains the question "What does the phrase 'to determine the will' mean?"

2. In 1980, while the present Code was still in draft form, Zenon Grocholewski pointed out that the phrase "to determine the will" is vague in that error could in fact determine the will but only for placing acts against indissolubility in general, i.e. not in regard to the particular marriage being entered. Grocholewski therefore recommended that the phrase "as long as it does not determine the will" be changed to "as long as it does not determine the consent" or "as long as it does not determine the object of consent". *(Periodica,* 1980, p. 588, h.).

   Although Grocholewski's specific recommendation was not, in fact, incorporated into the 1983 Code, the present canon is understood by virtually all commentators precisely as Grocholewski wanted it understood. It is, in other words, accepted that error about the essential properties or sacramentality of marriage vitiates consent only when it effectively specifies the object of the person's consent as something different from true marriage. When, for example, error about indissolubility brings it about, in one way or another, that the person enters a dissoluble marriage, then the

110

marriage is invalid; but when the error does not bring about that result, i.e. when the error does not determine the will, in some way or other, to enter a dissoluble marriage, then the marriage is valid.

This much, it seems, is not in dispute.

D. Determining Error - An Autonomous Ground?

While the basic notion of error determining the will is fairly clear and not a matter of dispute, the *manner* in which error determines the will, i.e. the *way* in which error exercises its efficacy, is very much in dispute.

Some canonists are of the opinion that error determines the will by *rejection*, i.e. by prompting the will to exclude, by a positive act of the will, an essential property or the sacramentality of marriage. A man, for example, is so thoroughly convinced of his right to divorce, that when he enters a specific marriage, he positively excludes indissolubility from the marriage contract. From a theoretical point of view, the proper ground of invalidity, according to this opinion, would be *simulation* (c. 1101 §2).

Other canonists are of the opinion that error determines the will by *election*, i.e. by prompting a person to enter the only kind of marriage he or she knows, namely one whose object is different from a valid marriage. A woman, for example, is firmly convinced that marriage is dissoluble, so when she marries, she positively elects to enter marriage as she knows it, i.e. as a dissoluble contract. From a theoretical point of view, the proper ground of invalidity, according to this opinion, would be *error of law* (c. 1099).

According to this second opinion, error of law is an autonomous ground; according to the first opinion it is not.

E. Canons 1099 And 126

1. Canon 126 says that an act placed from error results in invalidity in only two instances: a) when the error concerns an element which constitutes the substance of the act, or b) when it amounts to a conditio sine qua non.

2. As regards the former, it is understood that the term "the substance of an act" refers not to all the constitutive elements of something but only to those constitutive elements that must be positively intended by a human agent for the thing to exist (Michiels, *De Personis,* p. 657).

3. Canon 1096 §1, which describes the substance of the act of marriage, notes that marriage is a) a *permanent* consortium, i.e. a stable consortium, not necessarily a perpetual or indissoluble consortium, b) between a *man and a woman,* i.e.. a heterosexual consortium, not necessarily an exclusive or monogamous consortium (between one man and one woman).

It is understood, in other words, that although permanence and heterosexuality pertain to the substance of the act of marriage, indissolubility and unity do not, even though, by divine will (not human intention), they are the essential properties of marriage (c. 1056). In terms of the substance of the act, therefore, error about the permanence or heterosexuality of marriage invalidates, while error about the indissolubility or unity of marriage does not (31, 392; 60, 345; 67, 467; 69, 506 and 70, 438).

4.   If then error about unity or indissolubility is to invalidate a marriage, it must, according to c. 126, amount to a condition.

It is absolutely clear that according to the *first* opinion mentioned above (where error determines the will by *rejection,* i.e. by a positive act of the will excluding, say, indissolubility) the error amounts to a condition, since a condition, according to Staffa (see *De Conditione Contra Matrimonii Substantiam,* p. 10 and A 2, pp. 72, 78 and 85), is any "intrinsic limitation of the object of matrimonial consent", and that, of course, is precisely what a positive act of the will excluding indissolubility is.

While it is perhaps not so clear that according to the *second* opinion (where error determines the will by *election,* i.e. where the person enters marriage according to his or her own, erroneous lights) the error amounts to a condition, nevertheless the proponents of that position would say that it surely does since the erroneous concept of marriage determines the person's will to enter only that kind of marriage, e. g. a dissoluble marriage, and therefore it too amounts to an "intrinsic limitation of the object of matrimonial consent".

F.   Levels Of Intensity In Error

In terms of marriage invalidity there are two basic types of error of law: error that does *not* determine the will and error that *does* determine the will.

1.   Non Determining Error

   a.   *Simple Error.* Simple error, a term that was used in c. 1084 of the 1917 Code, refers to that error that remains, for the most part, in the intellect (it is sometimes called "speculative error") and does not substantially affect the will (Fellhauer, *Studia Canonica,* 1975, p. 107). A man, for example, believes that divorce and remarriage is, in general, acceptable if a first marriage proves to be unhappy; at present, however, he is deeply in love with his fianceé, and intends to enter a lifelong marriage with her. His speculative error clearly does not substantially affect his actual intentions in entering marriage. It was with this sort of case in mind that Heard, in a 1940 decision, wrote "Those general ideas which many people have about marriage, especially in those countries where divorce is common, almost always remain in the intellect and do not become a real act of the will" (32, 110).

b. *Non Prevailing Intransigent Error.* Intransigent error is a false judgment that exercises some substantial influence on the will (74, 194). It is most often called "error pervicax" in Latin, and is also known as stubborn, obstinate, radical or deep seated error in English.

Although it is virtually axiomatic that the more deeply entrenched the error, the more easily it will determine the will (see, for example, 63, 54), one cannot conclude that *all* intransigent error *necessarily* determines the will.

There are two basic reasons for this. The first is that error can be more or less intransigent, and that at least at the lesser levels, there must be some occasion or cause that prompts the person to carry that error into effect (Stankiewicz, *Periodica,* 1990, p. 478). In a given instance that *occasion or cause might be lacking.* A tribunal, for example, may determine that a woman not only entertains a general belief in the acceptability of divorce (simple error) but actually harbors a rather firm conviction that she has a right to obtain a divorce from a particular marriage (intransigent error). Nevertheless the tribunal may not conclude that intransigent error actually determined the object of the will unless it is also clear that some factor (e.g. a growing disenchantment with her fiancé prior to marriage) prompted the error to become activated in terms of this marriage.

The second reason why intransigent error might not determine the will is that even though the error be quite intransigent and actually enter the will as a strong tendency relative to the marriage in question, it *might not be the prevailing and efficacious intention.* Navarrete (*Periodica,* 1992, p. 482) offers the following observations and example on this point:

> The will tends to the object willed insofar as it is shown by the intellect. When the object contains elements that are *not* explicitly known, these elements can be intended only implicitly in the act of willing the object as it exists in all its complexity. This is especially true when it is a question of elements that are inseparably connected with the object. But if these elements *are* known and the will rejects one of them, then it automatically rejects the object to which the element is inseparably connected. In the event of a conflict between these two tendencies of the will, that tendency will prevail which is the stronger and more efficacious. If, for example, a man from America wishes to come to Milan, he implicitly wishes to come to Italy, even though he is unaware of the fact that Milan is in Italy, indeed even if he thinks Milan is in Switzerland. But if, in any way or for any reason, he intends, by a

prevailing and efficacious will, not to come to Italy, then by that very fact he intends not to come to Milan because it is a matter of inseparable objects of the will. In a conflict between the two tendencies of the will (not to come to Italy - to come to Milan), that tendency which is, in fact, stronger and more efficacious will prevail. For the person who intends to come to Milan but not to Italy would be intending a nonexistent and fictitious object.

Clearly the same can be true about the person in intransigent error who wishes, on the one hand, to enter a dissoluble marriage, but on the other, to enter a true, lifelong marriage with his or her beloved. In such a case that tendency will prevail which is the stronger and more efficacious, and the tribunal is left with the unenviable task of attempting to determine which one that is. Obviously it will not always be the error that prevails, in which case the tribunal must conclude that the error did not actually determine the will.

2. Determining Error

    a. *Prevailing Intransigent Error*

    There are two types of prevailing intransigent error: Less intense but with triggering factor, and more intense.

    1. *Less Intense With Triggering Factor.* As noted above there are cases where the error is truly intransigent (i.e. error that exercises some substantial influence on the will) but not so intense that it would, in and of itself, determine the object of the will. Such error, however, *can* determine the will when some extra factor (e.g. a growing disenchantment with one's intended spouse prior to the wedding) is present that prompts that intransigent error first to become activated in terms of the marriage and then to actually prevail over the intention to enter a true, lifelong marriage.

    2. *More Intense.* Sometimes error is *so* intransigent that is is difficult to imagine that it would not, by the sheer force of its intensity, determine the will. Suffice it to quote briefly from a few pertinent Rotal decisions:

    In a decision of February 28, 1950, *Felici* wrote:

    > But if opinions of this sort dwell so deeply in the person of the contractant that they become, as it were, part of his or her nature, and if there is no apparent reason why the contractant, in entering marriage, would depart from these opininons, and if furthermore a steadfast and shameful abuse of marriage along with other corresponding circumstances are proved, then a grave presumption (of invalidity) arises that would almost certainly result in moral certitude (42, 103).

114

Some four years later (July 13, 1954) *Felici* wrote:

> Error, which pertains to the intellect, is quite compatible with true matrimonial consent, which properly pertains to the will. Nevertheless if error is rooted in the person of the contractant so deeply that it constitutes, as it were, a new nature of that person, then dissent from that error is admitted only with difficulty: for generally a person acts in accord with his or her deepest perceptions, since according to the principle of motricity, the more vivid and profound an image or idea is and the more broadly it resonates within the person, the greater efficacy it enjoys, i.e. the more forcefully it impels the person to act (46, 616).

Filipiak, in a decision of March 23, 1956, said:

> At least an implicit intention (against indissolubility) is found in those people who, notwithstanding the Catholic teaching which they had learned, are so utterly convinced of their own right to divorce that they cannot completely depart from that conviction, (which has become, as it were, their second nature), especially when there is not present any particular reason why they ought to depart from that conviction in entering marriage (48, 256).

Sabattani, in a decision of December 11, 1964, said:

> But if one looks more deeply into the question of which path it is that leads the defect into the will, it will be clear that the defect is constituted by the fact that, given the presence of a very radical and therefore invincible error, all that the intellect presents to the will is a kind of dissoluble marriage, and it is to that that the will ultimately consents. In such a case, therefore, we should be speaking not so much of an "eroded will" as of "eroded freedom", and it is this that vitiates the will (56, 930).

In a decision of April 26, 1974, *Bruno* noted:

> Nevertheless if an error is so ingrained in the nature of a person that the person can only will or act in accord with that erroneous opinion then the error should be said to have entered the will and invalidated the consent (66, 290).

There are many other Rotal decisions as well that make the same point, namely that sometimes the error is so intransigent that the person cannot but act in accord with it. See, for example, the decisions coram *Pompedda* of 1/23/71 (63, 54); *Bruno* of 5/24/74 (66, 364-365) and of 12/19/84 (76, 648-650); *Anné* of 12/17/74 (66, 791-792); *Masala* of 3/15/83 (75, 109) and *Lanversin* of 2/28/84 (76, 145-146). See also LS, pp. 44-47.

Some of these auditors would hold that the intransigent error determines the will by rejection (i.e. simulation) and others that it determines the will by election (i.e. by the force of the error itself) but all of these auditors, and others as well, would recognize that error can sometimes be so intransigent that it almost inevitably determines the will and invalidates the marriage.

b. *Motivating Error*

Motivating error is that false judgment which prompts a person to marry, the precise reason why a person marries, the motive or reason on account of which the will is moved to contract.

Since it would be psychologically impossible for a person 1) to marry precisely because he or she thought marriage was, for example, dissoluble, and 2) to enter, at the same time, an *in*dissoluble marriage, it is generally accepted that motivating error of law amounts to a conditio sine qua non and is therefore invalidating (Navarrete, *Periodica,* 1992, p. 492).

G. Proof Of Determining Error

In order to prove a marriage invalid on the basis of c. 1099 two things must be proved, first that intransigent error is present, and secondly that that error determined the will.

"There is of course no doubt about the fact that those who reject the Church's teaching on the indissolubility of the bond create a presumption that they had intended to contract according to their own ideas. This, however, is only a presumption, not proof. It is a support by which simulation, if it is already proved by other means, can obtain confirmation.

" It should moreover be presumed that those people who had arranged for the celebration of their marriage in the Church, especially if they were Catholic, had intended to bind themselves to the law of Christ and the Church. This is why the presumption of law as stated in c. 1086 §1 of the 1917 Code: 'The internal consent of the mind is always presumed to be in agreement with the words or signs employed in celebrating matrimony' ought per se to prevail over the simple presumption drawn from the ideas of the contractants.

"In order to distinguish simple error from intransigent error it is necessary to determine to what degree the error entered into the mind and personality of the contractant.

"The judge, therefore, ought to inquire in each individual case whether it is a question of vague, futile and superficial opinions remaining in the intellect or of rooted persuasions that are constantly, seriously and openly manifested, and that exercise a serious influence on the will.

"This investigation ought to be carried out by weighing the prenuptial and postnuptial circumstances and facts which can reveal the true mind and will of the alleged simulator.

"People may not be said to have been induced by intransigent error if they declare that they had been in favor of divorce in certain circumstances when prior to marriage they had never been heard to explicitly disparage the indissolubility of their own marriage, or when, after the marriage finally broke down, they had no particular interest in obtaining a divorce and did not seek one through the intervention of others by exhibiting chagrin and grief.

"Similarly a disregard or contempt for religion, or threats of obtaining a divorce made theoretically either before or after the wedding, especially if there exists between the parties a profound and sincere love, do not, per se, imply intransigent error.

"Finally we should not forget the very great importance that the cause of simulating has in processes of this kind. The cause of simulating is the strongest argument, and when it is lacking, credence is not to be given to one admitting simulation.

"In the case of intransigent error, the cause of simulating is to be found in the error itself which, as is clear, determines the will to simulate consent" (from the decision of December 19, 1984 coram Bruno - 76, 649-650).

H. The Newness Of Error Of Law As An Autonomous Ground

Finally, an historical note.

The 1917 canon on error of law (c. 1084) is quite different from the 1983 canon on error of law.

The 1917 canon said only that "simple error about the unity or indissolubility or sacramental dignity of marriage, even though it is the cause of the contract, does not vitiate matrimonial consent". This canon was generally understood as follows: simple error, i.e. error as such, i.e. error that remains error, i.e. error that does not enter the will, at least in any substantial way, but rather remains, at least for the most part, in the intellect, does not vitiate. By implication once error did enter the will in a substantial way and prompted the will to exclude, by a positive act of the will, one of the essential properties of marriage or its sacramental dignity, then the marriage would be invalid. It was understood, however, that the invalidity was caused by the positive act of the will and not by the intellectual error since error, as such, was not invalidating.

The implication of the 1983 canon, however, is quite different. When the canon says that error that does not determine the will does not vitiate, it implies that error that does determine the will does vitiate and, as noted above, the will can be determined, according to some canonists, by the person electing the only kind of marriage he or she knows, e.g. a dissoluble marriage. According to these canonists, in other words, the will can be determined by the error itself, "vi et effectu ipsius erroris" (Sabattani's phrase, from his decision of December 11, 1964 - 56, 927-928).

In short, whereas the 1917 canon on error of law (c. 1084) did not readily lend itself to seeing error as an autonomous ground (though some jurists writing under that Code managed to go beyond the apparent gist of the canon and conclude that error of law could indeed be an autonomous ground), the 1983 canon (c. 1099) seems quite open to that interpretation, and it has, as a consequence, given considerable impetus to that position.

TOTAL SIMULATION

A. The Pertinent Canon

C. 1101 - CCEO, c. 824 - §1. The internal consent of the mind is presumed to be in agreement with the words or signs employed in celebrating matrimony.

§2. But if either or both parties through a positive act of the will should exclude marriage itself, some essential element or an essential property of marriage, it is invalidly contracted.

B. Distinction Between Total and Partial Simulation

1. The 1983 Code, like the 1917 Code, does not speak of a distinction between total and partial simulation. It speaks rather of excluding a) marriage itself, b) an essential element or c) an essential property. And to these three may be added, for the marriages of baptized Christians, d) sacramentality.

   a. *Marriage Itself.* Marriage is basically a consortium or partnership between a man and a woman (cc. 1055, 1096, 1098 and 1135). The person, therefore, who, in going through a marriage ceremony, excludes the idea of entering a consortium, is thereby excluding marriage itself.

   b. *Essential Elements.* The Relatio for the October 1981 meeting (*Communicationes*, 1983, 2, p. 234) noted that the essential elements of marriage "are to be determined by doctrine and jurisprudence, taking into consideration the definition of marriage (in c. 1055 §1) and, indeed, the whole of legislation and doctrine, both juridic and theological." For present purposes, however, it may be said that the essential elements of marriage are two: the procreational element and the personalist element. The procreational element involves the right to intercourse. The personalist element involves the right to self revelation, understanding and loving.

   c. *Essential Properties.* The essential properties of marriage are unity and indissolubility (c. 1056).

      Note: An element is a part; a property is a characteristic. The elements of water are hydrogen and oxygen. The properties are liquid and clear. The constitutive parts (the *elements*) of marriage are the rights to the joining of bodies and souls, which rights are to be exchanged (the *properties*) exclusively and perpetually.

   d. *Sacramentality.* While there is general agreement that, for the marriage of baptized Christians, sacramental dignity pertains to the essence of marriage (c. 1099), there is no consensus on how sacramental dignity should be categorized in law. Some (e.g. Faltin) are of the opinion that it is an essential *element* of marriage; some (e.g. De Luca) hold that it is an essential *property* of marriage; some (e.g. Navarrete) regard it as a *quasi property* of marriage; and a few (e.g. Burke) regard it as none of these but rather as *marriage itself*. See Mendonca, "Recent Trends", *Studia Canonica*, 1994, pp. 200-201; and Burke, "The Sacramentality of Marriage", *Monitor Ecclesiasticus*, 1994, p. 554.

2. A few rotal auditors, notably Felici (43, 370), Pinna (47, 678) and Rogers (61, 748) have held that there is no distinction between total and partial simulation, because, in effect, "whoever simulates, simulates totally."

3. Most jurists, however, do recognize a distinction between total and partial simulation (see the decision of 1/29/81 coram Stankiewicz in D2 pp. 140-143, and also *Periodica*, 1978, p. 286).

In general *total* simulation occurs when marriage itself, i.e. some basic consortium or partnership is excluded, while *partial* simulation occurs when an essential element or property or, in the marriages of Christians, sacramentality is excluded. See the chapter in this book entitled "Intention Against the Good of the Spouses" under C. 3 on p. 144.

The distinction has merit on two counts. First in the **psychological** order; since *total* simulators are often aware of the invalidity of the marriage they have feigned contracting externally, while *partial* simulators may think they have contracted a valid marriage, but one limited or defined according to the restricting intention. Secondly, in the **juridical** order; since, during the investigative process, it allows the court to focus on the specific area in which the defective consent actually exists.

4. Although the Code does not speak of a distinction between total and partial simulation, the distinction, because of its already noted psychological and juridical advantages, continues to be utilized in jurisprudence and is generally coordinated with the Code, with the "goods", "bona" or "blessings" of marriage, as follows:

Exclusion	Simulation	
Marriage Itself ————————————————		Total
Elements { Personalist ——	Coniugum	
Procreational ——	Prolis	
Properties { Unity ——	Fidei	Partial
Indissolubility ——	Sacramenti	
Sacramentality ——	Sacramentalitatis?	

120

5. The distinction between excluding marriage itself (total simulation) and excluding the bonum coniugum (partial simulation) deserves special mention. One excludes *marriage itself* when one excludes any sort of consortium or partnership; one excludes the *bonum coniugum* when one excludes the kind of partnership that is ordered to the good of the spouses, which involves the right to self revelation, understanding and loving.

C. Relationship Between Total And Partial Simulation

Although the Rota has, on at least one occasion (35, 637) given an affirmative decision on total simulation and a negative on partial simulation contra bonum prolis (because a specific intention against children had not been proved), there are surely many situations where a marriage declared invalid on the ground of total simulation (where, for example, a person intended never to cohabit with his or her spouse) is also clearly invalid on the ground of partial simulation (contra bonum prolis, for example - see 33, 692).

And, as we have seen, a few auditors, like Felici, Pinna and Rogers, would even argue in reverse, namely that if a marriage is invalid on the ground of partial simulation, it is also invalid on the ground of total simulation.

D. The Essence Of Total Simulation

1. Total simulation is the act of *externally* feigning consent during a marriage ceremony while *internally* excluding marriage or the right to a partnership.

2. True simulation always involves the finis operis (the inherent purpose of something) being excluded by and not just coexisting with the finis operantis (the purpose the individual has in mind, which is sometimes different from and extraneous to the finis operis).

   To use a homely, non marital example: the finis operis of a gun is to shoot or fire. A gun is for shooting. It may, however, be legitimately used as a decorative piece, and when so used the finis operantis of the gun is to decorate a room. These two purposes, fines or ends may coexist. It may also happen, however, that the finis operantis completely thwarts, frustrates and blocks the finis operis. This would happen implicitly if the firing pin of the gun were removed. It would happen explicitly if the gun were under sealed glass or somehow made unreachable so that, in effect, the finis operis could not be used. In such cases where the finis operis of the gun is explicitly or implicitly excluded, the object is no longer a real gun but rather a simulated, fake or imitation gun.

   The same can happen in marriage. The finis operis of marriage is a partnership. A person might have as his or her own finis operantis in entering marriage the attainment of wealth or prestige. And these two purposes (the purpose of marriage and the purpose of the individual) could plausibly coexist. When, however, a person, in going through a marriage ceremony, positively excludes a genuine partnership, then the finis operis of marriage is excluded, and such an arrangement is only a simulated, or invalid marriage (30, 344).

E. The Positive Act Of The Will

1. C. 1101 §2 notes that the exclusion must be by a "positive act of the will."

2. A positive act of the will may be either explicit or implicit but is certainly something more than a negative act of the will, that is to say, a non act. Perhaps another homely example will serve to illustrate. Before us on the table are two objects, one round, the other square. There are three ways for us to wind up without the round object. The first is to reject or discard it (a positive, explicit exclusion of the round object). The second is to select instead the square object (a positive, implicit rejection of the round object). The third is to do nothing, to choose neither (a negative exclusion of the round object).

3. The Code says that a positive exclusion of marriage as a partnership is invalidating. It implies that a negative exclusion is not invalidating but it does not actually say that. Accordingly, some jurists have suggested that an "inadequate commitment" to marriage may likewise be invalidating (for a discussion of this point, see the articles by Brown and by Humphreys which are listed in the Selective Bibliography). This suggestion, however, has not met with widespread acceptance.

F. Implicit Simulation

1. The excluding of marriage that is involved in simulation need not be actual or explicit to be invalidating. It suffices if the exclusion is virtual and implicit ("De Actu Positivo Voluntatis Quo Bonum Essentiale Matrimonii Excluditur" by Dinus Staffa in *Monitor Ecclesiasticus,* 1949, I, pp. 164-173). See also the chapter in this book entitled "Error of Quality" under D on pp. 100-102.

2. There are three principal ways in which marriage or the right to the partnership of life may be excluded implicitly:

    a. *By permanently excluding the right to cohabitation*

        Cohabitation and partnership are two different things. In one sense, perhaps the more obvious sense, partnership implies something more than cohabitation, since cohabitation is something merely physical whereas partnership is something personal. In another sense, however, partnership is something less than cohabitation, in that a true partnership can be attained without actually cohabitating. Absence can, given the right circumstances, make the heart grow fonder.

Nevertheless, in practice, when one positively and permanently excludes cohabitation, one implicitly excludes the right to a partnership and to marriage itself, and therefore totally simulates (29, 740 and 39, 8).

Though this point was not always so clear (see "Marriage and Cohabitation" in *The Jurist,* 1967, 85-89, and the second edition of *Annulments,* pp. 68-71) it no longer presents a problem in jurisprudence.

b.   *By going through a marriage ceremony solely for an extraneous reason*

Occasionally a person will go through a marriage ceremony only as a means to an end. He or she marries solely and exclusively for a reason that is extraneous to the finis operis of marriage. A man, for example, is in jail because of rape. He can gain release by marrying. He does go through the ceremony but only so that he can get out of prison (54, 50 coram Doheny). Or a man is in prison and in need of medical attention not available to prisoners. He marries only so that he can get out and obtain the desired medical treatment (58, 938 coram Filipiak). Or a woman marries solely to get away from home and escape the cruel domination of her father (52, 171 coram Lefebvre). Or a man marries a pregnant woman solely to escape the wrath of her family or friends (55, 44 coram Lefebvre). Such marriages can be declared invalid when it is proved that the finis operis of marriage was effectively frustrated.

It may also happen in such cases that the simulator enters marriage with a certain amount of repugnance. The repugnance, however, is not what invalidates the marriage. Repugnance, in itself, is not invalidating (36, 423). It is the implicit simulation that invalidates.

c.   *By substituting for true marriage one's own idea of marriage*

A person could simulate marriage by entering something different from marriage. In so doing he or she implicitly excludes the true essence of marriage. A man, for example, might view marriage purely as a contract by which he hires for himself an attractive social companion and hostess, and nothing more (see the decision of August 19, 1914 coram Sincero in AAS VII, pp. 51-56).

G.   Proof Of Simulation

The principal factors that would be pertinent to proving total simulation are the following: 1) Declarations of the Parties, 2) Affidavits, 3) Testimony of Witnesses, 4) Circumstantial Evidence, and 5) Motive.

1.   *Declarations of the Parties*

The value of the declarations of the petitioner and respondent in a marriage case is adequately summarized in the following canons:

C. 1535 - A judicial confession is a written or oral assertion against oneself made by any party regarding the matter under trial and made before a competent judge, whether spontaneously or upon interrogation by the judge.

C. 1536 §2 - In cases which concern the public good ... a judicial confession and the declarations of the parties which are not confessions can have a probative force to be evaluated by the judge along with the other circumstances of the case; but complete probative force cannot be attributed to them unless other elements are present which thoroughly corroborate them.

C. 1537 - Having weighed all the circumstances, it is for the judge to evaluate the worth of an extra-judicial confession which has been introduced into the trial.

C. 1538 - A confession or any other declaration of a party lacks all probative force if it is proved that it was made through an error of fact or if it was extorted by force or grave fear.

2. *Affidavits*

Many courts obtain information from people by affidavit rather than by formal testimony. In general it may be said that affidavits are considered to have the same basic value as judicial declarations and testimony. But see also P, pp. 45 and 53.

3. *Testimony of Witnesses*

As regards the value of testimony by witnesses, the pertinent canons read:

C. 1572 - In evaluating testimony, after having obtained testimonial letters, if need be, the judge should consider:

1° the condition and good reputation of the person;
2° whether the witness testifies in virtue of personal knowledge, especially what has been seen and heard personally, or whether the testimony is the witness' opinion, or a rumor or hearsay from others;
3° whether the witness is reliable and firmly consistent or rather inconsistent, uncertain or vacillating;
4° whether the witness has supporting witnesses or whether there is support from other sources of proof.

C. 1573 - The deposition of a single witness cannot constitute full proof unless a witness acting in an official capacity makes a deposition regarding duties performed ex officio or unless circumstances of things and persons suggest otherwise.

For a brief but interesting law section on the use of one witness, see the decision of June 19, 1972 coram Pinto (64, 354-355).

4.   *Circumstantial Evidence*

There is a whole range of circumstances which might lend plausibility or credence to the allegation of total simulation. The particular circumstances will depend on the case but some of the more common circumstances that might have relevance are: a certain amount of pressure being exerted on the alleged simulator, unhappy family relationships, a very brief marriage, the constant intent prior to marriage to marry someone else, a previously expressed intention never to marry, and a philosophy of life radically different from the Christian philosophy.

5.   *Motive*

Just as every effect must have a cause, so every act of simulation must have a motive. To identify that motive goes a long way towards proving that the simulation did in fact take place.

It is always important, though, to distinguish the motive for simulating from the motive for going through the ceremony. A man, for example, might marry a woman for her money. That's the motive for *contracting*. If, however, he has, at the same time, a strong aversion for the woman, that becomes his motive for *simulating*. The principal aim always is to identify the motive for simulating. If, however, the motive for contracting is unworthy or unsuitable, this is not at all irrelevant, and should be considered as important circumstantial evidence. See also 64, 181-182.

Some of the more common motives for simulating are that the person already loves somebody else, he or she doesn't love or has an aversion to the spouse, the spouses are of disparate social and educational classes, pre-marriage bickering, and occasionally just plain irresponsibility.

INTENTION AGAINST CHILDREN

A. The Pertinent Canon

C. 1101 - CCEO, c. 824 - §1 - The internal consent of the mind is presumed to be in agreement with the words or signs employed in celebrating matrimony.

§2 - But if either or both parties, through a positive act of the will, should exclude ... some essential element ... of marriage, it is invalidly contracted.

B. The Right To The Conjugal Act

1. The Code does not define what the essential elements of marriage are. It may, however, be deduced from c. 1055 §1, which states that the marital partnership is, "by its nature, ordered to the procreation and education of children," that one of the essential elements of marriage is the right to the conjugal act, i.e. to non-contraceptive intercourse. See also c. 1061 §1.

2. The title of this chapter, "Intention Against Children" is a popular and somewhat inaccurate phrase. The right to *children* is not really exchanged in marriage. When a sterile man marries, for example, he cannot really give the right to children. This, however, does not invalidate the marriage. The right that *is* exchanged in marriage is the right to the conjugal act, and the sterile man is perfectly capable of that.

3. The right to the conjugal act binds at all reasonable times. It is obvious that the right to have intercourse in public is not exchanged in marriage. That would not be a reasonable time. If, therefore, that were excluded at the time of marriage it would not invalidate the marriage. However the meaning of the phrase "at all reasonable times" is not always so clear. Would a man, for example, have the right to noncontraceptive intercourse with his wife when he had been advised that another child might endanger her life, or when the couple could only with great difficulty support any more children? A court is occasionally called upon to anwer such questions in its attempt to determine whether "the right to the conjugal act" had truly been excluded.

4. Besides the right to intercourse at all reasonable times, the term "the right to the conjugal act" also includes the obligation of not impeding procreation and life. If therefore a woman, for example, intended to perform the marital act in a natural way but also intended always to use spermicides or pessaries or to take the morning after pill or to practice abortion or infanticide, she would be marrying invalidly, because the obligation of not impeding procreation and life is implied in the "right to the conjugal act," a positive exclusion of which invalidates marriage (49, 81).

C. Excluding The Right To The Conjugal Act

Many couples entering marriage these days do so with an agreement to postpone children for a while. Such an agreement, however, does not usually involve an exclusion of "the right to the conjugal act." The following remarks are made, then, in an effort to clarify when the right is excluded and when it is not.

1. The essential terms of the marriage covenant are not determined by the parties. They are predetermined by God, nature and society. The marriage covenant therefore enjoys a certain constitutional integrity, even a sacred integrity or wholeness. Visually it may be represented by a perfect circle or pie, with one essential piece of the pie being the right to the conjugal act.

2. Generally when a couple enters marriage with an agreement to postpone children for a while, say for two years, their agreement leaves the covenant (the pie) untouched. The covenant remains whole and entire, and the right to the conjugal act (a piece of the pie) is therefore not excluded but exchanged. What the couple does is enter a kind of side agreement, extrinsic to the marriage covenant. At the same time, however, they realize the superiority and prevailing power of the marriage covenant so that in a showdown they would recognize that the rights exchanged in the marriage covenant prevail over their private, subordinate arrangement. If, therefore, one of the parties, say the wife, decided after six months or a year that she wanted children right away, it would be expected that her husband, recognizing that that was her marital right, would acquiesce. Perhaps he would do so reluctantly. Perhaps he would even remind her of their private agreement. But if he eventually acquiesced it would be a sign that he recognized the prevailing power of the marriage covenant (where the right to the conjugal act was granted) over the private agreement of the parties.

It is, at any rate, always presumed that the marriage covenant remained intact, even where there is evidence that the couple had made a premarital agreement to postpone children. Like all presumptions, this one of course cedes to the truth, but in the absence of contrary evidence, the covenant is presumed to have been entered intact, and the marriage therefore entered validly.

3. Occasionally, however, the intent of one or both parties is so firm, intense, inflexible, and non negotiable, that it can no longer be viewed as a side agreement subordinate to the marriage covenant. In such a case the intention of that person invades the heart of the covenant itself, excludes from it the right to the conjugal act (extracts that piece from the pie), and thereby distorts, truncates and intrinsically limits the terms of the covenant. Should a man with such an intention, having entered marriage with the understanding that children would be postponed for say two years, be asked by his wife for a child after only six months, it could be expected that he would see his wife's request as an illegitimate extension of her rights and some-

thing for which he had not really bargained in entering marriage.

This man would have truly excluded the right to the conjugal act and so entered marriage invalidly.

4. Where the right to the conjugal act is truly excluded by a positive act of the will, even if it is done only for a period of time, the marriage is invalid. See the decision coram Davino of 12/13/78 in D2, pp. 149-152.

5. The positive act of the will excluding the conjugal act can also be implicit. An implicit intention, however, must be distinguished from a presumed intention. An implicit intention is one that is expressed but not explicitly. A presumed intention is one that may or may not exist but is only conjectured to (56, 756-757 and p. 101 of this book). If, for example, no children were, in fact, born of the marriage and it was known that the woman was not particularly fond of children, one might presume that she had excluded children but one could not say that those circumstances alone amounted to an implicit intention. On the other hand, if there was an agreement before marriage to at least postpone children, if the woman was obsessed with her career, if she absolutely insisted on using contraceptives throughout the marriage even when the husband wanted to start a family, if she was cold towards the children of friends and neighbors and had no time for them etc.; if, in other words, the circumstances became sufficiently forceful and clear that it could be said that her behavior truly expressed, though perhaps implicitly, the woman's intention to withhold from her husband the right to children, then the marriage could be declared invalid because of her implicit intention contra bonum prolis.

D. Proof That The Right To The Conjugal Act Has Been Excluded

The principal factors that would be pertinent to proving an intention against children are the following: 1) Declarations of the Parties, 2) Affidavits, 3) Testimony of Witnesses, 4) Circumstantial Evidence, 5) Motive, 6) Presumptions.

1. *Declarations of the Parties*

The value of the declarations of the petitioner and respondent in a marriage case is adequately summarized in the following canons:

C. 1535 - A judicial confession is a written or oral assertion against oneself made by any party regarding the matter under trial and made before a competent judge, whether spontaneously or upon interrogation by the judge.

C. 1536 - §2 - In cases which concern the public good ... a judicial confession and the declarations of the parties which are not confessions can have a probative force to be evaluated by the judge along with the other circumstances of the case; but complete probative force cannot be attributed to them unless other elements are present which thoroughly corroborate them.

C. 1537 - Having weighed all the circumstances, it is for the judge to evaluate the worth of an extra-judicial confession which has been introduced into the trial.

C. 1538 - A confession or any other declaration of a party lacks all probative force if it is proved that it was made through an error of fact or it was extorted by force or grave fear.

2. *Affidavits*

Many courts obtain information from people by affidavit rather than by formal testimony. In general it may be said that affidavits are considered to have the same basic value as judicial declarations and testimony. But see also P, pp. 45 and 53.

3. *Testimony of Witnesses*

As regards the value of testimony by witnesses, the pertinent canons read:

C. 1572 - In evaluating testimony, after having obtained testimonial letters, if need be, the judge should consider:

1º   the condition and good reputation of the person;
2º   whether the witness testifies in virtue of personal knowledge, especially what has been seen and heard personally, or whether the testimony is the witness' opinion, or a rumor or hearsay from others;
3º   whether the witness is reliable and firmly consistent or rather inconsistent, uncertain or vacillating;
4º   whether the witness has supporting witnesses or whether there is support from other sources of proof.

C. 1573 - The deposition of a single witness cannot constitute full proof unless a witness acting in an official capacity makes a deposition regarding duties performed ex officio or unless circumstances of things and persons suggest otherwise.

For a brief but interesting law section on the use of one witness, see the decision of June 19, 1972 coram Pinto (64, 354-355).

4. *Circumstantial Evidence*

The court should take into consideration all those circumstances which, though not probative in themselves, nevertheless cast light on the intentions of the people. Some circumstances that might be relevant would be the following: the fact that the couple was quarrelling before marriage giving rise to doubts about the happy outcome of the marriage, an excessive concern for material things, being uncomfortable with children and showing impatience with them.

5. *Motive*

Simulation cannot be considered demonstrated unless it is apparent from the acts that there was sufficient motive for simulating. Motives for excluding children would be an inordinate fear of childbirth on the part of the woman or the fear of losing her figure, the fear of transmitting diseases, an aversion to children, being in love with another, the unwillingness to be tied down, the financial hardships that would result, a conviction that one should not contribute to an already overpopulated world.

Oftentimes the crucial question to be answered by the court is whether the agreement to postpone children was just a subordinate agreement or whether it was so intense that it actually entered into the central contract and altered the sacred terms of the covenant. As an aid to answering that question it is often helpful to determine the subjective importance of the motive for simulating and compare it with the motive the person had for marrying (48, 409).

6. *Presumptions*

Here again, since the crucial issue is often the intensity of excluding children, the following three presumptions are valuable as indicators of intensity:

a. *Cause*

This presumption involves the decision to marry. What is envisioned is a discussion before final marriage plans are made. One party, the alleged simulator, say the man, asks the woman to agree to a postponement of children; she, hypothetically, does not agree. If the man would then have decided to go through with the marriage anyway, this suggests that his desire to postpone children was not really very intense, and the presumption therefore is that the right to the conjugal act was not excluded. If, on the other hand, it is clear that the man would have called off the marriage had the woman not agreed to a postponement, then the indication is that the intention was very firm indeed, and the presumption favors the conclusion that the right was excluded.

b. *Perpetuity*

We have seen that whenever the right to the conjugal act is truly excluded, even if it be only for a time, the marriage is invalid. Nevertheless, the intent to exclude children only for a time suggests a lack of intensity, so that the presumption favors the validity of the marriage. Whereas if the intent was to exclude children forever, then the presumption is that the very right to the conjugal act was excluded (28, 445; 39, 590; 66, 72-76).

Where the exclusion refers to an indefinite period of time, one must judge from all circumstances whether it should be considered temporary or permanent. For example, the phrase, "We will have children only after your father dies" could, depending on the circumstances, be either temporary or permanent. If the father were ninety years old it would be equivalent to a temporary exclusion but if the father were forty it would amount to a permanent exclusion. See the following Rotal citations: 32, 465 and 36, 328; 34, 715 and 37, 245; and also 24, 158; 34, 225; 40, 115; 47, 151 and 48, 409.

c. *Tenacity*

A tenacity or prolonged resistance to a partner wanting children gives rise to a presumption that the original intention entered into the heart of the contract and was primary and involved an exclusion of the right, whereas giving in to the wishes of the party without grave pressure suggests that the agreement about postponing children should be viewed as a side, subordinate agreement, and the presumption therefore favors the validity of the marriage (26, 36).

INTENTION AGAINST FIDELITY

A. The Pertinent Canon

C. 1101 - CCEO, c. 824 - §1 - The internal consent of the mind is presumed to be in agreement with the words or signs employed in celebrating matrimony.

§2 - But if either or both parties, through a positive act of the will, should exclude ... an essential property of marriage, it is invalidly contracted.

B. The Right To Fidelity

1. C. 1056 notes that one of the essential properties of marriage is unity. Unity, however, at least in its strict sense, is a very basic right. It simply means that a person has the right to be the one and only spouse of the partner. The partner does not have the right to polygamy.

2. Fidelity is something different from unity. In the broad sense, marital fidelity refers to the trust, loyalty and support that spouses show each other. In the strict, juridic sense, it refers to sexual fidelity, i.e. having one's spouse as one's only sex partner. It means, therefore, that the partner lacks not only the right to have another spouse but the right to have another lover. The partner lacks the right not only to be a polygamist but to be an adulterer.

3. Historically, unity and fidelity have, in jurisprudence, always been seen as virtually identical. Over the past several decades, however, the link between the two qualities, though it has not been broken, has, as it were, been turned around. Or upside down. According to the older jurisprudence (33, 622; 39, 589; 51, 252) *fidelity was reduced* to mean unity; whereas, according to the newer jurisprudence (45, 641-642; 55, 717; 64, 101; 74, 359-360 and 83, 600-610) *unity was extended* to mean fidelity.

4. Consequently, when c. 1134 speaks of marriage creating a "bond which is, by its nature, exclusive," it implies a twofold obligation: of unity and of fidelity.

5. The right to fidelity excludes the partner's right to engage in the sexual act with any other person, whether of the opposite or of the same sex. A marriage involving one homosexual partner could therefore be heard on the ground of an intention contra bonum fidei if it could be shown that the homosexual was, at the time of marriage, firmly intent on engaging in homosexual acts.

6. Although the meaning of fidelity could, in theory, be extended to include the exclusive right to the joining of *souls,* it is difficult to imagine a case in which this would have any practical importance. In practice, therefore, fidelity always refers to the exclusive right to the joining of bodies. As regards

excluding the right to the bonum coniugum, however, see pp. 141-147.

C. Excluding The Right To Fidelity

1. According to the *older* jurisprudence, the bonum fidei was excluded only when unity was excluded, i.e. only when the right to the conjugal act was given, cumulatively, to two people. According to the *newer* jurisprudence (which seems more in accord with the traditional understanding of the bonum fidei - see Friedberg, I, 1065, and *Casti Connubii*, 19-39), the bonum fidei is excluded when fidelity is excluded, i.e. whenever one intends not to bind oneself to sexual fidelity. See "The Jurisprudence of the Sacred Roman Rota: Its Development and Direction After the Second Vatican Council" by Aldo Arena, in *Studia Canonica*, 1978, 2, pp. 265-293.

2. In order to result in invalidity, fidelity must be excluded as part of the marriage covenant. It may happen, for example, that in entering marriage a man foresees and even intends that he will have an extramarital affair should he have the opportunity. If, however, this remains casual and incidental, his intention does not invade, and therefore does not vitiate, the covenant. If, on the other hand, his intention is so intense and important to him that it actually becomes part of his central agreement or exchange of rights, with the result that he would regard his wife's demands that he be hers alone as an undue extension of the agreement he entered, then such a man excludes the very right to fidelity.

3. The positive act of the will by which fidelity is excluded can be hypothetical. If, therefore, a man intends as part of the marriage contract, to exchange the right to perpetual fidelity only if his wife remains sexually attractive to him, he contracts invalidly.

4. The positive act of the will can also be implicit. An implicit intention, however, must be distinguished from a presumed intention. An implicit intention is one that is expressed but not explicitly. A presumed intention is one which may or may not exist but is only conjectured to (56, 756-757). If, for example, a man had a lover both before and after marriage, one might presume that he did not intend to be faithful, but one could not say that those circumstances alone amounted to an implicit intention. On the other hand, if the man had a lover before marriage but was pressured into marrying someone else, openly expressed his aversion to marrying, spent more time, even in public, with his lover than with his wife, etc.; if, in other words, the circumstances became sufficiently forceful and clear that it could be said that his behavior truly expressed, though perhaps implicitly, the man's intention to withhold from his wife the right to fidelity, then the marriage could be declared invalid because of his implicit intention contra bonum fidei.

5. One's beliefs about free love and open marriage can be extremely influen-

tial in causing one to exclude, by a positive act of the will, the bonum fidei. C. 1099 notes that error concerning the unity of matrimony does not vitiate matrimonial consent so long as it does not determine the will. Which implies that it *does* vitiate marriage if it *does* determine the will. In a contra bonum fidei case, then, the beliefs of the alleged simulator and the intensity of those beliefs, should always be carefully investigated by the court. For more on this subject, see pp. 110-118.

6.   Bruno, in his decision of June 15, 1990 (82, 515-516) lists the following ways of excluding the right to fidelity:

    a.   by a direct exclusion of the right itself.
    b.   by attaching to the consent a condition contrary to the obligation of fidelity.
    c.   by granting to a third person the right to conjugal acts.
    d.   by an intention, even an implicit one, of excluding the obligation, by manifesting a firm intention of having sex with others, even with persons of the same sex.
    e.   by a rooted persuasion that, given our weak human nature, the observance of fidelity is impossible.
    f.   by restricting the right or obligation to a determined or indeterminate period of time.
    g.   by an intention of committing adultery that prevails over the giving and receiving of the obligation of fidelity.

D.   Proof That The Right To Fidelity Has Been Excluded

The principal factors that would be pertinent to proving an intention against fidelity are the following: 1) Declarations of the Parties, 2) Affidavits, 3) Testimony of Witnesses, 4) Circumstantial Evidence, and 5) Motive.

1.   *Declarations of the Parties*

The value of the declarations of the petitioner and respondent in a marriage case is adequately summarized in the following canons:

C. 1535 - A judicial confession is a written or oral assertion against oneself made by any party regarding the matter under trial and made before a competent judge, whether spontaneously or upon interrogation by the judge.

C. 1536 §2 - In cases which concern the public good ... a judicial confession and the declarations of the parties which are not confessions can have a probative force to be evaluated by the judge along with the other circumstances of the case; but complete probative force cannot be attributed to them unless other elements are present which thoroughly corroborate them.

C. 1537 - Having weighed all the circumstances, it is for the judge to evaluate the worth of an extra-judicial confession which has been introduced into the trial.

C. 1538 - A confession or any other declaration of a party lacks all probative force if it is proved that it was made through an error of fact or it was extorted by force or grave fear.

2. *Affidavits*

Many courts obtain information from people by affidavit rather than by formal testimony. In general it may be said that affidavits are considered to have the same basic value as judicial declarations and testimony. But see also P, pp. 45 and 53.

3. *Testimony of Witnesses*

As regards the value of testimony of witnesses, the pertinent canons read:

C. 1572 - In evaluating testimony, after having obtained testimonial letters, if need be, the judge should consider:

1° the condition and good reputation of the person;
2° whether the witness testifies in virtue of personal knowledge, especially what has been seen and heard personally, or whether the testimony is the witness' opinion, or a rumor or hearsay from others;
3° whether the witness is reliable and firmly consistent or rather inconsistent, uncertain or vacillating;
4° whether the witness has supporting witnesses or whether there is support from other sources of proof.

C. 1573 - The deposition of a single witness cannot constitute full proof unless a witness acting in an official capacity makes a deposition regarding duties performed ex officio or unless circumstances of things and persons suggest otherwise.

For a brief but interesting law section on the use of one witness, see the decision of June 19, 1972 coram Pinto (64, 354-355).

4. *Circumstantial Evidence*

Some of the circumstances that might be especially relevant in a contra bonum fidei case would be the moral and religious character of the person, whether the person was with his or her lover shortly before and shortly after marriage, whether he or she might have entered a marriage for an unworthy motive such as money, whether he or she might have been pressured into marrying, and whether promiscuity was present before and after marriage.

On this latter point see the decision of 7/15/71 coram Pinto (63, 688-691). Should the promiscuity involve actual nymphomania or satyriasis (Don Juanism), then besides an intention contra bonum fidei, another possible ground would be lack of due competence.

5. *Motive*

In order to regard an intention against fidelity as proved, the judge must be aware of the motive for simulating. Motives for excluding fidelity would be an attachment to a former lover, an inability to abandon a life of indulgence and promiscuity, and an aversion to one's spouse.

It is also helpful to compare the motive for simulating with the motive for entering a true marriage. Where the motive for simulating is very strong and the other weak, simulation may be presumed (48, 409).

INTENTION AGAINST PERPETUITY

A. The Pertinent Canon

C. 1101 - CCEO, c. 824 - §1 - The internal consent of the mind is presumed to be in agreement with the words or signs employed in celebrating matrimony.

§2 - But if either or both parties, through a positive act of the will, should exclude... an essential property of marriage, it is invalidly contracted.

B. The Meaning Of Perpetuity

1. The perpetuity of marriage refers to its indissolubility. It has been called the "bonum sacramenti" because of that special perpetuity enjoyed by the consummated *sacramental* marriage. Nevertheless, it is a property of all marriages, even non sacramental ones, since perpetuity belongs to the very essence of marriage (cc. 1056, 1057 §2 and 1134).

2. Perpetuity and permanence are two different things. Something is permanent when it is lasting or non-temporary. It is perpetual when it is everlasting or non-terminable (c. 1096 §1).

3. Permanence is a divisible notion. One could, for example, enter a permanent, that is, lasting contract, say for twenty-five years, with an option to cancel after fifteen years. The option to cancel does not destroy the permanence of the contract since fifteen years would, in itself, be sufficiently stable and enduring to be regarded as permanent. Permanence, in other words, admits of degrees.

   Perpetuity, on the other hand, is an indivisible notion. It does not admit of degrees. A thing cannot be moderately perpetual or somewhat indissoluble. If it is even one degree less than perpetual it is not perpetual.

C. Excluding Perpetuity

1. Since perpetuity is an indivisible notion, one cannot hedge on indissolubility. One could intentionally hedge on children or fidelity and still keep one's intention extrinsic to and subordinate to the integral marriage covenant (where the rights to children, fidelity and perpetuity are exchanged). A man, for example, can, in entering marriage, recognize that henceforth he is bound to be faithful to his wife, and he can, at the same time, intend perhaps to cheat if the opportunity presents itself. Or a couple may truly exchange the right to children and, at the same time, intend not to have the maximum number of children that the woman can physically bear.

   But if one intentionally hedges on perpetuity or indissolubility, the intention is automatically drawn into the covenant itself. If one decides that one will enter something less than an indissoluble, perpetual marriage, that decision or intention stands in direct and diametric contradiction to the terms of the marriage covenant. One cannot simultaneously intend on the one hand to enter an indissoluble marriage and on the other hand to enter a marriage that can be dissolved. One intention must necessarily cancel out the other. The two cannot exist side by side. A man cannot simultaneously give his wife a perpetual right to himself on the one hand and a terminable right on the other. The two are incompatible.

This means that, in excluding perpetuity, the intention need not have a special intensity, as it must in excluding children or fidelity. Because any genuine intention against perpetuity necessarily involves an intrinsic limitation or distortion of the marriage covenant.

2. Generally the exclusion of perpetuity is phrased hypothetically, as in "I plan to remain married for life if the marriage turns out to be a happy one." Even a hypothetical intention, however, suffices to invalidate a marriage (34, 809; 48, 256).

3. Perpetuity, furthermore, need not be excluded explicitly in order to result in invalidity. An implicit exclusion suffices (56, 930-931). An implicit intention is not to be confused with a presumed intention (56, 756-757) but sometimes the circumstances are so unusual and compelling that the only reasonable conclusion that can be drawn from them is that indissolubility was excluded. Where, for example, a non Catholic man, already on record as believing in divorce, marries a woman he doesn't love in order to make another woman jealous, and then leaves his wife shortly after marriage, one may legitimately conclude that he excluded perpetuity from his marriage. Actions, after all, speak louder than words (facta sunt verbis validiora - 16, 50; 25, 61). See D2, 160-163.

4. Finally a word about the effect that error about indissolubility might have on the validity of marriage. When a person begins by believing that divorce may and even should be utilized when a marriage is unhappy, what effect does that have on his or her intentions in entering marriage? To what degree does the intellectual error influence the will?

    C. 1099 says that error about the indissolubility of marriage does not vitiate matrimonial consent so long as it does not determine the will. Which implies that it *does* vitiate matrimonial consent if it *does* determine the will. In a contra bonum sacramenti case, therefore, the beliefs of the alleged simulator and the intensity of those beliefs, should always be carefully investigated by the court. For more on this subject see pp. 110-118.

D. Proof That Perpetuity Has Been Excluded

The principal factors that would be pertinent to proving an intention against perpetuity are the following: 1) Declarations of the Parties, 2) Affidavits, 3) Testimony of Witnesses, 4) Circumstantial Evidence, and 5) Motive.

1. *Declarations of the Parties*

The value of the declarations of the petitioner and respondent in a marriage case is adequately summarized in the following canons:

C. 1535 - A judicial confession is a written or oral assertion against oneself made by a party regarding the matter under trial and made before a competent judge, whether spontaneously or upon interrogation by the judge.

C. 1536 §2 - In cases which concern the public good ... a judicial confession and the declarations of the parties which are not confessions can have a probative force to be evaluated by the judge along with the other circumstances of the case; but complete probative force cannot be attributed to them unless other elements are present which thoroughly corroborate them.

C. 1537 - Having weighed all the circumstances, it is for the judge to evaluate the worth of an extra-judicial confession which has been introduced into the trial.

C. 1538 - A confession or any other declaration of a party lacks all probative force if it is proved that it was made through an error of fact or it was extorted by force or grave fear.

2. *Affidavits*

Many courts obtain information from people by affidavit rather than by formal testimony. In general it may be said that affidavits are considered to have the same basic value as judicial declarations and testimony. But see also P, pp. 45 and 53.

3. *Testimony of Witnesses*

As regards the value of testimony of witnesses, the pertinent canons read:

C. 1572 - In evaluating testimony, after having obtained testimonial letters, if need be, the judge should consider:

1° the condition and good reputation of the person;
2° whether the witness testifies in virtue of personal knowledge, especially what has been seen and heard personally, or whether the testimony is the witness' opinion, or a rumor or hearsay from others;
3° whether the witness is reliable and firmly consistent or rather inconsistent, uncertain or vacillating;

4° whether the witness has supporting witnesses or whether there is support from other sources of proof.

C. 1573 - The deposition of a single witness cannot constitute full proof unless a witness acting in an official capacity makes a deposition regarding duties performed ex officio or unless circumstances of things and persons suggest otherwise.

For a brief but interesting law section on the use of one witness, see the decision of June 19, 1972 coram Pinto (64, 354-355).

4. *Circumstantial Evidence*

Some of the circumstances that might be especially relevant in a case involving an alleged exclusion of indissolubility would be the religious background of the person, one's age, the culture in which one was reared, lack of love for one's spouse, a short lived marriage and subsequent remarriage and divorce, and, of course, the presence of an intensely held erroneous concept regarding indissolubility.

5. *Motive*

Among the motives that might make simulating plausible would be such things as being in love with a person other than one's spouse, a premarital realization that the couple is incompatible, a love of independence, and a deep seated conviction about the propriety of divorce as a solution to an unhappy marriage.

INTENTION AGAINST THE GOOD OF THE SPOUSES

A. The Pertinent Canons

Can. 1101 - CCEO, c. 824 - §1. The internal consent of the mind is presumed to be in agreement with the words or signs employed in celebrating matrimony.

§2. But if either or both parties through a positive act of the will should exclude marriage itself, some essential element or an essential property of marriage, it is invalidly contracted.

Can. 1055 - CCEO, c. 776 - §1. The matrimonial covenant, by which a man and a woman establish between themselves a partnership of the whole of life, is by its nature ordered toward the good of the spouses and the procreation and education of offspring; this covenant between baptized persons has been raised by Christ the Lord to the dignity of a sacrament.

B. The Right To The Good Of The Spouses

1. The phrase "the good of the spouses" is perhaps best known in its Latin form: the bonum coniugum.

2. In Roman law marriage was defined as "a union of a man and a woman and a partnership of the whole of life, a participation in divine and human law." (Digesta 23, 2, 1), and also as "a union of a man and a woman, involving an undivided sharing of life" (Instituta, 1, 9, 1).

3. Thomas Aquinas made the point that marriage is essentially a joining together, which is why it is called a "coniugium", i.e. a conjugal union (Suppl.q. 44, a. 2, Sed in contrarium).

4. The Second Vatican Council's Pastoral Constitution, *Gaudium et spes,* promulgated in 1965, said, in number 48:

   > The intimate community of life and conjugal love, which has been established by the Creator and endowed by him with its own proper laws, is rooted in the covenant of its partners, that is, in their irrevocable personal consent. Therefore the institute of marriage, made firm by divine law, arises, even in the eyes of society, by that human act by which the spouses mutually hand over themselves and receive the other; once entered, however, for the sake of both the *bonum coniugum* and the *bonum prolis,* as well as of society itself, the sacred bond no longer depends on human decision alone.

5. In his 1968 encyclical *Humanae vitae* Pope Paul VI said "Married love particularly reveals its true nature and nobility when we realize that it takes its origin from God, who 'is love', the Father 'from whom every family in heaven

and on earth is named'. Marriage, then, is ... in reality the wise and provident institution of God the Creator, whose purpose was to effect in human beings His loving design. As a consequence, husband and wife, through that mutual gift of themselves, which is specific and exclusive to them alone, develop that union of two persons in which they perfect one another, cooperating with God in the generation and rearing of new lives." (n. 8).

6. In the 1981 Apostolic Exhortation, *Familiaris consortio,* Pope John Paul II said (in n. 11) that "sexuality, by means of which man and woman give themselves to one another through the acts which are proper and exclusive to spouses, is by no means something purely biological, but concerns the innermost being of the human person as such. It is realized in a truly human way only if it is an integral part of the love by which a man and a woman commit themselves totally to one another until death. ... The only 'place' in which this self-giving in its whole truth is made possible is marriage, the covenant of conjugal love freely and consciously chosen, whereby man and woman accept the intimate community of life and love willed by God Himself, which only in this light manifests its true meaning." And also (in n. 19): "This conjugal communion sinks its roots in the natural complementarity that exists between man and woman, and is nurtured through the personal willingness of the spouses to share their entire life-project, what they have and what they are: for this reason such communion is the fruit and the sign of a profoundly human need."

7. Reflecting on such truths, Rotal jurisprudence has, in recent years, offered its own juridical observations:

    a. Anné, for example, in his decision of February 25, 1969 (61, 183-184 and D1, 99-100) said "It is true that in marriage 'in facto esse' the communion of life can be absent, but *the right to the communion of life* can never he absent ... the formal substantial object of this consent is not only the right to the body which is perpetual and exclusive for acts apt in themselves for the generation of children, excluding every other formal essential element, but it embraces also the right to the communion of life, i.e., the living together which is properly called matrimonial, and also the related obligations, i.e., the right to the intimate partnership of persons and of acts by which 'they perfect each other, so that they may cooperate with God in the generation and rearing of new lives.' (*Humanae vitae)."*

    b. In a widely quoted phrase from an April 11, 1988 decision, Pompedda said that "the bonum coniugum is understood and brought about by the right (and correlative obligation) to a communion of life understood in its broader meaning" (80, 202).

    c. Jarawan, in his decision of March 10, 1989 (81, 194-195) says that "without the acceptance of the obligations stemming from the bonum coniugum 'the intimate joining of persons and forces by which the spouses mutually extend to each other help and service is at least morally impossible' and 'the communion of life, i.e., the consortium of conjugal life in which marriage essentially consists is impossible'. "(quotations are from an unpublished decision by Pinto dated May 30, 1986).

d. Stankiewicz, in his decision of April 20, 1989 (81, 282-283) said, "The essential obligations of marriage, which the contractants must be capable of assuming at the time of the celebration of the marriage, take their canonical relevance from the essential object of consent, specifically from the essential goods of marriage as recognized by the jurisprudence of this tribunal.

"Within that general category there are *some* obligations which are contained in the three traditional goods of marriage, namely the obligation of observing conjugal fidelity (the bonum fidei), the obligation of observing the perpetuity of the conjugal partnership (the bonum sacramenti) and the obligation of accepting the conception of offspring brought about through acts performed in a natural way with the other spouse, and of rearing and educating those children once born (the bonum prolis); there are, however, certain *other* obligations stemming from the bonum coniugum, to which the conjugal partnership is , by its nature, ordered (can 1055 §1)."

e. Finally, the same jurist, Stankiewicz, in his decision of June 21, 1990 (82, 525) spoke of "the essential obligations inhering in the bonum coniugum which contribute in a substantial way to the establishment and perpetual maintenance of the communion of conjugal love of the spouses through mutual psycho-sexual integration."

8. For an argument in favor of the position that the essence of the bonum coniugum consists in the "ius ad amorem", i.e., the right that the other party not exclude from the covenant his or her obligation to be a loving spouse, see the 1986 article entitled "Refining the Essence of Marriage", included as Appendix three of this book. See also LS, pp. 26-27.

C. Excluding The Right To The Bonum Coniugum

1. The bonum coniugum, or good of the spouses, which all would agree has to do with the interpersonal relationship of husband and wife, has had its principal jurisprudential relevance in terms of c. 1095. The usual question raised regarding the bonum coniugum, in other words, has been whether a given person has or has not enjoyed either due discretion or due competence relative to the essential obligations stemming from the bonum coniugum.

The bonum coniugum can also be relevant, however, in terms of c. 1101. It is, in other words, possible for a person to exclude, by a positive act of the will, the essential rights and obligations of marriage stemming from the bonum coniugum, especially, as Anné would put it, "the right to the intimate partnership of persons" which is an essential part of the formal substantial element of marital consent (B 7a above). See *La Giurisprudenza dei Tribunali Ecclesiastici Italiani*, Vatican, 1989, pp. 283-294.

2.   The classic example of this is the case posed by Jemolo in 1941 about the man who married a woman so that he could be mean and cruel to her and make her pay for all the injuries committed by her family against him and his family. Clearly that man had excluded the bonum coniugum from his marriage.

While the Jemolo case may seem exceptional, it is an unfortunate and not uncommon fact that, when some men and women marry, they intend only to use and abuse their spouses and to take from them their money and services but to exclude any obligation on their own part to be loving, caring spouses. Such people are excluding the bonum coniugum, which is an essential element of the marriage covenant.

3.   Given the fact that marriage is essentially a relationship, a "partnership of the whole of life" (c. 1055 §1), it might seem that to exclude the relationship would be to exclude the marriage itself, and would therefore amount to total simulation. From an *ontological* point of view this is certainly true: to exclude the bonum coniugum is to exclude marriage itself. The same is true, however, of the bonum prolis, the bonum fidei, the bonum sacramenti and sacramental dignity. From an ontological point of view to exclude any of them is to exclude marriage, and would therefore amount to total simulation. From a *psychological* point of view, however, a person may intend to marry i.e., to enter some basic sort of partnership (and therefore not simulate totally) but also intend to exclude some essential element or an essential property of marriage (and so simulate partially). In this sense, which is the usual way of looking at simulation, when a person excludes the bonum coniugum, the proper ground is partial simulation rather than total simulation. See *Periodica*, 1978, p. 286, and the chapter in this book entitled "Total Simulation" under B 5 on p. 121.

4.   The positive act of the will by which the bonum coniugum is excluded can, as in other cases of simulation, be expressed implicitly, i.e. either by words which express the exclusion only indirectly or by actions that can have no other meaning but that an intention against the bonum coniugum was present motivating them. A man, for example, who, from the moment of marriage, did nothing but insult, curse, beat and treat as a slave his wife, without ever showing her the slightest affection or esteem, can be said to have excluded the bonum coniugum implicitly.

D. Proof That The Right To The Bonum Coniugum Has Been Excluded

The principal factors that would be pertinent to proving an intention contra bonum coniugum are the following: 1) Declarations of the Parties, 2) Affidavits, 3) Testimony of Witnesses, 4) Circumstantial Evidence, and 5) Motive.

1. *Declarations of the Parties*

The value of the declarations of the petitioner and respondent in a marriage case is adequately summarized in the following canons:

C. 1535 - A judicial confession is a written or oral assertion against oneself made by any party regarding the matter under trial and made before a competent judge, whether spontaneously or upon interrogation by the judge.

C. 1536 §2 - In cases which concern the public good ... a judicial confession and the declarations of the parties which are not confessions can have a probative force to be evaluated by the judge along with the other circumstances of the case; but complete probative force cannot be attributed to them unless other elements are present which thoroughly corroborate them.

C. 1537 - Having weighed all the circumstances, it is for the judge to evaluate the worth of an extra-judicial confession which has been introduced into the trial.

C. 1538 - A confession or any other declaration of a party lacks all probative force if it is proved that it was made through an error of fact or it was extorted by force or grave fear.

2. *Affidavits*

Many courts obtain information from people by affidavit rather than by formal testimony. It is perhaps true that well taken testimony is often a bit more thorough than an affidavit received from the same person. But it is also true that, given the time involved, a court tends to limit the number of testimonies taken, whereas, because of the ease with which they can be obtained, the number of affidavits are never or almost never restricted. In practice, therefore, a court, generally speaking, obtains more information through affidavits than it does through testimonies.

William Doheny, in his book *Canonical Procedure in Matrimonial Cases* (Vol. I, p. 400) says the following regarding the probative force of an affidavit:

In English-speaking countries affidavits are frequently resorted to as a means of documentary proof or evidence. These affidavits are written declarations or statements confirmed by oath or solemn affirmation. Since they are oftentimes presented in marriage cases, judges and other officers of the court should be warned not to ascribe to them more probative force than they purport to carry. An affidavit merely certifies that a specific person made a solemn affirmation confirmed by oath before a duly qualified notary public at a certain time. Obviously, such a statement, in itself, even though under oath does not constitute full proof in matrimonial cases. The inherent truth of the statement and the facts attested must be further investigated.

3. *Testimony of Witnesses*

As regards the value of testimony by witnesses, the pertinent canons read:

C. 1572 - In evaluating testimony, after having obtained testimonial letters, if need be, the judge should consider:

1°   the condition and good reputation of the person;
2°   whether the witness testifies in virtue of personal knowledge, especially what has been seen and heard personally, or whether the testimony is the witness' opinion, or a rumor or hearsay from others;
3°   whether the witness is reliable and firmly consistent or rather inconsistent, uncertain or vacillating;
4°   whether the witness has supporting witnesses or whether there is support from other sources of proof.

C. 1573 - The deposition of a single witness cannot constitute full proof unless a witness acting in an official capacity makes a deposition regarding duties performed ex officio or unless circumstances of things and persons suggest otherwise.

For a brief but interesting law section on the use of one witness, see the decision of June 19, 1972 coram Pinto (64, 354-355).

4. *Circumstantial Evidence*

Some of the circumstances that might be especially relevant in a contra bonum coniugum case would be the family background of the person, a background characterized by abuse, disrespect, selfishness and lack of affection; the personality of the alleged simulator, a personality characterized by a tendency to use people, self centeredness and a sense of entitlement; and the behavior of the person, especially after marriage, behavior characterized by the ignoring of the other spouse's needs and interests as though the other spouse were not important.

5. *Motive*

In order to regard an intention against the bonum coniugum as proved the judge must be aware of a reasonable, proportionate, adequate motive for simulating. Motives for excluding the bonum coniugum might be revenge (as in the Jemolo case), aversion to one's spouse, aversion to the opposite sex, or even the malice of the simulator.

It is also helpful to compare the motive for simulating with the motive for entering a true marriage. Where the motive for simulating is very strong and the other weak, simulation may be presumed (48, 409).

INTENTION AGAINST SACRAMENTALITY

A. The Pertinent Canons

C. 1101 - CCEO, c. 824 - §1. The internal consent of the mind is presumed to be in agreement with the words or signs employed in celebrating matrimony.

§2. But if either or both parties through a positive act of the will should exclude marriage itself, some essential element or an essential property of marriage, it is invalidly contracted.

C. 1055 - §1. The matrimonial covenant, by which a man and a woman establish between themselves a partnership of the whole of life, is by its nature ordered toward the good of the spouses and the procreation and education of offspring; this covenant between baptized persons has been raised by Christ the Lord to the dignity of a sacrament.

§2. For this reason a matrimonial contract cannot validly exist between baptized persons unless it is also a sacrament by that fact.

CCEO, c. 776 §2 - From the institution of Christ a valid marriage between baptized persons is by that very fact a sacrament, by which the spouses, in the image of an indefectible union of Christ with the Church, are united by God and, as it were, consecrated and strengthened by sacramental grace.

B. Total Simulation Or Partial Simulation?

1.	Regarding the exclusion of sacramental dignity, a tribunal may encounter two somewhat different situations. The *first* involves a person who, though baptized Catholic, had abandoned the faith by the time of his or her wedding but had a church wedding in order to please the family or for some other "profane" or social reason. The *second* involves a Protestant who marries before a priest, minister or civil official but who, in accord with the teaching of his or her own Church, does not recognize marriage as a sacrament. In either case the claim is made that the marriage is invalid on the ground that the person's lack of faith in the sacramentality of marriage carried with it an exclusion of sacramental dignity.

2.	For most of this century it was understood that an allegation of this sort could be heard only on the ground of *total* simulation. Gasparri (nn. 827 and 907), for example, said that in those circumstances the marriage would only be invalid if the person said, in effect, "I contract with you but I do not wish the sacrament, and if the sacrament were to come about, then I do not want marriage". For a recent defense of this position see Cormac Burke, *Monitor Ecclesiasticus*, 1994, IV, pp. 545-565.

3.   Especially since Zenon Grocholewski's 1978 article on the subject (*Periodica*, 1978, 283-295), however, it has come to be generally accepted that a case of this sort could be heard instead on the ground of *partial* simulation. Grocholewski argued that "it is a contradiction to affirm that a valid marriage between baptized people cannot exist without it being a sacrament, and then at the same time to say that a positive exclusion of sacramentality does not vitiate consent", and he further argued that "within the context of sacramental theology it is hard to admit that a person receives and adminsters a sacrament which, by a positive act of the will, he or she rejects." (p. 293)

According to this position it is not necessary, in order to prove invalidity, that a person positively reject the marriage itself rather than allow the sacrament to come into being; it is only required that a person positively exclude the sacrament, much as he or she might exclude the bonum prolis or fidei or sacramenti.

While this is not a new position (see, for example Schmalzgrueber, 4, 1, 1, 301-304) it is a position that was dormant for many years and has only recently been revived.

C. Partial Simulation Or Error Of Law?

1.   Once it became generally accepted that it was not necessary to prove total simulation in cases of this sort, then it gradually became clear that partial simulation was not the only alternative ground but that error of law might also be a possible ground where a person had rejected or abandoned the faith (and was thus in error about marriage being a sacrament).

2.   Some canonists favor such cases being heard on the ground of *partial simulation.*

It bears noting that, while the canon on simulation (c. 1101 §2) does not mention sacramentality or sacramental dignity specifically (see *Congregatio Plenaria*, pp. 452-460), it does mention it generically. The canon says that if a party should, by a positive act of the will, exclude "some essential element or an essential property of marriage" the marriage is invalid, and almost all authors agree that, for the baptized, sacramentality is either an essential element or an essential property (or the equivalent of same). See the chapter on Total Simulation under B 1 d on pp. 119-120.

Giuseppe Versaldi, a proponent of this position, says "Only if error carries with it a positive and formal act by which a person excludes sacramentality, i.e., only if simulation of consent is present, can the marriage be considered invalid". (*Periodica*, 1990, III-IV, p. 436).

3.   Other canonists favor *error of law* as the appropriate ground.

While the canon on simulation does not specifically mention sacramental dignity, the canon on error of law (c. 1099) does. The canon says that "error concerning the unity, indissolubility, *or sacramental dignity* of matrimony does not vitiate matrimonial consent so long as it does not determine the will", implying that error about sacramental dignity that *does* determine the will is invalidating. In accord with this canon and with all that has been said about determining error in the chapter of this book entitled "Determining Error (Error of Law)", some canonists would see intensely intransigent error about sacramentality as being, "by the power and working of the error itself", (56, 927), invalidating whenever it determines the will.

Mario Pompedda, the present Dean of the Rota and a proponent of this position, wrote that "a lack of faith, viewed juridically, can and indeed ought to be considered according to the category of 'error pervading the person', i.e. of error which, according to the terminology and positive norm of the Code of Canon Law, is such that it determines the will " (*Quaderni Studio Rotale*, 2 (1987), p. 56 and *Marriage Studies IV*, p. 51).

D. The Baptized Unbeliever As Recipient And Minister Of The Sacrament

1.   When two baptized people validly marry, they receive the sacrament of matrimony. As *recipients* of the sacrament it is only required, provided that they do not expressly exclude sacramentality, that they give marital consent; for by the very fact that they intend the matrimonial contract they also implicitly intend the sacrament. See c. 1055 §2 and Noldin-Schmidt, III, pp. 514-515.

Besides being the recipients, however, the baptized are also the *ministers* of the sacrament (see, for example, Pius XII's allocution to newlyweds of March 5, 1941 in *Papal Teachings, Matrimony*, pp. 320-321). Since, however, canon 11 of the Seventh Session of the Council of Trent said, "If anyone says that in ministers, when they effect and confer the sacraments, there is not required at least the intention of doing what the Church does, let him be anathema", it follows that when the baptized marry they must intend to do what the Church does.

2.   This gives rise to certain questions regarding a) Protestants who are aware that, according to the teachings of their own Church, marriage is not regarded as a sacrament, and b) baptized Catholic unbelievers who perhaps

left the Church with some animosity or had come to view the Catholic teaching on the sacraments as mere superstition, but who marry in Church for social reasons. Might these people (Protestants and baptized Catholic unbelievers alike), as prospective *recipients* of the sacrament, be prompted by their lack of faith in the sacramentality of marriage (which might be viewed as intransigent error) to exclude sacramental dignity? And perhaps more importantly, as *ministers* of the sacrament, would their lack of faith in the sacramentality of marriage, especially perhaps if they had actually become atheists or were antagonistic to the Church, be likely to dissuade them from intending to do what the Church does when they marry?

While it is axiomatic that "in order to contract a valid marriage faith is not necessary but only consent" (74, 247; 80, 89 and 83, 281) it must also be pointed out that the axiom alone does not provide an adequate answer to these vexing questions. More illuminating by far, and certainly more nuanced, are the following two quotations. Both are somewhat lengthy but are included here because of their critical importance. The first is from the *Propositions on the Doctrine of Christian Marriage,* issued in 1977 by the International Theological Commission (a consultative body to the Congregation for the Doctrine of the Faith); the second from *Familiaris Consortio,* the 1981 Apostolic Exhortation of Pope John Paul II.

Number 2.3 of the *Propositions* reads as follows:

> Just like the other sacraments, matrimony confers grace in the final analysis by virtue of the action performed by Christ and not only through the faith of the one receiving it. That, however, does not mean that grace is conferred in the sacrament of matrimony outside of faith or in the absence of faith. It follows from this - according to classical principles - that faith is presupposed as a "disposing cause" for receiving the fruitful effect of the sacrament. The validity of marriage, however, does not imply that this effect is necessarily fruitful.
>
> The existence today of "baptized nonbelievers" raises a new theological problem and a grave pastoral dilemma especially when the lack of, or rather the rejection of the faith, seems clear. The intention of carrying out what Christ and the church desire is the minimum condition required before consent is considered to be a "real human act" on the sacramental plane. The problem of the intention and that of the personal faith of the contracting parties must not be confused, but they must not be totally separated either.
>
> In the last analysis the real intention is born from and feeds on living faith. Where there is no trace of faith (in the sense of "belief" - being disposed to believe), and no desire for grace or salvation is found, then a real doubt arises as to whether there is the above-mentioned general and truly sacramental intention and whether the contracted marriage is validly contracted or not. As was noted, the personal faith of the contracting parties does not constitute the sacramentality of matrimony,

but the absence of personal faith compromises the validity of the sacrament.

This gives rise to new problems for which a satisfactory answer has yet to be found and it imposes new pastoral responsibilities regarding Christian matrimony. "Priests should first of all strengthen and nourish the faith of those about to be married, for the sacrament of matrimony presupposes and demands faith." (*Ordo Celebrandi Matrimonium, Praenotanda,* n. 7).

Number 68 of *Familiaris Consortio* says:

Precisely because in the celebration of the sacrament very special attention must be devoted to the moral and spiritual dispositions of those being married, in particular to their faith, we must here deal with a not infrequent difficulty in which the pastors of the Church can find themselves in the context of our secularized society.

In fact, the faith of the person asking the Church for marriage can exist in different degrees, and it is the primary duty of pastors to bring about a rediscovery of this faith and to nourish it and bring it to maturity. But pastors must also understand the reasons that lead the Church also to admit to the celebration of marriage those who are imperfectly disposed.

The sacrament of Matrimony has this specific element that distinguishes it from all the other sacraments: it is the sacrament of something that was part of the very economy of creation; it is the very conjugal covenant instituted by the Creator "in the beginning." Therefore the decision of a man and a woman to marry in accordance with this divine plan, that is to say, the decision to commit by their irrevocable conjugal consent their whole lives in indissoluble love and unconditional fidelity, really involves, even if not in a fully conscious way, an attitude of profound obedience to the will of God, an attitude which cannot exist without God's grace. They have thus already begun what is in a true and proper sense a journey towards salvation, a journey which the celebration of the sacrament and the immediate preparation for it can complement and bring to completion, given the uprightness of their intention.

On the other hand it is true that in some places engaged couples ask to be married in church for motives which are social rather than genuinely religious. This is not surprising. Marriage, in fact, is not an event that concerns only the persons actually getting married. By its very nature it is also a social matter, committing the couple being married in the eyes of society. And its celebration has always been an occasion of rejoicing that brings together families and friends. It therefore goes without saying that social as well as personal motives enter into the request to be married in church.

Nevertheless, it must not be forgotten that these engaged couples, by virtue of their Baptism, are already really sharers in Christ's marriage Covenant with the Church, and that, by their right intention, they have accepted God's plan regarding marriage and therefore at least implicitly consent to what the Church intends to do when she celebrates marriage. Thus, the fact that motives of a social nature also enter into the request is not enough to justify refusal on the part of pastors. Moreover, as the Second Vatican Council teaches, the sacraments by words and ritual elements nourish and strengthen faith: that faith towards which the married couple are already journeying by reason of the uprightness of their intention, which Christ's grace certainly does not fail to favor and support.

As for wishing to lay down further criteria for admission to the ecclesial celebration of marriage, criteria that would concern the level of faith of those to be married, this would above all involve grave risks. In the first place, the risk of making unfounded and discriminatory judgments; secondly, the risk of causing doubts about the validity of marriages already celebrated, with grave harm to Christian communities, and new and unjustified anxieties to the consciences of married couples; one would also fall into the danger of calling into question the sacramental nature of many marriages of brethren separated from full communion with the Catholic Church, thus contradicting ecclesial tradition.

However, when in spite of all efforts, engaged couples show that they reject explicitly and formally what the Church intends to do when the marriage of baptized persons is celebrated, the pastor of souls cannot admit them to the celebration of marriage. In spite of his reluctance to do so, he has the duty to take note of the situation and to make it clear to those concerned that, in these circumstances, it is not the Church that is placing an obstacle in the way of the celebration that they are asking for, but themselves.

Once more there appears in all its urgency the need for evangelization and catechesis before and after marriage, effected by the whole Christian community, so that every man and woman that gets married celebrates the sacrament of Matrimony not only validly but also fruitfully.

Deserving perhaps of special mention in these two quotations are the following statements: that "where there is no trace (vestigium) of faith ... then a real doubt arises as to whether ... the ... marriage is validly contracted or not" (from the *Propositions*), and that "when in spite of all efforts, engaged couples show that they reject explicitly and formally what the Church intends to do when the marriage of baptized persons is celebrated, the pastor of souls cannot admit them to the celebration of marriage" (from *Familiaris Consortio*).

One might, it seems, legitimately conclude from all this that when baptized unbelievers lack even a vestige or trace of faith, to the point where they clearly do not intend to do what the Church does in celebrating marriage, then the marriage should not be performed in Church because it would be invalid. Pompedda, indeed, has concluded that "a trace of faith (una traccia di fede) is necessary not just for the fruitful reception of the sacrament but for the validity of its reception." (*Quaderni Studio Rotale 2* (1987) p. 62 and *Marriage Studies IV*, p. 60). See also LS, pp. 42-44.

E. Proof Of An Intention Against Sacramentality

"If the juridic category under which the cases of baptized unbelievers who marry with a religious rite is simulation, then in the canonical process of a declaration of nullity of those marriages proof should be required according to the traditional triple way, i.e., through the confession of the simulator, a proportionate cause of simulation and antecedent, concomitant and subsequent circumstances.

"This requirement, in my judgement, is especially appropriate in these times when the so called divorce mentality or culture is widespread even among Christians: for many baptized people whose faith is weak and rarely observed do not wish to exclude a religious rite when they marry, but then, after living with their spouse for a time, they can desire, either because of real problems or because they failed to utilize the natural and supernatural means at their disposal, to break the marriage bond, and often indeed do break it by a civil action. Then, when they wish to enter a second marriage, they once more do not intend to exclude a religious rite and they attempt to obtain a declaration of nullity of their previous marriage on the ground of an exclusion of sacramentality from the conjugal covenant, claiming that the celebration of the sacrament had no religious meaning for them at all but only a profane meaning.

"In these cases a strictness in requiring the three elements of proof of partial simulation is, in my judgment, the only way that true cases of the exclusion of sacramental dignity can be distinguished from false cases, and abuses against the truth and against the true good of souls can be avoided. For if the marriages of baptized unbelievers are declared invalid with excessive ease, then the faith of those Christians is in no way strengthened and the credibility of the Church is indeed diminished since it would appear that a juridic process were being used to dissolve the marriage bond. But if the exclusion of sacramentality is proved in the proper manner, i.e., by way of partial simulation, then a declaration of nullity should certainly and promptly be pronounced on this autonomous ground but with certain safeguards being required regarding the simulator should he or she request a new sacramental celebration" (from the article by Versaldi in *Periodica*, 1990, pp. 438-439).

CONDITIONS

A. The Pertinent Canon

C. 1102 §1 - Marriage based on a condition concerning the future cannot (nequit) be contracted validly.

§2 - Marriage based on a condition concerning the past or the present is valid or invalid, insofar as the subject matter of the condition exists or not.

§3 - The condition mentioned in §2 cannot be placed licitly without the written permission of the local ordinary.

CCEO, c. 826 - Marriage based on a condition cannot (non potest) be validly celebrated.

B. Description Of A Condition

A condition, as the term is used here, is a circumstance attached to the marriage on which the validity of the marriage depends. In the *strict* sense it refers to a future circumstance which suspends the validity of marriage. In the *broad* sense is refers to any circumstance, past, present or future, which immediately renders the marriage either valid or invalid.

The 1917 Code (c. 1092, 3°) recognized a future condition as a condition in the *strict* sense, i.e. as suspensive of validity. The 1983 Code (c. 1102, §1) sees a future condition as a condition in the *broad* sense, i.e. as immediately invalidating.

Therefore, prior to November 27, 1983 (the effective date of the 1983 Code) a future condition only invalidated the marriage if the condition was unfulfilled. After that date, a future condition invalidates a marriage immediately, even if the condition is later fulfilled.

C. Conditioning A Marriage

Popularly one thinks of a condition as something highly explicit, as phrased, for example, by "I marry you on the condition that you come into your inheritance within the first year of marriage." In fact a condition can be far more subtle than that. In investigating a possible condition a court should keep the following points in mind:

1. *A condition may be placed implicitly.*

Etymologically an implicit intention is one which is contained "in plico," i.e.

in the folds of something else. In practice it refers to two different situations. The *first* is where the intention is expressed in words but only indirectly, as when a part is expressed in the whole, an effect in its cause, a species in its genus. When a man, for example, explicitly states that he will never cohabit with a woman, he implicitly simulates marriage. The *second* type of implicit intention is where the intention is expressed not in words but in actions, actions which can have no other meaning but that a certain intention was present motivating them. A man, for example, who says nothing but disappears immediately after the wedding ceremony never to be heard from again may be said to have excluded cohabitation implicitly (56, 929-931).

A condition, at any rate, need not be stated explicitly in order to invalidate marriage. An implicit condition suffices (49, 421).

2. *It is not required that a person placing a condition do so because of some doubt. Nor is a doubt required in order to prove a condition.*

Ordinarily, perhaps, it would not occur to a person to place a condition unless there were some suspicion about an important quality being missing. One would not usually say, for example, "I marry you only on the condition you are heterosexual" unless there was some doubt about the person's heterosexuality.

On the other hand, where a quality is extremely important to a person, he or she might want the validity of marriage to depend on that quality even without there being any real doubt about the existence of the quality. The Rota, for example, heard a case where the allegation was that the Catholic woman had married on the condition that the Calvinist man convert to Catholicism. Prior to the marriage the man promised her that he would become a Catholic, and she never doubted it. In fact the man never did convert. The Rotal judge, Monsignor Felici, judged that even without the doubt, the woman was such a good Catholic and having a Catholic husband was so important to her that the condition should be considered proved (48, 756).

While Stankiewicz, in his decision of January 30, 1992 (LS, p. 78), says that a doubt is, in fact, always required for the placing of a condition, he also says that "a neurotic obsession carries with it an impulse to doubt ... which, it seems, can provide a sufficient cause for attaching a condition". It would seem, therefore, that if, in the case judged by Felici, the conversion of the Calvinist man was *so* important to the Catholic woman that it could be considered obsessive, Stankiewicz too would consider that sufficient to precipitate a condition.

3. *A person may place a condition without realizing that it results in the invalidity of the marriage.*

On this point Monsignor Pinto said, in a decision of June 26, 1971 (63, 560):

> Jurisprudence, even Rotal jurisprudence, has sometimes held that a true condition can only be placed by a person who is aware of its invalidating effect. But this is not true. People are generally unaware of such legalities and in no way realize that entering marriage conditionally results in invalidity. All they know is that on occasion a particular circumstance is so important to them that they rate it higher than marriage itself and that, if they can't have the circumstance or quality, they don't want the marriage either. Now everybody agrees that that sort of mentality or intention conditions marital consent. And consequently Rotal jurisprudence, especially as it has evolved in recent years, holds that a true condition can coexist with ignorance of its invalidating effect as long as it is clear that the person would not have consented to marry unless the quality had been present.

4. *The value system both of society and of the individual is regarded as highly significant in determining the presence of a condition.*

In general jurisprudence has always recognized that, in order for a circumstance to be appropriate matter for a true condition, it ought to have a certain objective importance and it ought to be something that would play a significant part in the future life of the couple. Such circumstances would be, for example, the absence of venereal disease or of epilepsy or of sexual perversion.

Where, on the other hand, the circumstance is of only minor importance and would only indirectly affect conjugal life, such as a man's job or religion or social status, the presumption would be that a true condition is not present.

Our jurisprudence, though, has recognized too that sometimes the subjective estimate of a circumstance is not the same as the objective estimate. It may happen, for example, that a particular person regards his or her spouse's religion as extremely important. Wherever it is verified, therefore, that the circumstance is, in fact, of great importance to this particular contractant, then a true condition may well be present (40, 304; 49, 431; 50, 73).

5. *In a future condition (for marriages prior to 11/27/83) it suffices if the circumstance will occur moderately soon and if it is moderately specific.*

As regards the fulfillment date of a condition, it should be pointed out that, on the one hand, a person cannot suspend the validity of the marriage indefinitely or forever (31, 416-417), and , on the other hand, the circumstance need not occur so soon as to eliminate, for all practical purposes, most contingencies that might be of concern to a person entering marriage (48, 741). It would be reasonable to expect that a "few years" time might be the outside limit for the fulfillment or non fulfillment of a condition.

As regards the degree of specificity required, a circumstance on the one hand need not be ridiculously specific (I marry you if you inherit $10,956.23), and on the other hand should be something more than a vague generalization (I marry you if something really good happens). But the circumstance should have a moderate, measurable, verifiable, realistic specificity (I marry you if you receive a substantial inheritance within the next few years).

It is clear from all this that the conditioning of a marriage can be very subtle indeed. It can be done implicitly, i.e. stated indirectly or only conveyed by actions. A condition may be placed simply because a person regards a particular circumstance as extremely important. It does not have to occur to the contractant that the validity of the marriage is at stake, and the circumstance itself can be something that is only fairly precise and which may be verified within a few years' time.

Even though a condition may be subtle, however, it must, in order to be a true condition, fulfill the basic requirements of a genuine condition.

D. The Core Of A Condition

Put in its simplest terms a marriage is conditioned when people know that "a particular circumstance is so important to them that they rate it higher than marriage itself, and if they can't have the circumstance or quality, they don't want the marriage either" (Pinto decision of 6/26/71 quoted above). When, in other words, the marriage is subordinated to the quality in a "nexus subordinationis" (51, 117 coram Lefebvre) or when the circumstance prevails over the marital consent (42, 150 and 51, 631 coram Mattioli; 43, 569 coram Felici), then a true conditioning of the marriage exists.

E. Allied But Distinct Situations

There are four situations which in some ways resemble a condition but which do not invade the covenant and which leave marriage absolute. They are:

1. *Mode* - an obligation attached to the covenant by which one party makes some postnuptial demand on the other, e.g. "I marry you but afterwards you must stop drinking."

2. *Demonstration* - the expression of some quality which is taken for granted in one's spouse, e.g. "I marry you who are a virgin."

3. *Cause* - the reason or motive for the marriage, e.g. "I marry you because you will become a Catholic."

4. *Postulate* - otherwise called a prerequisite or presupposition.

   a. The postulate has often been confused with the *cause* but is, in fact, quite different. A cause remains in the intellect as the reason for the marriage whereas a postulate is in the will and is a true condition which refers primarily to the initial decision to marry. As, for example, when a man says "I take you as my fiancée on the condition that you are a practicing Catholic."

b.   The postulate has also been likened to a *prematrimonial condition* which does not influence the marriage itself. Some people have said, in other words, that the postulate is more a condition attached to the engagement than a condition attached to the marriage. Once the man, for example, is convinced that his intended is a practicing Catholic and takes her as his fiancée, then that is the end of the effectiveness of the prenuptial condition. It may not be presumed, they say, that the man further desires the validity of the marriage to depend on that past condition. For that, a new will act would have to be made. Perhaps it could be said that the engagement was invalid but it certainly would not follow that therefore the marriage was also invalid. Presumably the marriage was entered absolutely.

This, too, however, does not adequately express the true influence of the postulate.

c.   In point of fact the postulate is more correctly regarded as the *initial step* towards a matrimonial condition. In the real world, in other words, if a man becomes engaged to a woman only on the condition that she is a practicing Catholic, then more than likely, particularly if the prematrimonial condition was placed with considerable intensity, the postulate does influence, perhaps indirectly and secondarily, but nevertheless does influence the marriage itself (49, 420).

F.   A Personalist Condition

Everyone realizes that a great many people today enter marriage primarily for personal fulfillment. Personal fulfillment, it would seem, would enjoy a sufficient degree of specificity to qualify as a circumstance that might condition a marriage. It is, at least in many instances, measurable and verifiable. If, for example, it turns out, after a year or so of marriage, that a couple is hardly communicating at all except to argue, it can be reasonably concluded that personal fulfillment is lacking.

If, therefore, it can be shown in a specific instance that a party attached prevailing importance to personal fulfillment and subordinated marriage to it, that if personal fulfillment wasn't being realized within a few years after marriage the person didn't want the marriage either, such a marriage: 1) if it took place *before* 11/27/83 and the condition was unfulfilled, can be declared invalid by reason of c. 1092, 3°, 2) if it took place *after* 11/27/83, even if the condition was fulfilled, can be declared invalid by reason of c. 1102 §1.

159

G. Proof Of A Condition

In proving a condition the important factors to be considered are: 1) Declarations of the Parties, 2) Affidavits and Testimony of Witnesses, 3) Circumstantial Evidence, 4) Motive.

1. *Declarations of the Parties*

   The canons regarding the declarations of the parties as quoted in the four chapters on simulation are pertinent here. Also, although the exact words used by the contractant are important, nevertheless, since the word "condition" is so ambiguous (35, 793), and since, in general, actions speak louder than words (facta sunt verbis validiora - 16, 50; 26, 61) it is even more important to understand the total context and especially the mentality or mind set of the contractant (48, 742-743).

2. *Affidavits and Testimony of Witnesses*

   Here again the relevant canons can be found in any of the simulation chapters. It should be noted particularly, however, that if the witnesses relate the words of the contractant more forcefully than the conditioner himself or herself, then the testimony of the witnesses must be regarded as exaggerated, according to the axiom that there cannot be more water in the rivers than there is at the source (non potest plus esse in rivis quam in fonte - 18, 233).

3. *Circumstantial Evidence*

   Circumstances that might be important in proving a condition are whether the quality is objectively or only subjectively and perhaps idiosyncratically grave, the seriousness or solemnity used in expressing the condition, whether it was expressed only once or repeatedly, and whether there was an attempt to impose it on the other party (34, 819). The quickness of terminating the marriage and seeking an annulment once it is realized that the condition has not been fulfilled might also be important, but it should be realized too that some conditions are fulfilled only gradually and equivocally and sometimes involve injuring the reputation of the other party, and in such a case a delay is more than understandable (50, 74).

4. *Motive*

   The motive for conditioning a marriage is usually found in the extreme importance attached to the circumstance by the conditioner.

H. Relationship Between Condition And Error Of Quality (c. 1097 §2)

C. 1097 §2 says that when an error concerning a quality of a person is "directly and principally intended" the marriage is invalid. This is in no way different from a condition. The core of a condition, as noted above under D, consists in the marriage itself being subordinated to a quality in a "nexus subordinationis." A woman, for example, marries a man, erroneously thinking that he is a Catholic. If her *principal* intention is to marry a Catholic (and her "less principal" or *subordinate* intention is marriage) then the marriage is invalid. *From a logical or theoretical point of view* , therefore, the proper ground on which to hear such cases is not error but condition. Nevertheless, *from a systematic or structural point of view,* since the Code of Canon Law treats error of quality among the defects of the intellect (cc. 1095-1100) rather than among the defects of the will (cc. 1101-1103), such cases may be heard on the ground of error.

I. Relationship Between Condition And Imposed Error (c. 1098)

These two institutes are very closely allied (33, 529-530). When, for example, a man marries an alcoholic woman he may allege either that he was deceived or that he had placed a condition against marrying such a woman.

Circumstances, however, may suggest one or the other to be the preferable approach. For example, when deceit is high (the woman has completely concealed her problem) and awareness is low (he has no idea she has a problem) then ERROR is the likely ground. But where awareness is high (he has strong suspicions that she is alcoholic) and deceit is low (she has indicated to him that she drinks too much) then it would seem preferable to handle the case on the ground of a CONDITION.

J. The Eastern Canon

When one compares the form of marriage in the Latin Church (CIC, c. 1108) with the form of marriage in the Eastern Churches (CCEO, c. 828) it is clear that the Eastern Churches see the sacred rite, specifically the priestly blessing, as essential to the form of marriage while the Latin Church does not.

The law of the Latin Church has tended to emphasize the contractual aspects of marriage, with the consent of the parties making the marriage and with the priest (or even a deacon) acting only as the official witness requesting and receiving the consent. The Eastern Churches, meanwhile, have emphasized the spiritual, sacred aspects of marriage, and from ancient times have seen the blessing of the priest (not of a deacon) as necessary for a valid marriage.

Within this context the Eastern Churches have, for most of their history, seen "the placing of a condition on marriage as repugnant to the sacred character of the constitutive moment of marriage, which has always been considered a primarily religious event" (Joseph Prader, "Il consenso matrimoniale condizionato nella disciplina canonica latina e orientale" in *Iustus Iudex*, Essen, 1990, pp. 284-285). See also Robitaille, *Studia Canonica*, 1992, pp. 75-110.

This approach has now been embodied in the Eastern canon 826 which simply says that "marriage based on a condition cannot (non potest) be validly celebrated".

A. The Pertinent Canon

C. 1103 - CCEO, c. 825 - A marriage is invalid if it is entered into due to force or grave fear inflicted from outside the person, even when inflicted unintentionally, which is of such a type that the person is compelled to choose matrimony in order to be freed from it.

B. Force

1.   Force (vis) is the coercion (coactio moralis) which moves the will under the threat of an evil in such a way that the will, otherwise not about to consent, does, in order to avoid the evil, consent to the imposed action.

2.   When this definition is applied to marriage, it is clear that the true consent which is the efficient cause of marriage is presumed to be present (coacta voluntas manet semper voluntas) so that the question may well be asked, "Why, if the efficient cause of marriage is truly present, is the marriage invalid?" The answer basically is that, in a forced marriage, the full freedom of a person to choose one's own spouse, which is a basic human right, is not respected (*Gaudium et spes,* nn. 17, 26, 27, 29, 48 and 52).

C. Common Fear

Fear (metus) is the intimidation (trepidatio mentis) which results from the force. In order to invalidate marriage, the fear must be grave, extrinsic, and causative.

1.   *Grave*

In order to invalidate marriage fear must be grave. It may, however, be either absolutely or relatively grave. Fear is *absolutely* grave when it arises from an evil which is capable of compelling a well-balanced person to enter marriage against his or her will. Evils of this sort are threats of death, mutilation, imprisonment, exile, loss of great wealth and disinheritance. Lesser evils inflicted on more timid people can result in fear which is *relatively* grave but always there must be some objective gravity, at least prudently feared, for otherwise (if the gravity is a pure figment of one's imagination) the fear is not really extrinsic but intrinsic (27, 211; 35, 196; 35, 319).

2.   *Extrinsic*

a.   In its most obvious meaning this simply indicates that the fear is not invalidating if it is *intrinsic,* as for example, if it results from mere auto-suggestion or suspicion or moral or social obligation or from a scrupulous conscience.

b. It also means, however, that fear is not invalidating if it is caused by some *necessary* or *extra-human* agent, as for example, sickness, precarious economic situation or public infamy.

It should perhaps be noted here that when there is the intervention of an intermediary one must carefully ascertain whether he or she is advising the person of mere facts or of threats. If, for example, a doctor acts as a kind of intermediary in advising a woman that she is pregnant, the intervention of the doctor obviously does not make the fear extrinsic because it is not the doctor but the pregnancy which the woman fears. But if, on the other hand, it is the woman's brother, for example, who is advising her of the father's threats, then extrinsic fear is indeed present. See the following Rotal decisions: 17, 240; 18, 176; 26, 81; 31, 26; 35, 74.

3. *Causative*

a. In order to invalidate a marriage the fear must not only be grave and extrinsic; it must also be causative. That is to say, one must have been compelled to marry in order to free him or herself from the force and fear. Marriage, in other words, must be the effect, of which the cause (the principal and determining cause) was fear, so that if the fear (the cause) were not present, marriage (the effect) would not take place. It is clear then that to invalidate a marriage, fear ought not to be merely the occasion of marriage (so that one marries *cum* metu) but the real cause (so that one marries *ob* metum vel *ex* metu).

b. If there is another remedy besides the marriage to the threatened evil, which remedy is not utilized, then it is presumed that there was another cause for the marriage, that fear was not the cause and that the marriage was not entered ex metu.

c. The force need not be inflicted *directly* for the purpose of extorting consent. It is sufficient if the force is present and *indirectly* causes the marriage, e.g., when the father of a pregnant woman threatens, in anger, to kill the woman's lover, whereupon the lover offers to marry the woman. This was stated *implicitly* in the 1917 Code (in that it rejected a draft canon requiring direct force - see Coronata II, para. 479) and is stated *explicity* in the 1983 Code (by the phrase "even when inflicted unintentionally - etiam haud consulto incussum" - see *Communicationes* 1983, 2, p. 234 and D2, p. 179).

d. It should be noted, furthermore, that the words of the Code, "the person is compelled to choose matrimony," do not indicate a compulsion to a particular marriage with a specific person but to marriage in general. If, therefore, a person is truly compelled to marry in order to avoid some evil, the marriage is invalid even if some choice of spouses is offered.

e.   In an interesting case decided before Mattioli on January 23, 1957, the Rota declared a marriage invalid in which the force exerted on the woman to go through a civil ceremony was regarded as virtually perduring and influencing the religious marriage four years later (49, 37).

f.   Perhaps the best criterion for judging whether a marriage was entered ex metu or simply cum metu is the presence of aversion. This *could* mean a physical aversion for the person but need not; it suffices that there be an aversion to *marrying* this person. This type of aversion obviously could exist simultaneously with liking the person as a friend since there is a vast difference between wanting the person as a friend and wanting him or her as a spouse. But unless there is some sign of this minimal type of aversion, the marriage must be considered valid.

The ordinary signs or symptoms of aversion are crying and complaining before marriage, sadness and denial of the signs of affection. The absence of such signs after marriage proves nothing since it is then presumed that one is making the best of a bad situation.

Where there *are* these signs, where there is aversion, fear is presumed, *only* presumed however and not with a certainty which would invalidate marriage. Ultimately it is not merely aversion but fear that must be proved.

D.   Reverential Fear

1.   *The Notion*

When the extrinsic force exerting the influence is a parent or some superior, the whole question of reverential fear and its special considerations comes into play. It is not that the net result of reverential fear is something different from the fear mentioned in c. 1103. It is simply that where we start off with a relationship of subjection, we have a kind of breeding ground, we have the ideal conditions for the existence of fear.

2.   *The Object*

Obviously where the subject has a built-in respect, reverence and obedience for the superior, he or she is especially fearful of offending the superior and most of all of arousing the superior's indignation. It is important to note that it is this indignation and not any concomitant threats of evil which is the specific object of reverential fear. Thus, if a daughter is threatened by her father with expatriation, we have two evils which are exerting force - the indignation of the father and expatriation. If the daughter marries to avoid indignation, she is marrying out of *reverential* fear. But if she marries to avoid expatriation, she is marrying out of *common* fear. It is not always easy, of course, to determine whether the expatriation is the *principal* motive for marrying, a *subsidiary* motive or just a *sign* of the father's indignation but it is an important area to be investigated by the court.

3. *The Degree*

This indignation which is the specific object of reverential fear would, in itself, be considered force or coercion but would per se be considered only slight coercion. If, however, it were or probably would be harsh or long lasting, it could easily be serious or grave coercion and could result in grave, invalidating fear.

4. *Parental Behavior*

This indignation is an abuse of authority and of the filial reverence offered by the children and is a luxury in which no parent has a right to engage. This is not to say, of course, that parents have no right to assist their children in choosing a partner, that they cannot offer them advice and even warnings, that they cannot attempt to persuade their children to marry this or that partner, even to the extent of using some moderate, proportionate force as long as it remains parental. All of this, indeed, may prompt the subject to sacrifice his or her own happiness and, in order to comply with the wishes of the parent, agree to marry, perhaps "non libenter sed libere tamen."

But this is quite different from inflicting a fear of harsh and long lasting indignation on one's child. Here the means are not the moderate urgings and exhortations mentioned above but severities, cruelties, absolute and imperious commands, threats, curses, a grim and gloomy mien, angry badgering, ceaseless and uncivil complaining, constant and annoying requests. These remove from the child the possibility of marrying "non tantum libenter sed etiam libere" (not necessarily eliminating free consent altogether but greatly diminishing the actual freedom and making the choice at best a voluntarium secundum quid, something which would not have been willed at all were it not for the fear).

5. *Another Remedy*

As regards the element of causality (C 3b), it should be noted that, in the case of reverential fear, the real evil present is the parental indignation, not the actual content of concomitant threats. In the case then of the woman who marries to avoid not the *expatriation* but the *indignation* of the parent, the question to be asked is not whether there was another remedy to expatriation but whether there was another remedy to indignation; not whether if she hadn't married, she could have avoided the *expatriation* but whether, if she hadn't married, she could have avoided by any other remedy the *indignation* of her father.

166

6. *Extreme Force*

It should likewise be noted that if the force exerted on the subject is so grave that it would give rise to intimidation even in the non subject, then the resulting fear is not really reverential fear at all but common fear. It is clear, therefore, that not all fear exerted by parents is reverential fear. Reverential fear and common fear differ in two ways: by reason of the *object* (indignation vs. something else) and by reason of *degree* (the amount likely to be exerted on a loved one vs. the kind used on a well balanced person who owes no reverence).

E. Proof Of Force And Fear

There are two basic arguments in a force and fear case: the direct argument (proving coercion) and the indirect argument (proving aversion).

In developing both arguments a tribunal should of course look to the declarations of the parties and the testimony of witnesses (the relevant canons can be found in the chapters on simulation), to all the circumstantial evidence (the age, sex and temperament of the one being forced, relationship to the person exerting the coercion, etc.) and to a motive for the coercion.

F. Applicability Of The Canon

The Code Commission, having determined apparently that the nullity caused by force and fear is of the natural law (for Rotal decisions on this matter see 40, 327-328; 56, 650 and 61, 284), has declared that c. 1103 can apply to non-Catholics as well as Catholics (*Communicationes,* 1987, 1, p. 149). For more on this question see *The Jurist,* 1991, 1, pp. 119-137.

DEFECTIVE CONVALIDATION

A. The Pertinent Canons

C. 1156 - CCEO, c. 843 - §1. To convalidate a marriage which is invalid due to a diriment impediment, it is required that the impediment cease or that it be dispensed and that at least the party who is aware of the impediment renew consent.

§2 - This renewal of consent is required by ecclesiastical law for the validity of the convalidation even if both parties furnished consent at the beginning and have not revoked it later.

C. 1157 - CCEO, c. 844 -The renewal of consent must be a new act of the will concerning a marriage which the person who is renewing consent knows or thinks was null from the beginning.

C. 1158 - CCEO, c. 845 - §1 - If the impediment is a public one, the consent is to be renewed by both parties according to the canonical form, with due regard for the prescription of canon 1127 §2.

§2 - If the impediment cannot be proven to exist, it is sufficient that the consent be renewed privately and in secret by the party who is aware of the impediment, provided the other party perseveres in the consent already given, or by both parties when each of them knows about the impediment.

C. 1159 - CCEO, c. 846 - §1 - A marriage which is invalid due to a defect of consent is convalidated when the party who had not consented now gives consent, provided the consent given by the other party still exists.

§2 - If the defect of consent cannot be proven it is sufficient that the party who did not consent gives consent privately and in secret.

§3 - If the defect of consent can be proven it is necessary that the consent be given according to the canonical form.

C. 1160 - CCEO, c. 847 - With due regard for the prescription of canon 1127 §2, a marriage which is invalid due to a defect of form must be contracted anew according to canonical form in order to become valid.

B. Those Bound By Ecclesiastical Law

The rules for determining who is and who is not bound by ecclesiastical law are, as we shall see, of some import in this area. In terms of a possible convalidation they may be summarized as follows:

1. *Under the 1917 Code*

   a. A Catholic was bound (c. 12).
   b. A baptized non-Catholic was bound (c. 12).
   c. A non-baptized person was bound only when marrying a baptized person (c. 1016).

2. *Under the 1983 Code*

   a. A Catholic is bound (c. 11).
   b. A baptized non-Catholic is bound only when marrying a Catholic (c. 1059).
   c. A non-baptized person is likewise bound only when marrying a Catholic (c. 1059).

C. The Division Of The Canons

The canons on convalidation are divided into three sections, treating, namely, marriages which are invalid due to a:

1. Diriment Impediment (1156-1158)

2. Defect of Consent (1159)

3. Defect/Lack of Form (1160)

D. Convalidating Marriages Invalid Because Of A Diriment Impediment

The canons of both the 1917 and the 1983 Codes indicate that when a marriage is invalid because of a diriment impediment, it is validated by a) the cessation of the impediment, b) the person being aware that the marriage was invalid because of the impediment and c) the renewal of marital consent, i.e. a new decision to marry (expressed, when required, according to the norms of law) which involves the exchange of the essential marital rights in view of the fact that those rights had never before been exchanged, at least effectively.

The canons further indicate that the latter two factors (knowledge of invalidity and renewal of consent) are required only by ecclesiastical law and are not therefore relevant when the marriage involves people not bound by that law.

There are then the following practical possibilities:

a. *Marriage Involving Two Unbaptized Parties* - Two Jewish people, for example, marry after one of them obtains a divorce from a previous spouse. The impediment of ligamen is present invalidating the union. Should the previous spouse die, however, the present marriage is ipso facto validated by the cessation of the impediment. Consequently, should the second marriage later break up and one of the parties wish to marry a Catholic, that second marriage could not be declared invalid on the grounds of a defective convalidation (or even of prior bond).

This has been the operative jurisprudence under both Codes.

b.   *Marriage Involving Two Non-Catholics, at least One of Whom is Baptized*

1)   *Under the 1917 Code* - Were one or both of the people in the case outlined above not Jewish but Protestant, then by reason of their baptism, they would, in order to validate their union on the death of the former spouse, first have had to recognize its invalidity and secondly have had to renew their consent (though not according to any particular form). Both of these requirements, though, would have been so unlikely to be met by a non-Catholic that once the initial marriage was proved invalid, its invalidity may be presumed to have perdured despite the cessation of the impediment.

2)   *Under the 1983 Code* - After the 1983 Code went into effect this type of marriage followed the same rules as those that had previously applied to a marriage involving two unbaptized people (as in a. above). For example: two Protestants, Jack and Jane married in 1982 and were divorced in 1983. In 1984 Jane married Tarzan, another Protestant. That marriage was invalid by reason of ligamen. When, however, Jack died in 1985 the marriage of Jane and Tarzan was automatically validated.

c.   *Marriages Involving at least One Catholic Party* - When a Catholic is involved it is less likely that a marriage will take place with a diriment impediment being present. It is conceivable, though, that a couple might marry with one of them, for example, being unbaptized or under age without a dispensation having been granted. In that event, if the impediment is *demonstrable* (public) then the marriage may be declared invalid informally unless and until consent is renewed in the proper form; and if the impediment is *not demonstrable* then the marriage cannot be declared invalid at all.

E.   Convalidating Marriages Invalid Because Of Defect Of Consent (Or Force And Fear)

It is consent that makes marriage. When consent is flawed the marriage is invalid. There is no substitute for consent. (c. 1057 §1). This is a matter not just of ecclesiastical law but of the natural law itself.

Therefore, when a marriage is invalid because of a defect of consent, i.e. because of some defect mentioned in the Code under the heading "De Consensu Matrimoniali" (embracing CC. 1095-1107), then the natural law would require that a genuine marital consent be elicited, which, as c. 1157 points out, would entail the person recognizing the invalidity of the first ceremony.

Consequently, whatever the baptismal or ecclesial status of the parties, were a marriage invalid because of, let us say, force and fear, it would not be ipso facto validated when the force and fear ceased but knowledge of invalidity and renewal of consent would be required in order to validate it.

It was indeed on this very basis that the famous Vanderbilt-Marlborough marriage was declared invalid by the Rota. See 18, 286 and, for a similar case, 28, 714.

F. Convalidating Marriages Invalid Because Of Lack Of Form

C. 1160 is clearly speaking about marriages that involved at least one Catholic in which the form was neither observed nor dispensed. In convalidating such marriages, as noted in Section B, even the non-Catholic party has, under both the old and the new Code, been obliged to observe ecclesiastical law. In such cases, therefore, it is required that both parties a) personally recognize the invalidity or at least the probable invalidity of the former marriage and b) transfer the marital right to their partner, i.e. not merely confirm or reiterate a former exchange of rights but actually give a new marital consent distinct from the former inefficacious one.

This does not usually involve a problem where both parties are Catholic but these requirements demand more than can reasonably be expected of most non-Catholics. Consequently many convalidations involving a non-Catholic can be proved invalid on the ground that the non-Catholic party either failed to recognize the original union as invalid or failed to give new consent.

Finally, it must be remembered that in these cases it is not necessary to prove simulation, i.e. exclusion of marital consent by a *positive* act of the will; but it is only necessary to prove the *negative* omission of the new consent required for a valid convalidation. See the decision of January 21, 1969 coram Rogers (61, 64-65) in D1, p. 144, and the decision of June 30, 1988 coram Funghini (80, 440-444) in LS pp. 88-93.

G. Proof Of Defective Convalidation

The declarations of the parties and the affidavits and testimony of witnesses (see the canons in the simulation chapter) are important in proving a defective convalidation. All records should likewise be obtained so that it is clear that a genuine convalidation is being considered. Also the circumstances that might be relevant, such as the religion of the parties, what, if any prenuptial preparation was given, the person's attitude toward the Catholic Church, the reason for the convalidation, how soon after the first marriage it occured, and whether the parties were getting along well at the time.

APPENDICES

APPENDIX ONE

When Is An Invalid Marriage Null?

Introduction

For years tribunals have been issuing what are popularly called annulments. For years we have been declaring marriages null, or perhaps even null and void, which is a kind of double whammy.

But over the past decade or so many of us have become increasingly uncomfortable calling marriages null. For most people, after all, their marriage was the most important event in their lives. It may have been the most humiliating, devastating, destructive, depressing, painful, frustrating experience of their lives and, almost incredibly, it may, at the very same time, have included the most romantic, enjoyable, rewarding, happiest times they can remember. But whatever the mix, their marriage was, for almost everybody, the most significant, the most important event of their life. So how can we say it never existed? Isn't that what "null" means?

People, in other words, are intuitively offended by having their marriages declared null. I guess we have always understood that but, at the same time, we felt we had to be honest and "tell it like it is". And our traditional understanding was that an invalid marriage was not a true or real marriage and that, in truth, it didn't really exist as a marriage.

In recent years, however, more and more canonists have begun to question the accuracy of that position. They have begun to ask, "Are the terms invalid and null really synonymous? If not, are some invalid marriages also null? And if so, which ones?"

This paper attempts to answer those questions. It does so by discussing what I see to be the four basic positions that have evolved over the years on the subject. These positions are: 1) All invalid marriages are null; 2) Only those marriages that are invalid due to lack of form are null; 3) Only those marriages that are invalid due to a defect of consent are null; and 4) The only marriage that is null is the one that never took place.

The first three positions I shall discuss rather briefly; the fourth somewhat more at length.

The Four Positions

Position One - All invalid marriages are null.

This, it would seem, is the most popular position. According to this opinion the terms "invalid" and "null" are perfectly synonymous. Gasparri noted that in common parlance the two terms, invalid and null, are used interchangeably[1], and both the 1917 and 1983 Codes likewise seem to use "invalidity" and "nullity" as synonyms. The 1983 Code, for example, refers to marriages being null or to the nullity of a marriage more than a dozen times[2] so, over the years, we have all become quite used to looking upon an invalid marriage as null, that is to say, as nothing or nonexistent, or as not really existing, at least as a marriage.

It is an approach that goes back to Roman Law. In the *Digest* of the "Corpus Iuris Civilis", for example, Paulus, who wrote somewhere around the year 230, is quoted as saying that if a teacher marries his young student without her father's permission, "non est matrimonium - it is not a marriage", or "there is no marriage".[3] And the *Institutes*, which was promulgated by the Emperor Justinian in the year 533 as a brief, elementary textbook in Roman Law (it usually prints to about fifty pages), gives, at one point, a long list of people who are disallowed from marrying each other due to consanguinity, affinity or some other reason, and then concludes with these words, "But if, contrary to these precepts, people join together then nec vir, nec uxor, nec nuptiae, nec matrimonium, nec dos intelligitur - you have neither husband nor wife nor nuptials nor matrimony nor dowery".[4] In other words, you've got nothing. You've got not just an invalid marriage but a matrimonium nullum, a null marriage, or no marriage.

Fast forward six hundred years and we see Gratian, in Cause 29, say that one who is in error about the person he or she is marrying does not really consent, and without consent, says Gratian, "there can be no marriage - nullum matrimonium esse potest".[5]

So this first opinion seems, at least at first glance, a fairly solid one. If a marriage is invalid, it's null. That's what invalid means. The Code of Canon Law seems to endorse this opinion, and there is adequate precedent for it in both Roman and medieval canon law, of which I have given but a few examples.

Position Two - Only those marriages that are invalid due to lack of form are null.

Although Cardinal Gasparri had noted that the terms invalid and null are, in common parlance, used interchangeably (or, as he said, "promiscuously") he also pointed out that, *properly* speaking (si proprie loqui velimus), the two terms are *not* synonymous. Properly speaking, according to Gasparri, the term "null" should be reserved for those marriages that are invalid because a required form of marriage was not in any way followed. So if, for example, a Catholic married before a Justice of the Peace without a dispensation from form, that marriage would, according to Gasparri, be properly called "null". Such a marriage would lack even the "species seu figura matrimonii - the appearance or figure of matrimony" and would not therefore be a real marriage. It would, rather, be a non marriage. Canon 1014 of the old Code and c. 1060 of the new say that "matrimonium gaudet favore iuris", but the marriage of a Catholic before a Justice of the Peace is, according to Gasparri, a matrimonium nullum or no marriage, and therefore *non* gaudet favore iuris - it does not enjoy the favor of law.

Viewing a civil marriage by a Catholic as nonexistent is, as we know, considered harsh today. In *Familiaris Consortio*, Pope John Paul II said: "There are increasing cases of Catholics who, for ideological or practical reasons, prefer to contract a civil marriage, and who reject or at least defer religious marriage. Their situation cannot of course be likened to that of people simply living together without any bond at all, because in the present case there is at least a certain commitment to a properly defined and probably stable state of life." [6] And Monsignor Funghini, in his decision of June 30, 1988 concluded from the Pope's remarks that we should not therefore regard such marriages as nonexistent but rather as juridically inefficacious.[7]

But calling the civil marriage null or nonexistent was only half of Gasparri's position. The other half (and in terms of our present discussion the more important half) was that any other invalid marriage should not be called nullum but just invalidum or perhaps irritum, that is to say, ineffectual or without effect. If, therefore, a marriage was invalid due to a diriment impediment or a defect of consent, such a marriage, according to Gasparri, should not, properly speaking, be called null but rather invalid or ineffectual.

This approach is not without its own tradition. In the *Decretals of Gregory IX* (published in 1234), for example, Pope Gregory himself is quoted as saying: "If conditions against the substance of marriage are placed; if, for example, one says to the other, 'I contract with you if you avoid having children' . . . then the matrimonial contract, however favorable it might otherwise be, nevertheless lacks effect - caret effectu".[8] Gregory, it should be noted, did not say that such a marriage would be null; rather he said it would be ineffectual.

And this, according to Gasparri, was the proper way to describe any invalid marriage except for the one which altogether lacked the species seu figura matrimonii, namely the lack of form marriage.

Position Three - Only those marriages that are invalid due to a defect of consent are null.

It is consent, as we all know, that makes marriage. This is perhaps the most enduring and most basic principle in the canon law of marriage. In Roman Law, Rule of Law number 30 was "Nuptias non concubitus sed consensus facit - it is not cohabitation but consent that makes marriage,"[9] and, in a slight variation of that, an ancient writer once thought to be St. John Chrysostom said "Matrimonium non facit coitus sed voluntas - it is not intercourse but the will that makes marriage".[10] The same point is made over and over again throughout the history of canon law right up to the 1983 Code which says, in c. 1057, "The legitimately manifested consent of legally qualified parties makes marriage."

So since it is consent that makes marriage, it is understandable that some canonists would take the position that, where valid consent is lacking there is no marriage. One canonist who took that position was Robert Harrigan who, in his 1938 Catholic University doctoral dissertation, noted that marriages that are invalid due to a diriment impediment or to a defect of form should be called simply "invalid", whereas marriages that are invalid due to a defect of consent, and only those marriages, should be called "null". Harrigan pointed out that "whereas the word *null* implies nonexistence the word *invalid* simply indicates that although something exists it is lacking in legal force." Harrigan's bottom line conclusion was, in effect, this: that, since it is consent that makes marriage, where valid marital consent is lacking, there is literally no marriage. Where, in other words, valid consent is lacking the marriage is truly null.[11] More specifically, what Harrigan had in mind was a situation where the consent was vitiated by fear or error or condition or simulation or ignorance or some sort of mental incapacity. In such cases, Harrigan would say, the marriage was truly null in the strict sense of the word, that is to say, nonexistent.

Harrigan's position, it must be pointed out, was never widely accepted. Monsignor, later Cardinal, Giacomo Violardo, my own wonderful professor of marriage law at the Lateran University back in the 1950s, rather summarily dismissed it, saying simply, "If such marriages were really nonexistent, then there would be no need for the sentence of a judge terminating them. This, however, is not allowed by the Code which requires a double conforming affirmative decision in order for a marriage to be declared invalid, even a marriage that has been entered into as a joke."[12]

Although Violardo did not go into any detail on this matter, I think I do not misrepresent him when I say that he had long ago intuitively or implicitly accepted as normative what might be called the three basic though unwritten, derivative rules that stem from the axiom that consent makes marriage. I would construct those rules as follows: 1) valid consent makes a valid marriage; 2) flawed consent makes a flawed marriage (that is, an invalid marriage); and 3) no consent makes no marriage (that is, a null or nonexistent marriage).

The error in Harrigan's position, as I see it, was that he tried to blend together rather than to keep separate rules two and three. Instead of accepting the fact that a flawed consent makes a flawed marriage and no consent makes no marriage, he tried to say that flawed consent makes no marriage.

Is there an example of no consent making no marriage? Sure. A couple schedule a wedding date, make all arrangements with the local priest, hire a hall and so forth but then cancel at the last minute. The wedding may even be reported in the local newspaper. But in fact, of course, there is no marriage because there was no consent.

Harrigan, however, went beyond this scenario and claimed that, even when the couple actually exchange consent to marry according to form, the marriage must be regarded as nonexistent whenever the consent is flawed or defective, as might happen, for example, where a party lacks due discretion. It was, in effect, this undue extension of rule two that Violardo found objectionable and that caused him to reject the Harrigan position as untenable and unacceptable.

Or, to put it another way, Violardo belonged to the Gasparri school and clearly not to the Harrigan school.[13]

Position Four - The only marriage that is null is the one that never took place.

The opening canon, canon 1134, of the section in the Code entitled "The Effects of Marriage", repeats verbatim the old canon 1110, and reads as follows: "From a valid marriage there arises between the spouses a bond, which, by its nature, is perpetual and exclusive."

The first thing to be noted about this statement is that both the new and the old canon are speaking in terms of cause and effect. The valid marriage is the cause; the indissoluble bond is the effect.

Many of the commentators on the 1917 Code used this cause and effect approach as a way of defining both the valid and the invalid marriage. Gasparri[14] and Wernz[15], for example, defined a *valid* marriage as one that produces an indissoluble bond. And Wernz[16] and Coronata[17] defined an *invalid* marriage as a marriage in which something obstructs its value or validity - matrimonium cuius valori aliquid obstat.

In an invalid marriage, in other words, the cause is present but not the effect; the marriage is present but not the indissoluble bond, because something (either an impediment or a defect of form or a defect of consent) prevents the cause from having its normal effect.

As already noted, this was basically the approach of Pope Gregory IX when he said that a conditioned marriage "caret effectu - it lacks its effect", namely an indissoluble bond.

According to this fourth opinion, then, the only marriage that should be called null is some sort of mock or make believe ceremony in which not only the effect but the cause itself is lacking. If, for example, a marriage takes place as part of a movie or stage production, it is understood that this is not a real marriage but rather a fictional or theatrical one. But such a marriage is not really a marriage. It is, in other words, no marriage, a matrimonium nullum.

When dealing with the real, as opposed to this fictional, world, however, there are, according to Bender three and only three pertinent juridic states. In ascending order these are: 1) concubinage, 2) an invalid marriage, and 3) a valid marriage. The invalid marriage, in other words, is the middle ground between the two extremes of a valid marriage on the one hand and concubinage on the other.[18]

So what precisely is an invalid marriage? It has, I think, been most accurately de-scribed, again by Father Bender, as follows: "a reciprocal, external act of a man and a woman which is, per se, a manifestation of matrimonial consent but which, because of some accidental obstructing cause, has no effect."[19]

The phrase in this description which perhaps needs some explanation is that the act is *per se a manifestation of matrimonial consent.* This, according to Bender, means simply that the bride says to her groom in these or similar words "I take you as my lawful husband" while the groom takes his bride as his lawful wife. Nothing more than that. Just enough so that those present and witnessing the ceremony would conclude that a marriage has just taken place.

Once that is done you have a marriage, a *valid* marriage if no obex obstructs the indissoluble bond, an *invalid* marriage if something prevents that effect from coming into being. But in either case there is a marriage.

Let me summarize this fourth opinion this way: in the world of *fiction* there can be a marriage which is no marriage and which the entire audience recognizes as such; but in the world of *fact* every marriage is a marriage whether it is valid or not.

Four arguments may be offered in support of this position:

1. *The Authority of the Manualists*

> Following Gasparri[20] there is widespread agreement on the part of the commentators on the 1917 Code that to refer to an invalid marriage as "null" when the invalidity is due either to an impediment or to a defect of consent, is to use the word "null" in an improper or broad sense. Mörsdorf[21], Payen[22], Sipos[23], Cappello[24], Violardo[25] and Bánk[26], all take this position. For all of these authors, when a marriage is invalid due to an impediment or to a defect of consent, it should properly be called not null but either invalid or ineffective (irritum in Latin).

> Seen in isolation, of course, this argument seems to favor the second position, that of Gasparri, rather than this fourth position. Presumably, however, all of these authors, were they writing today, would be in agreement with the already quoted paragraph 82 of *Familiaris Consortio* where Pope John Paul stated, in effect, that the civil marriage of a Catholic, even though it is invalid due to a lack of form, is nevertheless not only a marriage but a marriage that produces a certain bond between the couple and obliges them to fulfill their commitment to each other. It seems fair to conclude, therefore, that all of these authors, were they writing in this post *Familiaris Consortio* era, would be proponents of this fourth position and would consider it incorrect and improper to refer to any invalid marriage as "null", irrespective of whether the invalidity was caused by an impediment or by a defect of consent or by a defect of form.

> Moreover, using the term "null" to describe these marriages is not only improper but also misleading and disadvantageous. The words "null" and "nullity" upset people. People find them offensive and offputting. How, they wonder, can the Church say that their marriage never existed when they know it did? And doesn't this make the children illegitimate? The word "invalid" has, I think, quite a different connotation from the word "null", and does not generally convey or reinforce these mis-

conceptions about the marriage being nonexistent and the children illegitimate; and since, according to most of the authors, "invalid" is the proper and more precise term anyway, why not use it?

2. *The Nature of a Convalidation*

John, a divorced man, and Jane, a single woman, marry. They are both Protestants. We would regard that marriage as invalid due to the impediment of ligamen or prior bond. After some years, however, John's former wife dies and the impediment therefore ceases. According to c.1156 the marriage is then automatically convalidated.

How does one explain that? If one holds that the initial marriage of John and Jane was, because of the impediment, truly null, that is to say, nonexistent, then one, I think, would be hard pressed to explain it. It would, after all, seem absurd to claim that, on the occasion of the death of John's first wife, his marriage to Jane just suddenly sprang into existence out of thin air, out of nothing, ex nihilo, so to speak.

But if, on the contrary, one holds that the marriage was there all along but had simply been juridically inefficacious due to the obex, the obstacle, the impediment of ligamen, then, of course, it makes perfect sense that, when the obstacle ceased to exist, the marriage was then able to achieve its normal effect of creating an indissoluble bond between the couple.

This is why the chapter heading in the Code dealing with convalidation is entitled "On the Convalidation of *Marriage - De Matrimonii* Convalidatione", because what is convalidated must always be a marriage. It can never be anything less than an existing marriage. Concubinage, for example, cannot be convalidated. And neither can a nonexisting or null marriage, at least if the word "null" is used in its proper and accurate sense.

3. *The Standard Terminology used in Describing an Invalid Marriage*

Another argument that favors this fourth opinion is based on the Latin words that have been used over the centuries to describe marriages that are not valid. Apart from the word *nullum* (which, as we have noted, is used only improperly in this context) the three words that have been traditionally employed to describe invalidity are *invalidum*, *irritum* and *vitiosum*, all of which point not to nonexistence but rather to some defect in an existing marriage.

First the word *invalidum*. The root word here is the noun *valetudo*, which means health, or the verb *valere*, which means to be healthy, well or strong. When, therefore, something is valid, it not only exists but is, moreover, strong or healthy or well. And conversely when something is invalid, it does not mean that the subject is nonexistent but rather that it is lacking strength or wellness. It is, in other words, infirm. It bears noting, incidentally, that, in English the adjective inválid and the noun ínvalid, that is to say, one who is wounded or injured or ill, are one and the same. It is also significant that both Schmalzgrueber[27] and the *Decretals of Gregory*[28] speak of the possibility of an invalid marriage "convalescing" and becoming a valid marriage. The *Decretals*, for example, speak of a marriage that had originally been entered under coercion as convalescing or recovering its health through spontaneous cohabitation.

Secondly the word *irritum,* which means fruitless, vain, ineffectual, or ineffective. The idea here is not that the marriage is nonexistent but rather that it does not produce its primary intended effect which, as c. 1134 says, is the perpetual bond. The *matrimonium irritum may* produce, indeed usually *does* produce, a bond, that is to say, certain obligations between the spouses and towards any children born of the marriage, but, because it is invalid, it does not produce the perpetual bond, the *vinculum perpetuum* that is the primary effect of marriage.

And finally the word *vitiosum,* which means faulty, defective, unfit or unsound. The Code uses the word "vitiate" only once, namely in c. 1099, but the authors frequently speak of a marriage being vitiated by an impediment or by a defective consent. What should always be kept in mind, however, is that the verb "to vitiate" means to damage, injure or corrupt. It does not mean to erase, eradicate or to render nonexistent.

4. *The Practice of the Congregations for the Sacraments and for Doctrine on the Impediment of Prior Bond.*

Both the Congregation for the Sacraments and the Congregation for the Doctrine of the Faith have, over the years, issued decisions that imply that an invalid marriage not only exists but in fact produces a very significant canonical effect, namely the impediment of prior bond or ligamen.[29]

A typical case would be this: Margaret and James, both single and both Protestant, marry before a Justice of the Peace and divorce a couple of years later. Some years after that Margaret falls in love with Robert, a single Catholic, and they make arrangements to marry. Robert is aware of Margaret's previous marriage but both of them are under the impression that the marriage doesn't count as far as the Catholic Church is concerned because it was between two Protestants before a Justice of the Peace. So either they don't mention it to the pastor at all, or they do mention it and he mistakenly agrees that that marriage really didn't count. So Margaret and Robert marry and everything goes along fine until Margaret decides she wants to become a Catholic and enters an RCIA program where she learns to her dismay that her marriage to James is a presumably valid marriage. At that point she immediately submits the case to the local Tribunal where, fortunately, the marriage is found to have been invalid and is declared so by the required two concordant decisions.

So now everything is OK and nothing further need be done, right? Well, it depends. If the affirmative decisions by the Tribunal of first instance and its court of appeals really meant that the marriage was null, that is to say, that it never existed, then sure, nothing further needed to be done because the "declaration of nullity" meant that, when Margaret married Robert, she was entirely free to marry. In effect she had never been married before so when she married Robert before his pastor, it was a perfectly valid marriage. No further action had to be taken. Nothing further needed to be done.

According to the Congregations for the Sacraments and for the Doctrine of the Faith, however, something more *did* have to be done. Based on how these Congregations have handled such cases in the past, a radical sanation would be granted for the marriage of Margaret and Robert because that marriage, contracted before Robert's pastor, was, according to these Congregations, invalid due to the diriment impediment of prior bond. This has been the practice of these two congregations - to grant a radical sanation in such cases.

In terms of the case under discussion the principal implication of this practice is that, when the marriage of Margaret and James was declared invalid, that declaration clearly did not mean that the marriage of Margaret and James never existed, because if it never existed, it could not, of course, have been an impediment to Margaret's second marriage.

What the practice of the two Congregations is saying, therefore, is that the impediment of ligamen can be caused not just by a valid marriage but also by an existing invalid marriage, provided that the two parties (in this case Margaret and James) were free to marry and then married according to whatever form that was required of them[30], and also, of course, provided that the marriage had not already been *declared* invalid by the Church.

This practice of the two Congregations, therefore, supports this fourth position in that it recognizes that an invalid marriage truly exists, indeed not only exists but exists to the point where it produces the significant juridic effect of giving rise to an impediment.

In short, whether or not we agree with this practice of these two prestigious Congregations, the fact is that the practice tends to corroborate the position that the only marriage that is null is the one that never took place. Any marriage that did take place, by that very fact, exists and is not therefore null in the proper sense of the word[31].

Conclusion

If we agree with this fourth position, what is it that we really do when we declare a marriage invalid? If we are not declaring it null or nonexistent, what are we saying?

We are saying that the marriage suffered from some substantial defect that prevented it from achieving its principal effect of creating between the spouses a perpetual bond. We are saying that, from its inception, the marriage did not enjoy the kind of wholeness or integrity or soundness or health that the Church, at a given point in history, requires for a marriage to be considered perpetually binding. These standards have, as we know, changed over the years. St. Thomas Aquinas, for example, explained at considerable length how the degrees within which consanguinity has been an impediment to marriage have varied according to various times, and how the Church has the right to determine which degrees would, in a given era, be considered as diriment impediments[32]. And, in our own time, due in no small part to the Second Vatican Council, we have seen both jurisprudence and legislation alter the minimum standards for validity in a host of areas including impotence, ignorance, psychic incapacity, error of quality, imposed error, determining error, intention against fidelity, intention against sacramentality and defective convalidation.

In all of these areas, it seems to me, the Church is not questioning the existence of marriages tainted with one or another of these factors, but is simply setting new criteria for determing at what point a given marriage fails to meet minimum standards of marital health that are appropriate for our age. It is, in other words, a matter of quality, not of existence.

The Tribunal, therefore, serves a kind of "quality control" function. When petitioned, a Tribunal investigates whether a given marriage meets the minimal standards for validity established by the Church for our time, and when the Tribunal is morally certain that it does not, it declares the marriage to have been invalid. This, as I understand it, is what we are about.

ENDNOTES

1. Petrus Card. Gasparri, *DeMatrimonio* (Rome, Typis Polyglottis Vaticanis, 1932) n. 45
2. Canons 1100, 1123, 1157, 1160, 1432, 1673, 1677 § 3, 1682 §§ 1 and 2, 1683, 1684 § 1, 1685, 1686, 1690, 1700 § 2 and 1702. See also cc. 1085 and 1087-1090.
3. *Digesta* 23, 2, 66
4. *Instituta* 1, 10, 12
5. Decretum C. 29, q. 1
6. *AAS,* LXXIV (1982) 183, 82
7. *ARRT Dec.* 80, 442. For a translation of the Funghini law section see Wrenn, *Law Sections,* pp. 88-93
8. X, 4, 5, 7
9. *Digesta* 50, 17, 30
10. *Opus Imperfectum in Matthaeum,* c. 1, C. xxvii, 2; P.G. 56, 802
11. Robert J. Harrigan, *The Radical Sanation of Invalid Marriages* (Washington, The Catholic University of America, 1938, n. 116) pp. 99-100
12. G. Violardo, *De Matrimonio,* pp. 108-109
13. Ibid. p. 106
14. Gasparri, op. cit. n. 39
15. Franciscus Wernz and Petrus Vidal, *Ius Matrimoniale,* (Rome, Universitas Gregoriana, 1946) n. 22
16. Ibid. n. 22
17. Matthaeus Conte a Coronata, *De Matrimonio* (Italy, Marietti, 1957) n. 30
18. L. Bender, "Matrimonium Invalidum" in *Angelicum,* 1941, p. 301. See also Th. Vlaming and L. Bender, *Praelectiones Iuris Matrimonii* (Bussum, Paulus Brand, 1950) p. 43
19. Bender, op cit. p. 309 and Vlaming-Bender, op cit., p. 43
20. Gasparri, op cit. n. 45
21. K. Mörsdorf, *Die Rechtssprache des Codex Iuris Canonici* (Paderborn, 1937) pp. 222-223
22. G. Payen, *De Matrimonio* (Zikawei, Tousewe, 1935) n. 139
23. Stephanus Sipos, *Enchiridion Iuris Canonici* (Rome, Herder, 1954) n. 100, 1
24. Felix Cappello, *De Matrimonio* (Italy, Marietti 1961) n. 48
25. Violardo, op cit. p. 106
26. Joseph Bánk, *Connubia Canonica* (Rome, Herder, 1959) p. 53
27. Franciscus Schmalzgrueber, *Ius Ecclesiasticum Universum,* 4, 1, 1, 3, 3, nn. 458-459
28. X, 4, 1, 21
29. CLD 5, 551-552 and *Studia Canonica,* 1996, 492-494
30. It is true that, had James been a Catholic when he married Margaret before the Justice of the Peace, the Congregations would not have considered that ceremony as giving rise to the impediment of ligamen. This is not to say, however, that the Congregations would, in practice, be in disagreement with the sentiments of John Paul II expressed in the already quoted passage from *Familiaris Consortio,* or that they would, in effect, be endorsing the old Gasparri opinion which held that the civil marriage of a Catholic would be truly null. Rather it would merely be saying that the Congregations would recognize the unique status of the lack of form marriage as a marriage that exists but not as the kind of marriage that would produce the impediment of ligamen.
31. Contrary to the practice of these two Congregations, the Rota and the Signatura hold that only a *valid* marriage gives rise to the impediment of ligamen (*The Jurist,* 1987, pp. 358-370). To these two tribunals, therefore, the question of whether an *invalid* marriage exists or does not exist is, in terms of the matter under discussion, irrelevant since in neither case does it give rise to the impediment.
32. St. Thomas, *Suppl.,* Q.54, a. 4

APPENDIX TWO

Canon 1095: A Bird's Eye View

I. INTRODUCTORY REMARKS

Canon 1095 is a new creature; the 1917 code contained nothing like it. Basically it says that people who are not psychologically equipped for marriage cannot enter a valid marriage.

Canon lawyers, especially judges, are happy to have the canon. It is one of the important innovations in the new code. At the same time, however, it is quite clear that the canon, in and of itself, says almost nothing. It is very much like saying that one must be strong enough for the task. Well, of course! But the question is: what is the task?

In much the same way, canon 1095 tells us that a person must be strong enough for marriage. But the question is: what is marriage? It is a question that has been asked for centuries. The answer has not always been the same.

II. MARRIAGE BEFORE VATICAN II

There are two basic elements to marriage: the *procreational* element called the *"bonum prolis,"* and the *personalist* element, called the *"bonum coniugum."*

As the subject of marriage has been investigated over the centuries by various civil lawyers, canon lawyers and theologians, some have tended to emphasize the *procreational* element while others have emphasized the *personalist* element. Let us look briefly at a few examples of each.

A.   *Those Favoring the* Bonum Prolis

1.   *St. Augustine* (d. 430). St. Augustine, as Theodore Mackin has pointed out, [1] was "caught in a kind of crossfire." He lived at a time when two extremist positions were tearing society apart. One opinion said, in effect, that all sex was bad, the other that all sex was good. Augustine attempted to find orthodoxy somewhere in between. Sex, he said, was sometimes good and sometimes bad. Usually bad perhaps. But sometimes good, namely when it is had within marriage for the purpose of procreating offspring. [2] Procreation, for Augustine, was the main point of marriage. Etymologically, he noted, the word matrimony is derived from the Latin word for mother -mater. [3] Mater-matrimony. When a couple marries, in other words, the woman becomes not so much a wife as a mother. Procreation is what counts. Indeed, in his final essay on marriage, Augustine spelled it out quite clearly. He said: "Therefore the propagation of children is the first, the natural and the legitimate purpose of marriage."[4]

This Augustinian attitude and theory on marriage was, as we know, immensely influential for hundreds and hundreds of years.

2. *Gratian* (1140). When Gratian composed his *Decretum,* he phrased the question in more legal terms than had Augustine but his conclusion was basically the same. In Cause 27 (the opening cause on the subject of marriage) he wrote, "Let us ask ourselves the question: which sort of consent constitutes marriage? Is it consent to cohabitation or to intercourse or to both?"[5]

    Gratian's anwer was that the consent that constitutes marriage is the consent to intercourse. Even the Virgin Mary, he said, consented to carnal intercourse. If she had not, he implied, she would not have been truly married. [6] Not that the Virgin actually *had* intercourse (because she also had a vow of virginity) but she consented to it at the time of marriage and that, says Gratian, is what constituted the marriage.

    So once again, an extraordinarily influential author had endorsed the position, even on the basis of the toughest possible case, that the essence of marriage consists not in its personalist but in its procreational aspects.

3. *Duns Scotus* (circa 1300). The Scottish Franciscan, John Duns Scotus, in his commentary on the *Sentences* of Peter Lombard, could hardly have been more explicit or more direct in lending his support to the Augustinian position. He defined marriage itself, the contract of marriage and the sacrament of marriage as follows:

    > Marriage is an indissoluble bond between man and woman arising from the mutual transferral of power over each other's body for the procreation and right education of offspring.

    > The contract of marriage is the mutual transferral by man and woman of their bodies for perpetual use in the procreation and right education of offspring.

    > The sacrament of marriage is the expression of certain words of man and woman, signifying the mutual handing over of power over each other's body for the right procreation of offspring, efficaciously signifying by divine institution the conferral of a grace which is beneficial to each of the contractants for their mutual joining of souls.[7]

4. *Wernz* (1904). In the years just prior to the 1917 code, the idea that marriage consisted basically in the right to intercourse was generally accepted. The Jesuit, F. X. Wernz, reflected that acceptance when he described, in his Ius Decretalium, what pertained to the *essence,* to the *integrity* and to the *perfection* of marriage. He wrote:

    > As regards the matrimonial contract, the *material object* is the persons

themselves while the *formal object* (i.e., the aspect under which it is viewed) is the undivided sharing of life. This sharing of life consists principally and *essentially* in the mutual, equal, exclusive and perpetual right and duty over the spouse's body for the generation and education of offspring, not for any other purposes, but always with the wife being subject to the husband who is her head. Then, in order that that essential communion attain its *integrity,* the communion of bed and board is necessary but can sometimes be absent without detracting from the essence of marriage. Finally, the *union of souls* through the mutual love of the spouses, although it is a condition for a happy marriage, nevertheless is not part of the *object of the matrimonial contract,* nor indeed, could the *marriage bond* consist in so fickle an element.[8]

5.   *The 1917 Code.* Given the fact that Wernz was reflecting what, by that time, was the common opinion, the actual wording of the pertinent canons in the 1917 code came as no surprise. Canon 1013 referred to the procreation and education of offspring as the "primary end of marriage" and canon 1081, §2 said that "Matrimonial consent is an act of the will by which each party gives and accepts a perpetual and exclusive right over the body for those acts which are per se apt for the generation of offspring."

With the promulgation of the 1917 code the Augustinian position became "official" and dominated Catholic thought for the next several decades.

B.   *Those Favoring the* Bonum Coniugum

1.   *Roman Law* (circa 235). Although there have always been influential proponents for the position that marriage is *primarily procreational,* it is also true that there has always existed a solid tradition in favor of the other position, namely that marriage is, at least in part, *essentially personalist.*

In classical Roman law (and it is, after all, axiomatic that for many centuries, "Ecclesia vivit lege Romana"), there were two commonly accepted definitions of marriage, but neither of them even alluded to children. Both of them spoke only of the personalist aspects of marriage.

The definition in the *Digest,* attributed to Modestinus, said that "marriage is a union of a man and a woman and a partnership of the whole of life, a participation in divine and human law."[9] The definition in the *Institutes,* attributed to Ulpian, was quite similar. It said that "marriage, or matrimony, is a union of a man and a woman, involving an undivided sharing of life."[10]

Seeing marriage as primarily personalist was, therefore, firmly rooted in Roman law.

2.   *Hugh of St. Victor* (d. 1141). Although Hugh of St. Victor has been referred to as the "second Augustine" because of his great indebtedness to the bishop

of Hippo, Hugh and Augustine had quite different notions of marriage. David Fellhauer summarized Hugh's position this way. "Hugh," he said,

> distinguished between *coniugium* and *officium coniugii*. The latter remained the obligation of mankind to propagate the human race, which required sexual intercourse. But the former, simple *coniugium*, was the marital society in itself, in which carnal copula was neither required nor always to be desired. In Hugh's theory the distinction between *coniugium* and *officium coniugii* was so pronounced that marriage actually involved two acts of consent, one of the marital society of two persons who lived in a communion of hearts and minds and who loved each other (spiritually, but not necessarily sexually); the other consent was directed to sexual intercourse. These two acts of consent, *consensus coniugalis* and *consensus coitus,* ordinarily coincided. But they need not. No one was bound to engage in marital copula, at least when its exclusion was mutually agreed upon. Thus the marriage of the Blessed Virgin and St. Joseph was a complete marriage. And more, it was the perfect marriage, the ideal, in Hugh's opinion. Mary and Joseph were united in a love which was without imperfection; they entered a conjugal society of exquisite closeness and mutual care; and they did not have sexual relations.
>
> What was, then, for Hugh of St. Victor the object of matrimonial consent? It was the *coniugalis societas,* the community of conjugal life and love. The copula was not necessary; it was not even - if one wished the perfect marriage - desirable. And it did not belong to the essence of marriage.[11]

Hugh's position, it is clear, was extremely and unrealistically spiritual. It would have to be modified before gaining any sort of widespread acceptance. It was Peter Lombard who took up that work of modification.

3. *Peter Lombard* (1158). Peter Lombard completed his *Book of Sentences* in 1158, became the Archbishop of Paris the following year, and died the year after that. His *Book of Sentences* was the standard theology text book in the Middle Ages. Most of the major theologians over the next few centuries wrote commentaries on it. It postdated Gratian's *Decretum* by seventeen or eighteen years.

    Peter disagreed with Gratian on the subject of marriage and he stated his disagreement directly. He took Gratian's key question "Which sort of consent constitutes marriage? Is it consent to cohabitation or to intercourse or to both?" and he gave it a different answer. Gratian, as we saw, answered the question by saying that it was consent to carnal intercourse that makes marriage. Peter's response was that "neither the consent to cohabitation nor the consent to carnal intercourse make marriage but rather the consent to the conjugal society."[12]

So the issue was clearly joined in the twelfth century. It was one giant against another: Gratian against Peter Lombard. Gratian would eventually win, but more eventually, Peter too would have his day.

4.   *Thomas Aquinas* (1256). Thomas was one of the many theologians who wrote a commentary on Peter Lombard's *Book of Sentences,* and it is principally in that commentary that we find Thomas' teaching on marriage. Thomas wrote his commentary early in his career while he was lecturing in Paris on the *Sentences.* He was only about thirty years old. The *Sentences* had been written about a hundred years earlier.

When Thomas arrived at distinction 28, where Peter had posed the question (which Gratian before him had posed) about which sort of consent constitutes marriage, consent to cohabitation or to intercourse or to both, Thomas came down firmly on the side of Peter. "It seems," he said, "that the consent which makes marriage is the consent to intercourse," and then Thomas gives four reasons to support that statement. "But in fact," he says "the contrary is true.... The effect should respond to the cause. But consent is the cause of marriage. Since, therefore, intercourse does not constitute the essence of marriage, it seems that it is not the consent to intercourse that causes marriage. The truth of the matter is this: that the consent that makes marriage is the consent to marriage because the proper effect of the will is the thing willed....Marriage, however, as noted above, is not essentially the carnal union but rather a certain association of the husband and wife."[13]

Thomas, therefore, said essentially the same thing as Peter. For Peter the consent that makes marriage is the consent to conjugal society; for Thomas it is the consent to marriage itself, but to the whole of marriage and not just the carnal part of it.

5.   *Thomas Sanchez* (1605). Although Sanchez may properly be listed in this grouping of "Those Favoring the *Bonum Coniugum,*" his endorsement of this position is rather ambiguous and equivocal, and thus symbolizes the waning strength of this viewpoint. On the one hand, Sanchez defined marriage as "the undivided, persevering sharing of life so that the purpose of marriage, which is cohabitation, may be attained,"[14] but on the other hand, he spoke of "the mutual giving over of bodies" as that "in which marriage consists" and the "increase of the human race," he intimated, was "the principal end of marriage."[15]

It would seem, therefore, that Sanchez considered the *personalist* aspects of marriage, "the undivided, persevering sharing of life" as very important, almost as important as the *procreative* aspects, but not quite. And not quite essential either.

It was a sign, perhaps, that the battle was virtually over. But not the war, of course.

III. PSYCHIC REQUIREMENTS FOR VALID MARRIAGE BEFORE VATICAN II

A. General Remarks

Let it be clear, first of all, that if the essence of marriage consists only in the right to those acts with are per se apt for the generation of offspring, then there can be only one kind of constitutional incapacity for marriage, and that is *impotence*. If, however, the essence of marriage also includes the right to an interpersonal relationship, then there is a second kind of incapacity, namely *incompetence*.[16] To this extent, at least, there is a direct connection between a society's notion of marriage and the psychological requirements for marriage.

But even beyond that, even within the narrower limits of the "incapacitas praestandi consensum" itself, [17] one would have to assume that all things being equal, the following would be a legitimate rule of thumb: *the more sophisticated a society's notion of marriage, the higher will be the psychological aptitude level demanded of the participants.*

Historically, of course, all things have *not* been equal. At certain times and in certain societies, for example, divorce has been quite acceptable while at other times and places, the damage done by divorce to the immediate and extended family and to society as a whole has been so apparent and so frightening as to make divorce almost unthinkable. Then too, there has been over the centuries a growing appreciation of how emotional disorders impair a person's ability to relate to others. Obviously factors such as these (and many others as well) will exert a strong influence on legislators in their determination of the psychological aptitude levels of marriage that would be appropriate to their own societies.

One would expect, therefore, that the rule of thumb would suffer many exceptions. And so it has. By and large, however, the rule seems to be a generally valid one. In practice, wherever marriage has been viewed as consisting essentially only in the *procreative* aspect, the psychological requirements for marriage have tended to be low; but where the essence of marriage has also included a *personalist* element, the requirements have, as a rule, been higher.

The opinions of various authors, jurists and legislators over the centuries regarding the psychological aptitude for marriage fall generally into three categories: the rationality norm, the puberty norm, and the proportionality norm.

B. *The Rationality Norm*

During most of the Church's history, the rationality norm prevailed. This meant that when a person enjoyed the use of reason, he or she was considered *capable* of marriage; when, however, a mental disorder deprived a person of the use of reason, that person was considered *incapable* of marriage.

The following are the highlights in the history of this position.

1. *Roman Law* (circa 230). Although Roman Law saw marriage as essentially interpersonalist, its knowledge of mental disorders was quite limited and, largely as a result of that, Roman Law settled on the rationality norm and apparently found it adequate. Among the Romans a person, it seems, was either sane or insane, i.e., mad or "furious," as they said. Sane people possessed the use of reason and could marry. "Furious" people could not. The rule was stated succinctly in what eventually became an axiom, usually attributed to the jurist Paulus. It read "Neque furiosus neque furiosa matrimonium contrahere possunt sed contractum matrimonium furore non tollitur",[18] i.e., "Neither the insane man nor the insane woman can enter marriage but once the marriage is contracted, it is not invalidated by subsequent insanity."

The axiom itself did not appear in the *Corpus Iuris Civilis* but the clear and exact sense of it was stated in slightly different words in the *Digest*,[19] and it is quite apparent that that was the only rule the Romans had to regulate psychological aptitude for marriage.

Given their total culture it appears to have been sufficient.

2. *Gratian* (1140). Gratian's theory, as we have seen above, was that marriage is constituted by the consent of the parties to intercourse. He obviously found the "Neque furiosus" axiom quite compatible with this theory and so, in treating of the psychological requirements for marriage, Gratian simply quoted the ancient axiom (more or less) without explanation of any kind.[20] Gratian too, in other words, found it sufficient.

In quoting the axiom, incidentally, Gratian, like Burchard of Worms before him,[21] took the liberty of ascribing it to Pope Fabian, a contemporary of Paulus, rather than to Paulus himself. Gratian did this, no doubt, because it better suited his grand purpose of exalting clergy over laity, but according to Daniel J. Boorstin, such a practice was quite acceptable in the Middle Ages. The age of modern historical criticism had not yet arrived and so certain liberties were apparently still permissible. Boorstin writes "Forgery was a prosperous medieval art. . . . Forgery of documents to support an acknowledged authority was generally considered an act of piety or patriotism. Before falsifying historical documents could have the opprobrium of forgery, it was necessary to believe that the historical past was not a flimsy fabric of myth and legend but had a solid definable reality."[22]

Gratian, at any rate, agreed with the third century axiom and found it sufficient. Unless a person was violently insane, he or she was capable of marriage.

3. *Innocent III* (1205). In the year 1205, Pope Innocent III issued the decree *Dilectus*[23] in which he said that, if it was really true, as Rufina and her father claimed in the case at hand, that Rufina's husband, Opizo, "suffered from a continuing madness - *continuo furore laborat*", then clearly "a legitimate

190

consent could not occur - *legitimus non potuerit intervenire consensus"* and the couple could separate.

The decision of Pope Innocent is one of the few examples we have over a period of many centuries of an allegation of marriage nullity on the grounds of defect of consent due to a mental disorder. Innocent, like his predecessors, used the simple rationality test.

4.   *Thomas Sanchez* (1605). Not surprisingly, the position of Sanchez on this point is not entirely clear. As he was ambiguous regarding the essence of marriage, he is likewise ambiguous regarding the psychological requirements for marriage. On the one hand, Sanchez has long been considered not just a proponent but indeed the *chief* proponent of the simple rationality norm; on the other hand there are certain indications in his writing that he was more inclined towards the puberty norm. It is unclear, for example, whether Sanchez was distinguishing between deliberation and discretion. It is also unclear whether he was applying the rationality norm just to betrothal or to marriage as well. William Van Ommeren discussed the matter at considerable length in his 1961 dissertation.[24]

It is all quite confusing; but the fact is that, deservedly or not, the name of Thomas Sanchez has always been associated with the simple rationality test.

5.   *Buratti* (1624). In his book, *Power to Dissolve*, John T. Noonan, Jr. indicates that, very likely, no marriage sanity case had been presented to the Roman Curia between 1205 (when Innocent III issued his *Dilectus* in the case of Rufina vs. Opizo) and 1763 (when the Sacred Congregation of the Council, as we shall see under number 6, took up the case of Jose and Ana).[25] Van Ommeren, however, does mention one case heard before the Rota in 1624 in which the ponens, Buratti, lent his full support to the simple rationality norm by writing "The madman, the captive in mind and the person destitute of senses are unable to contract marriage if, being entirely deprived of reason or sense, they suffer from permanent insanity or from a defect of sense."[26]

Buratti's wording was extremely cautious, as though to close off any possibility of moving beyond the simple rationality test. For Buratti, it seems, only the absolute madman was incapable of marriage.

6.   *Sacred Congregation of the Council* (1763). In the chapter entitled "Captive in Mind," Noonan discusses the case of Jose Ponce de Leon vs. Ana Guzman heard before the S.C.C. in 1763. The marriage of Jose and Ana had actually taken place in 1728 when Ana was 22 years old. There was a great deal of evidence pointing to Ana's insanity. One witness, a stranger to Ana, testified that about a year before the wedding Ana had suddenly approached him, and, with shrill cries and and laughs, told him that the devil would carry him

off. Just prior to the wedding, rumors reached Jose's family that Ana "was crazy, had always been crazy and at the present was without improvement." On the wedding night, Ana totally surprised Jose by announcing that she had made a vow of virginity and could not have sex with him. During the months following the wedding, Ana indulged in all sorts of bizarre behavior, including screaming obscenities, running naked in the sight of the household and, while naked, making piles of snow in the garden.

The decision of the S.C.C. was "non constat." The nullity of the marriage had not been proved since Ana might have been enjoying the use of reason at the moment she exchanged consent.[27]

Even within the limits of the rationality norm, this was an extremely narrow reading.

7. *Parrillo* (1928). The simply rationality test seems archaic and medieval to us today but it was vigorously defended, as recently as 1928 by Franciscus Parrillo, the rotal auditor. In a long, thirteen page law section of a negative sentence dated February 16, 1928, Parrillo argued the position in a way that was remarkably similar to the S.C.C. decision of 165 years earlier.[28] The simple rationality test was not dead yet.

C. *The Puberty Norm*

The puberty norm was proposed fairly early on but for many years failed to gain the kind of widespread practical acceptance that the simple rationality norm did, despite the immense authority of its principal proponent, namely:

1. *Thomas Aquinas* (1256). In his commentary on Peter Lombard's *Book of Sentences,* Thomas was crystal clear in stating his position regarding the degree of psychological strength required for various actions, including the entering of marriage.

He divided a person's early life into three seven year periods and then said:

> Before the end of the first septennium people are not capable of entering any sort of contract, but at the end of that first septennium they begin to be capable of promising certain things in the future, particularly those things to which natural reason more inclines them, but not of obliging themselves to a perpetual bond since they do not have a firm will; and therefore people are able to contract engagements. But at the end of the second septennium people can oblige themselves to those things which pertain to their own person like entering either religion or marriage. And after the third septennium they can even oblige themselves to those matters that concern other people as well, and after the age of twenty-five people are empowered, in accordance with the law, of disposing of their own belongings.[29]

Thomas' position that marriage involves obligations that pertain only to one's own person and not to others, seems puzzling to us now. But puzzling or not, the position of Thomas was at least firm and clear: the maturity of at least a fourteen year old was required for entering marriage.

2. *Schmalzgrueber* (1719). Among the Romans it was understood that a young person should have reached the age of puberty before marrying,[30] and this norm, which had been generally accepted by the Church, eventually found its way into the Decretals of Gregory IX.[31]

   Initially the point of requiring puberty for marriage was, of couse, that marriage essentially involved intercourse and it is at the age of puberty that one becomes reasonably capable of procreative intercourse.

   Schmalzgrueber, however, noted that there were two reasons for requiring puberty as a minimum age for marriage:

   a. Because marriage induces a greater and firmer obligation than does engagement; and consequently it demands a greater maturity of judgment and a greater freedom of consent.

   b. It has been said that the use of reason is sufficient, and that the use of reason is generally present at the end of the seventh year; for marriage, however, besides the use of reason, there is also required the power of generating, that is to say, the capacity for perfect carnal intercourse.[32]

   For Schmalzgrueber, therefore, the degree of discretion usually attained around the age of puberty was required in order to enter marriage.

3. *Wernz* (1904). Like Schmalzgrueber, Wernz in his pre-code commentary discussed the degree of discretion required for marriage under the general heading of the age required for marriage. He wrote:

   > The canonical impediment of age in celebrating marriage is a double defect, namely the defect of discretion of judgment for conjugal consent and the defect of actual potency for generating.[33]

   Wernz then went on to observe that the discretion of intellect sufficient for a valid and licit marriage is presumed present in the boy of fourteen and the girl of twelve.

   Wernz, therefore, clearly endorsed the puberty norm, which meant logically that if a person were deprived by a mental disorder of *that* degree of discretion at the time of marriage, the marriage would be null.

D. The Proportionality Norm

1. *Gasparri* (1891). Gasparri wrote the first edition of his treatise on marriage more than a decade before Wernz. Like Wernz, Gasparri too treated the matter of discretion under the impediment of nonage. Unlike Wernz, however, Gasparri broke new ground. He went off in a new direction. He left behind the old puberty norm and demanded instead what he called "due discretion - debita discretio," i.e., a degree of discretion that would be proportionate to marriage and which would require in the contractant a sufficient understanding of the nature, importance and essential qualities of marriage.[34]

   Gasparri's new direction must have seemed, at the time, fairly insignificant. In practice, after all, there was probably little difference between the degree of discretion enjoyed by the ordinary fourteen year old and the degree of discretion proportionate to Gasparri's idea of marriage (which essentially involved only the joining of bodies). Within seventy-five years, however, Gasparri's idea of marriage would be supplanted by Vatican II's idea of marriage (which included the joining of souls), and the degree of discretion proportionate to that sort of marriage would be far greater than Gasparri or any of his contemporaries even imagined.

2. *Sincero* (1911). In a rotal decision dated August 28, 1911, Luigi Sincero endorsed Gasparri's idea of due discretion (though Sincero did not consider it germane in the case at bar) and thereby contributed to the dissemination and acceptance of the Gasparri position.[35]

3. *Prior* (1919). In a rotal decision of November 14, 1919, Prior rejected the Sanchez rule, as he called it (the simple rationality norm), noted that Thomas Aquinas demanded more than Sanchez (the puberty norm), and then himself went on to quote and endorse the Gasparri position (the proportionality norm).[36]

   After Prior, more and more jurists came to accept the proportionality theory as appropriate and reasonable. As long, however, as the object of the proportionality was marriage seen as a procreative union only, the potential of the theory was severely limited. Only if marriage could be seen as both procreative and personalist would the theory be able really to expand and blossom.

   To do that, however, it would take an ecumenical council.

IV. THE SECOND VATICAN COUNCIL

The Pastoral Constitution on the Church in the Modern World, *Gaudium et spes,* was promulgated by Pope Paul VI on December 7, 1965.

The Constitution saw marriage as consisting essentially of both a procreative and a personalist element; both the *bonum prolis* and the *bonum coniugum,* it said, are at the heart of marriage. The council, in other words, rejected the position of Gratian that had been dominating Catholic thought for so long and embraced instead the position of Peter Lombard.

In number 48 of the constitution, for example, we read:

> The intimate community of life and conjugal love, which has been established by the Creator and endowed by him with its own proper laws, is rooted in the covenant of its partners, that is, in their irrevocable personal consent. Therefore the institute of marriage, made firm by divine law, arises, even in the eyes of society, by that human act by which the spouses mutually hand over themselves and receive the other; once entered, however, for the sake of both the *bonum coniugum* and the *bonum prolis,* as well as of society itself, the sacred bond no longer depends on human decision alone.[37]

And number 50 concludes with these words:

> But marriage is not merely for the procreation of children: its nature as an indissoluble covenant between two people and the *bonum prolis* demand that the mutual love of the partners be properly shown, that it should grow and mature. Even in cases where, despite the intense desire of the spouses, there are no children, the marriage still perdures as a sharing and communion of the whole of life and remains valid and indissoluble.[38]

The general tenor of the constitution regarding marriage is well known. In 1965 it was a call to the whole Church to rethink what had become its accustomed position regarding the essence of marriage. The essence of marriage, said the constitution, consists not just in a procreative element but in a personalist element as well.

Besides this fundamental point, however, two other, rather incidental matters deserve mention.

First I suspect that it is not entirely accidental that the very council which promoted collegiality (i.e., decentralization) is also the council which promoted *personalism* in marriage, whereas Gratian, whose goal was to strengthen the papal hand (i.e., centralization), promoted *procreationism* in marriage. There is a certain sense, in other words, in which the more monarchical type governments tend to emphasize the *institution* (where procreation is a prime virtue) whereas the more democratic type governments favor the *individual* (where personalism is stressed). This, however, is more a sociological than a canonical question.

A second point is this. It is well known that many churchmen, including even some bishops who participated in the Second Vatican Council, vigorously resisted applying *the teaching of the council* on marriage to *the canon law* on marriage. The remarks of the council, they said, were pastoral in nature and were never meant to be uprooted and transplanted into a legal or juridical setting. To do so would be to do them violence and would come to no good. History, however, has never been tolerant of such compartmentalization, and before long the inevitable began to happen. Beginning with Lucien Anne's decision of February 25, 1969, there were over the next fifteen years a host of decisions by the Rota and other courts around the world, directly translating the conciliar teaching into jurisprudence. The Commission for the Revision of the Code was, meanwhile, taking the same tack. Father Peter Huizing, the chairman of the Marriage Committee, reported in the 1971: 1 issue of *Communicationes:*

> As regards the question of how the personal relationship of the spouses along with the ordering of marriage to procreation should be expressed ... to accord with the Second Vatican Council's description in the Pastoral Constitution on the Church in the Modern World, *Gaudium et spes,* the majority of the committee finally agreed in affirming the nature of marriage as an intimate joining of the whole of life between a man and a woman which, by its nature, is ordered to the procreation and education of offspring. Following the same constitution, the committee decided that the notion of the primary ... and secondary ends (of marriage) ... should no longer be used.[39]

So the stage was now set for the drafting of a new Code of Canon Law.

V. THE CODE OF CANON LAW

A. *On Marriage*

Once the committee agreed to the general philosphy as reported by Huizing, the task was then to incarnate that philosophy in appropriate canons.

This was accomplished particularly in the following areas.

1. *Nature of Marriage.* Canon 1055 of the new code (the opening canon on marriage) notes that marriage is, by its nature, ordered to both the *bonum coniugum* and the *bonum prolis.* Interestingly, the *bonum coniugum* is listed first. The same canon refers to marriage as a "partnership of the whole of life," and notes that it is entered by means of a "covenant." The opening canon on marriage of the old code (c. 1012), used the word "contract" rather than "covenant" and offered no description of marriage whatsoever.

2. *Ends of Marriage.* The second canon on marriage in the old code (c. 1013, §1) listed the procreation and education of offspring as the primary end or purpose of marriage. The new code simply omits a comparable canon.

3. *Object of Consent.* Canon 1057, §2 of the new code states that matrimonial consent is an act of the will by which a man and a woman, through an irrevocable covenant, mutually give and accept each other. The parallel canon in the old code (c. 1081, §2) described matrimonial consent as an act of the

will by which each party hands over and receives the perpetual and exclusive right to the body for those acts which are per se apt for the generation of offspring.

4.   *Ignorance.* Canon 1096, §1 of the new code says that for matrimonial consent to be valid, it is necessary that the contracting parties at least not be ignorant that marriage is a permanent consortium.[40] The parallel canon in the old code (c. 1082, §1) required that the contractants recognize marriage not as a consortium but simply as a society.

5.   *Effects of Marriage.* Canon 1135 of the new code notes that each of the spouses has equal obligations and rights to those things which pertain to the partnership of conjugal life. The parallel canon in the old code (c. 1111) referred, instead, to the rights and obligations of the spouses "for those acts which are proper to conjugal life."

All five of these examples, especially when seen in constellation, clearly demonstrate that the vision of marriage held up by the Fathers of the Second Vatican Council has been effectively incorporated into our present Code of Canon Law.

B.   *On the Psychic Requirements for Marriage*

The 1917 code contained no canon that required any particular degree of maturity or psychic health for a person to enter marriage. There was, of course, a canon on the impediment of nonage (c. 1067) and also the canon on ignorance just mentioned (c. 1082), but the old code contained no canon that stated any sort of minimum psychological aptitude required for marriage. As late as 1928, as we saw, one rotal auditor was still applying the old simple rationality test.

In accordance, however, with the rule of thumb mentioned above under III, A, that the more sophisticated a society's notion of marriage the higher will be the psychological aptitude level demanded of the participants, it was clear by 1970 that it would be absolutely imperative for the new code to contain such a canon.

That canon, as eventually promulgated, is canon 1095 and reads as follows:

Canon 1095 - They are incapable of contracting marriage:

1° who lack the sufficient use of reason;

2° who suffer from grave lack of discretion of judgment concerning essential matrimonial rights and duties which are to be mutually given and accepted;

3° who are not capable of assuming the essential obligations of matrimony due to causes of a psychic nature.

In *Annulments* and *Decisions* I have referred to the three numbers of the canon as (1°) lack of due reason, (2°) lack of due discretion, and (3°) lack of due competence. Each number deserves a brief comment here.

1. *Lack of Due Reason.* The tripartite division found in canon 1095 had acutally been devised very early on. In the 1971:1 issue of *Communicationes,* Father Huizing reported that in its early discussions the Marriage Committee had agreed on the following:

> Although the principles regarding the incapacity for eliciting valid matrimonial consent are implicitly contained in the present law, it was considered appropriate that they be more distinctly and clearly expressed in the new law. The division would be as follows: the total incapacity of eliciting marital consent because of a mental disorder or disturbance by which the use of reason is impeded; incapacity stemming from a grave defect of discretion of judgment about the matrimonial rights and duties that are to be mutually exchanged; and the incapacity of assuming the essential obligations of marriage due to a serious psychosexual anomaly.[41]

It is worth noting that Father Huizing referred to lack of due reason as a "total incapacity," as it truly is. It is, indeed, precisely because of this that the ground is virtually ignored by tribunals in their day-to-day practice. Courts tend to resist trying to prove the superfluous, and it is superfluous to show the "total" incapacity of 1° when 2° recognizes that, for an affirmative decision, it suffices to show the "partial" (or, at least, "the not so total") incapacity which comes from lack of due discretion.

Despite what seems a practical tautology, however, the tripartite division has, nevertheless, found its way into law.

2. *Lack of Due Discretion.* The English word "discretion" refers to both the intellect and the will. When we say that we leave a matter to another person's discretion, we mean that it is left to both the judgment and the free choice of that person.

The Latin word has traditionally had the same meaning. If one looks up "Discretio iudicii" in Palazzini's *Dictionarium Morale et Canonicum,* it says see "Capacitas intelligendi et volendi" and when one turns to that heading, it begins by noting that "discretio iudicii" (which is the same phrase used in 1095, 2°) consists of two elements: understanding and willing.[42]

The meaning of discretion is, therefore, quite clear. It means first of all that a person must understand the duties that are to be assumed, and that secondly he or she freely choose to assume those understood duties.

3. *Lack of Due Competence.* The statement was made earlier (above, III, A) that when the essence of marriage was understood to consist only in the right to intercourse, then there would be only one sort of constitutional incapacity for marriage, namely the incapacity for intercourse, i.e., impotence. This was

certainly logical and was clearly implied in the opening pages of Gasparri's work on marriage.[43]

It should be remembered, however, that the 1917 code recognized not only the *essence* of marriage (the right to intercourse) but also two *essential properties* of marriage (unity, i.e., fidelity, and indissolubility). If, therefore, it were recognized that a person could be psychologically incapable of fidelity or indissolubility, then besides *impotence* there would be a second kind of constitutional incapacity, namely *incompetence*. So understood, incompetence would, of course, have an extremely limited scope; it would apply only to people who were truly incapable of either fidelity or perpetuity, usually the former.

The concept seems to have been used for the first time by the Rota in a decision given by Alberto Canestri on February 21, 1948. At the time Canestri referred to incompetence as "moral impotence," a term which gained fairly wide acceptance for a time but was eventually discarded. Canestri wrote:

> There are men and women who, by reason of an atavistic or hereditary imperfection, or because they are mired in vice or have been poisoned by breathing in the fumes of a corrupt society, are so depraved, especially in the area of sexual desire, that they are rendered incapable of marriage by a kind of impotence, not a physical but a moral impotence.[44]

Given this background, that incompetence or moral impotence as understood from 1948 on referred primarily to an incapacity for fidelity due to hyperaesthesia, it is understandable that the 1970 draft and even the 1975 draft of canon 1095 spoke of people being incapable of assuming the obligations of marriage *due to a psycho-sexual anomaly*. Once it was realized, however, that the very essence of marriage included the right to an interpersonal relationship, then it was obvious that the phrase "due to a psycho-sexual anomaly" was unduly restrictive and the phrase was dropped. The 1980 draft changed "psycho-sexual anomaly" to "psychic anomaly," and the 1983 code spoke only of "causes of a psychic nature."

According to the present code, therefore, a marriage is rendered null by any psychological reason (even though it is not a "disorder" or "anomaly") whenever that reason or cause renders a spouse incapable of assuming the essential obligations of marriage, especially the obligation of engaging in an interpersonal relationship.

VI. CONCLUDING REMARKS

Canon 1095 of the new Code of Canon Law, taken in context, says certain things but leaves other things unsaid.

It says that in order to enter a valid marriage, a person must enjoy sufficient discretion and sufficient competence for a marital consortium.

Left unsaid, however, is the precise nature of a consortium. Also left unsaid is the meaning of "sufficient discretion" and "sufficient competence"; but it is clear that these latter terms are essentially relational to the former, so that if we knew the precise meaning of the term "consortium" then we would, at least, be well on our way to understanding how much discretion and how much competence would be "sufficient."

The special task for the jurist in our time, therefore, is to determine as precisely as possible the essential elements that go to make up a consortium. We could start, for example, with the dictionary definitions and look to the right of one spouse to the (1) company, (2) affection, and (3) help of the other. Or we could consider Ombretta Fumagalli Carulli's three "constitutive elements" of conjugal love: (1) recognizing the other as a person endowed with his or her own identity, (2) regarding the other as a person with whom one wants to establish a common life, and (3) wishing the other well.[45] My own three components of (1) self revelation, (2) understanding, and (3) loving, which were adapted from Eugene C. Kennedy's "signs of life in marriage,"[46] seem to me to be the basic practical skills one must enjoy in order to enter a stable, intimate relationship. And there are several other approaches that deserve consideration as well.[47]

Above all, perhaps, we should be reading and listening to what married men and women are saying about what it really takes to make it in marriage. Male celibates are not without their own insights into marriage but it certainly makes no sense to listen only and exclusively to them, as we have in fact done for so many years.

Canon 1095 is a useful canon but it leaves much to the "discretion," i.e. to the insightful decisions, of the judges. Not all of us, of course, will understand the canon in exactly the same way but all of us must, at least, be as knowledgeable and as equitable and as responsible and as charitable as, with God's grace, we can be.

ENDNOTES

[1] Theodore Mackin, *What is Marriage?* (New York: Paulist, 1982), p. 128.
[2] St. Augustine, *De Bono Coniugali,* c. 6; PL 40: 377-378.
[3] St. Augustine, *Contra Faustum Manichaeum,* lib. 19, c. 26; PL 42: 365.
[4] St. Augustine, *De Coniugiis Adulterinis,* lib. 2, c. 12: PL 40: 479.
[5] *Decretum,* C. 27, q. 2, c. 2.
[6] *Decretum,* C. 27, q. 2, c. 3.
[7] Duns Scotus, Quaestiones in quartum librum Sententiarum, dist. 26, q. unica *(Omnia opera,* Vol. 19, p. 186).
[8] Francesco Xav. Wernz, S.J., *Jus Decretalium,* Tomus IV (Romae: Typographia Polyglotta S.C. De Propaganda Fide, 1904), p. 48.
[9] *Digesta,* 23, 2, 1.
[10] *Instituta,* 1, 9, 1.
[11] David Fellhauer, "The 'Consortium Omnis Vitae' as a Juridical Element of Marriage," *Studia Canonica* 13 (1979) 58-59.
[12] Peter Lombard, *Libri IV Sententiarum,* lib. IV, dist. 28.
[13] St. Thomas, *In IV Sent,* d. 28, art. 4
[14] Thomas Sanchez, *De Sancto Matrimonii Sacramento,* lib. 2, disp. 1, n. 8.

[15] Ibid., lib. 2, disp. 4, n. 3.

[16] Lawrence G. Wrenn, *Annulments* p. 7 under B5.

[17] As opposed to incompetence, which is the "incapacitas praestandi obiectum consensus."

[18] *Fontes Iuris Ante Justiniani*, II, 345.

[19] *Digesta*, 23, 2, 16.

[20] *Decretum*, C. 32, c. 26.

[21] Burchardus, X, 28-29; PL 140: 819.

[22] Daniel J. Boorstin, *The Discoverers* (New York: Random House, 1983), p. 576.

[23] *X*, 4, 1, 24.

[24] William M. Van Ommeren, *Mental Illness Affecting Matrimonial Consent* (Washington: Catholic University of America Press, 1961), pp. 105-132. See also John R. Keating, *The Bearing of Mental Impairment on the Validity of Marriage* (Rome: Gregorian University Press, 1964), pp. 123-143.

[25] John T. Noonan, Jr., *Power to Dissolve* (Cambridge: The Belknap Press of Harvard University Press, 1972), pp. 154-155. "Apart from Innocent III's decision incorporated in the decretal *Dilectus*, neither the advocates of the parties nor the Secretary of the S.C.C. were able to refer to any instance of marriage attacked for insanity before any court of the Curia. It would be rash to say that no marriage sanity case had gone to Rome since *Dilectus* had been issued in 1205, but where precedent is unknown it is as good as nonexistent."

[26] *S.R.R.D., coram* Buratti (Rome, 1624), annot. ad decis. 763, as quoted in Van Ommeren, p. 38.

[27] Noonan, pp. 136-158.

[28] *S.R.R.D.* 20: 58-71

[29] St. Thomas, *In IV Sent,* d. 27, q. 2, a. 2, n. 7.

[30] *Instituta 1,* 10.

[31] *X,* 4, 2-3.

[32] Franciscus Schmalzgrueber, *Ius Ecclesiasticum Universum,* tom. 4,pars 1, tit. 2. See also tom. 4, pars 1. tit 1, n. 14.

[33] Wernz, p. 469

[34] Gasparri, *De Matrimonio* (Paris, 1891), n. 777. In Gasparri's 1932 edition, see n. 783.

[35] *S.R.R.D.* 3: 450.

[36] *S.R.R.D.* 11: 173. See also *AAS* 13 (1921) 56.

[37] *Gaudium et spes,* no. 48.

[38] *Gaudium et spes,* no. 50.

[39] *Communicationes 3* (1971) 70.

[40] The word "consortium" is a legitimate word in the English language but, except for this one canon, the CLSA translation has translated it "partnership." See cc. 1055, 1098 and 1135. The *American Heritage Dictionary* gives, as one of its meanings for the word consortium, "a husband's right to the company, help and affection of his wife (and) the right of the wife to the same." *Webster's New Collegiate Dictionary* defines consortium as "the legal right of one spouse to the company, affection and service of the other."

[41] *Communicationes 3* (1971). See also *Communicationes 7* (1975) 41 for the actual 1970 draft. Regarding Huizing's statement about the *implicit* presence of the notion of incapacity in the 1917 code, see cc. 1035 and 1081, §1.

[42] Petrus Palazzini, *Dictionarium Morale et Canonicum,* 4 vols. (Rome: Catholic Book Agency, 1962), vol. 2, p. 103 and vol. 1, p. 536.

[43] Gasparri, §7.

[44] *S.R.R.D.* 40: 64.

[45] Ombretta Fumagalli Carulli, "Essenza ed esistenza nell'amore coniugale: Considerazioni canonistiche," *Ephemerides Iuris Canonici* 36 (1980) 216-218.

[46] Eugene C. Kennedy, "Signs of Life in Marriage" in *Divorce and Remarriage in the Catholic Church,* ed. Lawrence G. Wrenn (New York: Newman Press, 1973), pp. 121-133.

[47] See, for example, *Decisions,* first edition, p. 60.

APPENDIX THREE

Refining The Essence Of Marriage

This paper will consist of five sections. The first section will discuss the Jemolo case, which was a hypothetical case devised some years ago to test the common understanding of marriage that prevailed at the time. The Jemolo case states the problem. The next section, "Some Preliminary Observations," consists of a half dozen points which try to keep us on the straight and narrow, and so facilitate our attempt to come up with a solution to the problem. The third section attempts to define with some reasonable degree of precision the nature and essence of the marital relationship. This section might be called "A Solution" or perhaps more realistically "Towards A Solution." In the fourth section we will discuss several possible objections to the solution proposed. And finally, some practical applications of the theory will be considered, at least briefly.

A. The Jemolo Case

Forty-five years ago the Italian jurist, A. C. Jemolo, asked his students and his readers to think hard about a hypothetical marriage case.[1] An honest pondering of the case, Jemolo implied, would necessarily involve a thorough rethinking of the then current understanding of marriage.

The case that Jemolo posed was this: a man marries a woman not primarily out of love or to have a family or for any of the usual reasons; rather he marries her primarily to carry out a vendetta. His principal interest is to be mean and cruel to his wife and to make her pay for all the injuries committed by her family against him and his family.

Is it possible, asked Jemolo, that such an arrangement could ever be considered a valid marriage? The question was, at the time, an intriguing and troublesome one. Under the old code marital consent consisted in the exchange of rights to those acts which are per se apt for the generation of offspring. If in an individual case those rights *were* exchanged, and if at the same time neither of the essential properties of marriage (unity and indissolubility) were excluded, then a valid marriage would occur.

In terms of the *bona matrimonii* (the goods or blessings of marriage), all three *bona* (the *bonum prolis,* the *bonum fidei,* and the *bonum sacramenti)* could conceivably be present in such a case. Indeed in the scenario posed by Jemolo, the man did intend to have children; he did intend to be faithful to his wife (in the minimal sense that he was not reserving to himself the right to have a lover on the side); and he did intend to cohabit with his wife until death. The man, furthermore, was quite capable of fulfilling all those obligations.

In other words the man did, first of all, have the capacity for marriage as it was then understood, and secondly, he did not simulate marriage either totally or partially. *Technically*, therefore, he entered what would have to be regarded as a valid marriage.

Yet common sense told Jemolo that such an arrangement could not possibly be called a marriage. This kind of hate-filled vendetta was absolutely and unequivocally unworthy of being considered a marriage, let alone a *sacrament* of marriage. It is much more like a *Mafia* contract than a *marriage* contract; certainly it is not a marriage *covenant.*

The obvious implication, of course, was that if the Church judged that man's vendetta-inspired union to be a valid marriage, then there was something radically wrong with the Church's understanding of marriage. The essence of marriage needed reexamination. Something important, indeed something essential must have been overlooked and omitted. There must be something above and beyond the *bonum prolis,* the *bonum fidei,* and the *bonum sacramenti.* And that was the problem: if the marriage of the man bent on vendetta is *not* a marriage, and surely it is not, then *why* is it not? In canonical terms, what essential element was lacking in that arrangement which rendered it non-marital, that is to say, something less than a marriage?

B. Preliminary Observations

1. First I should like to point out what the missing element is *not.* The missing element is not to be found by looking at a person's *motive* for marrying. Jurisprudence has always held that an otherwise valid marriage is never rendered invalid simply by an unworthy motive. A person, for example, may marry for money or prestige, or to gain citizenship in a desirable country, or to escape from an unhappy home life, or for countless other less than noble reasons. Such motives, however, do not in themselves invalidate a marriage. Such motives can only affect validity when and if they also exclude the essence of marriage. If, for example, a Polish man married an American woman in order to gain entry into the United States, that motivation would not ordinarily invalidate the marriage. It could invalidate the marriage, if say, the man intended to divorce the woman as soon as he obtained his citizenship, but ordinarily and of itself it would not vitiate the marriage.

    It has always been understood, in other words, that the *finis operis* (in this case the purpose of marriage itself) and the *finis operantis* (the motive of the spouse in marrying) do not necessarily have to coincide. It is probably nice if they do but they do not have to. All that is absolutely required is that the spouse, for whatever reason, consent to the essence of marriage. This is what is known as the principle of the irrelevancy of motive.

    In the Jemolo case the man's motive for marrying was, of course, immoral; but despite this, he did not exclude the essence of marriage as it was understood at the time. He consented to the three *bona* of marriage and that made the marriage valid. In other words, when we look for the missing

203

element in the Jemolo case, we should look not at the *finis operantis* but at the *finis operis;* we should look to the essence of marriage itself.

2. My second observation flows from the first and is really the other side of the coin. It is the flip side of the principle of the irrelevancy of motive. It is this: just as generally speaking the presence of a bad motive does not result in invalidity, so it is equally true that the absence of a good motive likewise does not result in invalidity.

    This, I think, is an important point because it means that if jurisprudence were eventually to conclude that some specific element, for example *love,* is essential to marriage, then the love that would be at issue would *not* be the love that motivates people to marry. Courts would not, therefore, declare a marriage null because it had been shown that one or both of the spouses were not "in love" when they married or that they failed to marry for reasons of love. Again, motivation is basically irrelevant. Rather, the love that would be at issue would be something intrinsic to marriage itself. It would be part of the object of consent. It would be something the parties consent to.

    If, therefore, jurisprudence were eventually to conclude that love is essential to marriage then it would be expected that when people marry, they would agree - even if they were not marrying for reasons of love - that they would be loving persons to each other for the rest of their lives. If therefore love comes to be accepted as essential to marriage, this and only this will be the love we are talking about.

3. My third observation is a direct, if rather vague and quite general, response to the question raised by the Jemolo case. In the Jemolo case the man consented to the *bonum prolis,* the *bonum fidei* and the *bonum sacramenti* and therefore seemed to enter a technically valid marriage. The question is: was there another element, essential to marriage, an element to which the man did not consent, which rendered the marriage invalid? In light of the Second Vatican Council and of the 1983 code, the answer is crystal clear. The answer is that besides the three *bona* recognized prior to Vatican II, we now know that there is a fourth *bonum* which is equally essential to marriage, namely the *bonum coniugum.*

    Canon 1055, §1, the opening canon on marriage, makes this very clear. It reads: "The matrimonial covenant, by which a man and a woman establish between themselves a partnership of the whole of life, is by its nature ordered to the *bonum coniugum* and to the procreation and education of offspring..."

    Common sense told us all along, of course, that this was the basic problem in the Jemolo case. The man was not intending to be his wife's *helpmate* but rather her *antagonist,* and that is what rendered his union a non-marriage. This was not so clear in 1941 as it is now. Now it is clear that there are not

204

three essential *bona* but four. The precise, exact, detailed meaning of the *bonum coniugum* we shall try to clarify during the course of these remarks, but for the present I would simply like to make the point that the *bonum coniugum*, whatever it involves, is definitely and certainly an essential element of marriage.

4.   I would note, fourthly, that, except for indissolubility, it is really inaccurate to say that the *bona matrimonii* themselves pertain to the essence of marriage. It is rather the right, the ius ad bona matrimonii, that pertains to the essence. Take the *bonum fidei*, for example. It is not really fidelity but rather the *right* to fidelity that pertains to the essence of marriage. If this were not so, if fidelity itself pertained to the essence of marriage, then part of the essence of marriage and therefore the marriage itself would cease to exist whenever a spouse was unfaithful; that, or course, is not true.

The same is true of the *bonum coniugum*. Strictly speaking it is not the *bonum coniugum* but the right to the *bonum coniugum* exchanged at the time of the wedding that belongs to the essence of marriage. It is, therefore, the actual pledge of the spouses to contribute to their mutual welfare that is essential and constitutive of a valid marriage. If at some later time the actual, de facto *bonum coniugum* should dissipate - if, for example, the couple's love for each other should turn to hate - that disappearance of the *bonum coniugum* would not invalidate or dissolve the marriage. What is essential is not the *bonum coniugum* but rather the right to the *bonum coniugum*.

5.   A fifth preliminary observation is this. The specific components of the *bonum coniugum* might differ from culture to culture. It is quite possible, for example, that conjugal love would be considered an essential component of the *bonum coniugum* in the twentieth century whereas it would not have been regarded as absolutely essential in the eighteenth century.

This was a point made by Lucien Anné in his famous decision of February 25, 1969.[2] It strikes me as a valid and practical observation. It means, for example, that as we turn our attention to the task of determining the precise components of the *bonum coniugum*, it is not necessary that we arrive at some sort of pure, universal essence that would be applicable for all places and for all times. Rather it would suffice if we could identify with reasonable preciseness the components of the *bonum coniugum* for this time and this place, that is to say, for our own culture and our own civilization.

6.   My final preliminary observation is a simple word of caution, namely that in our attempt to locate and identify the exact dimensions of the *bonum coniugum* for our culture, it is important that we avoid being either too generous or too stingy, too inclusive or too exclusive.

The Jemolo case made it clear that the 1917 code had sinned by being too exclusive, that in excluding the *bonum coniugum* from the essence of marriage it had artificially truncated the notion of marriage and deprived it of some of its essential richness. The canonists of the early twentieth century fell into a trap regarding the essence of marriage. Now that that error has been corrected we do not want to fall into a similar trap, this time regarding the essence not of marriage itself but of the *bonum coniugum*. On the one hand we *do not want to say*, "Yes, the *bonum coniugum* is essential but the *bonum coniugum* means only that the spouses should be civil to each other." On the other hand, neither do we want to say, "The *bonum coniugum* is essential and that means that the spouses must be madly in love with each other or there is no marriage." These two extremes must be avoided. The challenge will be to find the truth, which will not necessarily be exactly in the middle but should, at least, be somewhere between the two extremes.

C. Towards A Solution

Over the years jurisprudence has defined with reasonable precision the sense of the three traditional *bona*. The *bonum prolis* refers to the right of the parties to non-contraceptive intercourse; the *bonum fidei* refers to the right of the parties to be their spouse's only sex partner; the *bonum sacramenti* refers to the indissolubility of marriage.

The essence of the fourth *bonum*, the *bonum coniugum*, however, is not yet so clear. Does it refer to the right of the parties to simple, basic goodwill from their spouse? Or does it go so far as to include a right to a romantic, passionate love?

As with the other *bona*, a clarification of this issue will come gradually through the work of jurisprudence. But in this section of the paper I would like to discuss six of the more obvious qualities that might constitute the essence of the *bonum coniugum*. They are partnership, benevolence, companionship, friendship, caring, and finally love.

1.   *Partnership*

Since marriage is a consortium and the usual translation of "consortium" is partnership, and since canon 1135 says that "each of the spouses has equal obligations and rights to those things which pertain to the partnership of conjugal life," it might seem that that quality of partnership constitutes the nucleus of the *bonum coniugum*.

Justice Story defined a partnership as "a relation existing between two or more competent persons who have contracted to place their money, effects, labor and skill, or some or all of them, in lawful commerce or business with the understanding that there shall be a communion of profit among them." In a more general sense a partner is anyone who has a part in something. A partner is a partaker, a sharer, a participant, an associate, or a colleague.

In light of all this it is clear, I think, that partnership is a pretty impersonal, business-like arrangement. Still there is something to be said for it. In terms of the Jemolo case one would be hard pressed to say that the man in that case recognized the woman as a true partner. On the contrary, he treated her not as a partner but as a victim. Certainly he did not intend her to share in what Justice Story called the "communion of profit among them." So even if jurisprudence had, in those days, recognized that much, namely that the essence of marriage required a true partnership, then the union proposed by Jemolo could easily have been declared null according to the then accepted rules of jurisprudence.

Mere partnership would therefore seem to have solved the Jemolo case. But that was forty-five years ago and since then the question has shifted somewhat. What we want to know now is whether it can be said that partnership is the special quality that constitutes the nucleus of the *bonum coniugum*. The answer, I think, is no. Since the Second Vatican Council, it seems to me, mainstream jurisprudence has concluded that mere partnership, that is, merely being a colleague, is not enough; some interpersonal relationship is required as constitutive of the essential nucleus of the *bonum coniugum*. Mere partnership therefore is too impersonal and too business-like to qualify even as the bare minimum that would be required for a valid marriage.

2.   *Benevolence*

Benevolence, otherwise known as goodwill, seems to suffer from the same basic defect as partnership: it is too impersonal to constitute the essence of marriage. Marriage is now recognized as being an interpersonal relationship of some depth and intensity. But this is not what benevolence is.

Benevolence is defined in Webster's as the "kindly disposition to do good and promote the welfare of others: goodwill." Given that definition it would seem that the people who would appropriately exercise benevolence would be, not husband and wife toward each other, but rather benefactors and philanthropists toward their beneficiaries. Benevolence, I take it, can be present and even practiced without even knowing who the beneficiary is. It seems evident, therefore, that mere benevolence or goodwill would necessarily fall far short of what is required in order to have a true *bonum coniugum*. It is not enough, in other words, for husbands and wives to treat each other as beneficiaries. Some degree of personalism is absolutely essential in marriage.

Thomas Aquinas, incidentally, made a clear distinction between love on the one hand and goodwill or benevolence on the other. Love, he said, involves much more than simply wishing a person well. Goodwill, he said, is neither friendship nor love but just the beginning, just the first step or groundwork of friendship, the *principium amicitiae*.[3]

One would of course expect spouses to exercise goodwill toward each other, but one would also expect more. Mere benevolence is not enough to constitute a real marriage.

3. *Companionship*

Companionship is more personal than benevolence and to that extent is closer to what might constitute the nucleus of the *bonum coniugum*. The word "companion" comes from "cum" and "panis". A companion, therefore, is one with whom you break bread. He or she is not some nameless beneficiary of your kindness but rather an acquaintance with whom you spend time and share experiences on the great journey of life.

C. S. Lewis suggests that companionship is a product of the gregarious instinct in human nature, and notes that it might also he called "clubbableness" since companionship is the kind of thing shared by men and women at the golf club or even in the barroom.[4] Companionship, however, is something less than friendship. It is, you might say, the matrix of friendship in that given the right people and a shared interest, friendship might grow and develop out of it. But companionship is not so rich or so deep as friendship. Friendship is gold; companionship is silver.

But the jurisprudential question is whether the *bonum coniugum* could be said to be present if, at the time of the wedding, the spouses consented not to love one another or even to be friends, but simply to be companions. The famous decision of November 29, 1975 of the five Signatura judges in the Utrecht case answered in the affirmative.[5] In the opinion of those judges *communio vitae* meant nothing more than the *communio thori, mensae et habitationis* of the old canon 1128. In that view, in other words, a spouse was precisely a companion, or more precisely a sexual companion, that is 'to say, one with whom the other party broke bread and had sex, one with whom bed and board were shared.

Since that time, however, mainstream jurisprudence has, I think, come to require more than that. The present view is that spouses must share not just bed and board but they must share their whole lives as well. Marriage is a *consortium totius vitae,* as canon 1055 says. It is a sharing not just of externals but of the internal lives of the spouses as well, a sharing of their thoughts and feelings and, in some way, of their very selves.

Mere companionship, therefore, is not enough to constitute the *bonum coniugum.*

4. *Friendship*

St. Thomas says that there are five things that pertain to friendship: we should wish our friends well (benevolence); we should wish them to be and to live;

we should take pleasure in their company (companionship); we should make choice of the same things; and we should grieve and rejoice with them.[6]

Clearly for Thomas friendship includes such things as benevolence and companionship, but it is also something over and above those things and is distinct from both of them. Friendship, furthermore, is likewise distinct from love, at least from the love of lovers. C. S. Lewis notes the following differences between friendship and love. First, lovers are always talking to each other about their love, whereas friends hardly ever talk to one another about their friendship. Second, lovers are normally face to face, absorbed in each other, whereas friends tend to stand side by side, absorbed in some common interest. Third, love is an exclusive relationship between two people only, whereas in friendship two friends delight to be joined by a third, and three by a fourth. "True friendship," says Lewis, "is the least jealous of loves."[7]

So once again we come to the jurisprudential question: what is it that constitutes the essence of the *bonum coniugum*? Is it enough if the spouses pledge to be each other's lifelong friend, even each other's *best* friend forever?

Friendship, as we noted, is golden. It is a *wonderful*, noble thing and has been extolled by many of history's greatest poets and philosophers. But in spite of that, the right to friendship, it seems to me, still falls short of what is necessary for a valid marital relationship, principally because the marital relationship must have a certain exclusive quality about it whereas friendship, by definition, is not exclusive but inclusive.

Spouses should certainly be friends, just as they should be benevolent partners and companions. But none of those qualities, taken either separately or together, is sufficient to constitute the essential nucleus of the *bonum coniugum*. For that something more is required.

5. *Caring*

The verb "to care" has many meanings. It is, first of all, often used as a synonym for love. Morton T. Kelsey, for example, has written a book which has as its title *Caring*, but as its subtitle, *How Can We Love One Another?* In fact, this book entitled *Caring* is really all about *loving*. Second, caring can denote a burdensome sense of responsibility and solicitude, or trouble caused by duties, and in that sense we speak of a "careworn face." Third, it can mean to have charge of or to be responsible for, as a doctor or nurse cares for a patient and a shepherd or pastor cares for the flock. In this sense it is the opposite of apathy.

The classic, popular discussion of the subject is in a little book called *On Caring* written by Milton Mayeroff. Mayeroff, in effect, adopts the third meaning of the term, namely to be responsible for something or someone.

More precisely, Mayeroff defines caring as "helping the other grow,"[8] which is basically what the doctor, nurse, shepherd and pastor do. Rollo May, in his book *Love and Will,* adopts this same meaning of the term. May writes, "if I care about being, I will shepherd it with some attention paid to its welfare."[9]

Seeing care as "helping the other grow" is, in fact, a very ancient way of viewing care. Martin Heidegger recounts this ancient parable in which care is portrayed as a shaper and molder of the human being, or to use Mayeroff's expression, as one who helps another grow:

> Once when "Care" was crossing a river, she saw some clay; she thought-fully took up a piece and began to shape it. While she was meditating on what she had made, Jupiter came by. "Care" asked him to give it spirit, and this he gladly granted. But when she wanted her name to be bestowed upon it, he forbade this, and demanded that it be given his name instead. While "Care" and Jupiter were disputing, Earth arose and desired that her own name be conferred on the creature, since she had furnished it with part of her body. They asked Saturn to be their arbiter, and he made the following decision, which seemed a just one: "Since you, Jupiter, have given its spirit, you shall receive that spirit at its death; and since you, Earth, have given its body, you shall receive its body. But since 'Care' first shaped this creature, she shall possess it as long as it lives. And because there is now a dispute among you as to its name, let it be called homo, for it is made out of humus (earth)."[10]

In saying that care "shall posses it as long as it lives," this ancient parable implies that the human being is essentially and irrevocably constituted as a caring person. This is certainly an upbeat, optimistic anthropology that sug-gests that our common vocation as human beings is to help one another grow. We are all called to care for one another. Caring is seen, therefore, as a kind of primordial human disposition.

But having said that, let us return once again to the jurisprudential question. In order to exchange the right to the *bonum coniugum* what precisely is it that the spouses pledge to do? Is it that they pledge themselves to be caring spouses to each other?

I think it is not, and the reason I think it is not is this. In order to bring about the *bonum coniugum* it is essential that the spouses not only care for each other, that is, help each other grow; it is also necessary that they allow themselves to be cared for. Caring, in other words, is only half the process. In the helping professions and in many other situations as well, caring alone works fine and can be a beautiful thing. But in close interpersonal relation-ships including marriage, caring alone (without a corresponding openness to be cared for) can be destructive.

Woody Allen's movie *Hannah And Her Sisters is*, I think, a clear illustration of this. *Hannah And Her Sisters,* as the title implies, is about the relationship of Hannah (played by Mia Farrow) with her two sisters, Lee and Holly. But it is also about Hannah's relationship with her two husbands, her first husband being Woody Allen, her second Michael Caine.

Hannah is a charming, efficient, accomplished, caring, thoughtful, considerate, self-sufficient, wonderful person. She has given up a career on the stage in order to have a family but in the course of the movie returns to do a single play on Broadway for which she gets rave reviews. She also deserves rave reviews as a homemaker and mother and she is, in general, a marvelous person, totally in control of her own life and always willing to help others.

The only problem is that she somehow manages to undermine everybody around her. Hannah and her first husband, Woody Allen, (as we see in flashbacks) are unable to have children and when they go to a doctor in an attempt to remedy the situation they find that Woody is incurably sterile. Hannah's second husband, Michael Caine, is deeply in love with Hannah. But at one point he says to her "It's impossible to live with someone like you, who is so giving but who has no needs of her own," and he goes out and has an affair with Hannah's sister Lee. Lee is a good person but is so overwhelmed by Hannah's flawlessness that she first lives with a totally antisocial, intellectual artist, and then has her fling with Michael Caine. Then there is Holly who, like Lee, is overpowered by Hannah and becomes a drug addict and can never figure out what she wants to do with her life. Interestingly, though, before the movie ends, Holly marries Woody Allen and, lo and behold, she becomes pregnant by Woody who, when he was with Hannah, was regarded as incurably sterile.

The message, I think, is clear; namely, in close interpersonal relationships, caring alone is not enough. Unless, indeed, it is coupled with a willingness to be cared for, caring alone can be a destructive and sterilizing thing in an institution like marriage. When, however, caring is in fact coupled with an openness to being cared for, then it is no longer called caring but something else, namely love.

6.   *Love*

Love, as we know, is a many splendored thing; but in our context, at least, it may be defined as an affective tendency toward another person which is dialogical in nature and which involves union with the other.

To descibe love as an "affective tendency" is to distinguish it immediately from infatuation. A tendency is just an inclination or a propensity, and connotes perhaps a strong and eager but nevertheless a somewhat gentle movement, whereas infatuation involves a kind of dizzy, careening, uncontrolled, raging flame of desire. Etymologically the word infatuation comes from the Latin *fatuitas,* which means "foolishness"; love, on the other hand, is the most unfoolish thing in the world.

The phrase "affective tendency" also distinguishes love itself or simple love from romantic love. In her book *The Theology of Romantic Love, A Study in the Writings of Charles Williams,* Mary McDermott Shideler notes that romantic love always begins with the shock of an intense personal experience and then causes the lover, both in body and mind, to function as a whole person, as an integrated entity, focusing all his or her powers on the beloved. It is the kind of love that Dante had for Beatrice and, in our century, the kind of love that Wally Simpson and King Edward VIII seem to have had for each other. But as Shideler points out, that kind of romantic, heroic love is not the only love. "Sweetness and serenity," she says, "quiet affection and gradual development, belong as truly to the Kingdom of Love as do the tumults of the romantic encounter. The absence of the romantic response to experience implies no disparagement, because this can be a difference in style of loving, rather than a difference in degree or depth of love."[11]

Finally, the term "affective tendency" also distinguishes love from a completely cooled down, business-like experience that pertains only to the mind and the reasoning faculty. Love is affective. It involves the heart and the emotions. St. Thomas treats of love under the heading of the soul's passions[12] along with hatred, desire and aversion, joy and sorrow, hope and despair, fear and daring, and anger. Love, said St. Thomas, pertains to the appetite,[13] is rightly classified as a passion,[14] can easily lead to ecstasy,[15] and involves a "union of affection, without which," he says "there is no love."[16]

Love, therefore, is neither infatuation nor romantic love on the one hand, nor is it a kind of intellectual esteem or respect on the other. It is rather an affective tendency.

The second part of the definition of love notes that is is dialogical in nature. Unlike caring, therefore, which in itself is a kind of monologue, love is seen rather as a conversation, a dialogue. It involves two axes or poles in each person around which the love flows.

These two poles were called by Aquinas *amor concupiscentiae* and *amor benevolentiae,*[17] which Karl Rahner translates respectively as love of desire and love of generosity.[18] Love of desire, as the term implies, involves desiring the other as a source of legitimate self-fulfillment, whereas love of generosity involves wanting the best for one's beloved for the beloved's own sake. In all healthy human love, however, both poles coexist and are more or less constantly active. In all healthy human love there must be both giving and receiving. Love is essentially an exchange. Contrary to the axiom, the fact is that it is not always more blessed to give than to receive.[19] Human love, at any rate, cannot exist without both.

Finally let me mention briefly the third element in the definition of love, namely that it involves union with the other. Thomas devotes a separate article to this, noting that every love is a unitive force and that both poles, the love of desire and the love of generosity, are each in its own way creative of a unity between the lover and the beloved. Love is always a bonding force that makes for communion and, in some sense at least, makes two people one.[20]

If one were to list reasons in favor of the position that the essence of the bonum coniugum consists in the ius ad amorem, this perhaps would be the first, namely that both marriage and love have the same effect. They both create a bond between people; in both cases, the two people become one. In marriage they become one flesh which is not necessarily true in all love. But this, I think, is the point. Whereas it is all right for two people to become one without being one flesh, it is not all right for two people to become one flesh without their first having become one. It is all right, in other words, for two people to love each other without being lovers, but it is not all right for people to become lovers unless they love each other. In marriage the spouses have a right to have intercourse, but there is something wrong (and probably immoral) if they have intercourse without loving each other.

This is the fundamental reason why the bonum prolis and the bonum coniugum go hand in hand and are inseparable: because the essence of the bonum coniugum is the ius ad amorem, and unless that is present it is not right to have intercourse. It perhaps even explains why in canon 1055, §1, the bonum coniugum is mentioned first and the bonum prolis second: because people should commit themselves to loving each other before they make love.

A second reason in support of the essentiality of the ius ad amorem is the importance assigned to love in papal encyclicals, notably Casti connubii (n. 23) and Humanae vitae (nn. 8-9). In the former Pius XI referred to love as that "excellent soil" in which conjugal faith has rooted and he noted that "love of husband and wife ... pervades all the duties of married life and holds pride of place in Christian marriage." In the latter Paul VI noted that marital love was part of God's loving design, and that its characteristic features are that it be fully human, total, faithful, exclusive and fruitful.

A third reason for saying that the bonum coniugum consists in the parties pledging to be loving persons to each other is found in the Second Vatican Council's Gaudium et spes (nn. 48-50) which assigns to love an absolutely central and pervasive role in marriage, and which describes marriage as "an intimate community of life and love."

A fourth reason is the one developed by Theodore Mackin. He points out that if love is not essential to marriage, then the sacrament of matrimony is lacking a matrix.[21] St. Paul pointed out in the fifth chapter of Ephesians that the love of wife and husband in marriage is the symbol of the love between Christ and the Church. Marriage is a sacrament precisely because it images the love of Christ and the Church, but unless love or the right to love is

213

regarded as essential to marriage, then marriage is incapable of performing that imaging function, and without the imaging function there is no sacrament. To put it another way, how can a couple symbolize the love of Christ and the Church unless they pledge to love one another?

Finally, a fifth reason is that marital consent, as defined in canon 1057, §2, is, as Urban Navarrete said, "essentially an act of love."[22] The canon says that "matrimonial consent is an act of the will by which a man and a woman, through an irrevocable covenant, mutually give and accept each other (*sese mutuo tradunt et accipiunt*) in order to establish marriage."

The canon, it should be noted, does not say simply that the parties mutually *give* themselves to each other. Rather it seems to go out of its way (as did *Gaudium et spes*) to state quite exactly that parties "mutually *give and accept* each other" which, as we have seen, is precisely what love is. It seems quite clear, therefore, that, according to canon 1057, what the parties consent to at the time of marriage is to love each other.

So much for a brief statement of the position. Let us look now at some possible objections.

D. Some Objections

1. A first objection to love ever being regarded as essential to marriage is that Pope Paul VI, in his allocution to the Rota on February 9, 1976, [23] seemed to indicate that that can never be the case. Pope Paul took issue, in that allocution, with those people who "consider conjugal love as an element of such great importance in law ... that they subordinate to it the very validity of the marriage bond" and he also noted that "conjugal love is not included in the province of law."

    When, however, the entire allocution is read, it is clear that there is no real conflict between the position of Paul VI and the position taken in this paper. Paul was making the point that it is consent and only consent that makes marriage, and once that consent is given an indissoluble bond is created. Whether the parties are in love prior to marriage or whether they fall out of love afterwards is juridically irrelevant.

    That, of course, is entirely true but in no way does it differ from our position. Our position does not claim that love is essential to marriage. Rather it claims first that *the right* to the *bonum coniugum* is part of the essential object of marital consent, and second that the *bonum coniugum* consists not in partnership, companionship, caring, etc., but rather in the love of the parties for each other.

    Once, however, the parties consent to marry and pledge to love each other, the marriage is then valid; it remains valid, of course, even if their commitment to love later disappears.

2.   Another objection to our position is that whatever is consented to in marriage must be under the control of the will; love, however, is an affection or an emotion and, as such, is not under the control of the will. This is a point made by Bishop Zenon Grocholewski, Secretary of the Signatura, in his 1979 *Periodica* article.[24] How, he asks, can people oblige themselves to be affectionate? Either we are affectionate or we are not. We cannot just decide to be affectionate and then be so. Human nature does not work that way.

   St. Thomas, however, states quite clearly that human nature in fact does work that way. Thomas takes up the question in several places[25] and he concludes that love may be viewed as residing either in the sensitive appetite or in the rational appetite. Even when it is in the sensitive appetite, however, love is under the command of the will. Thomas concludes, in other words, that a person's love is free and voluntary and can, indeed, even be measured. He notes, for example, that a man should love his wife more intensely than he does his parents, but he should love his parents with greater reverence than he does his wife.

   It would seem, therefore, at least according to Thomistic psychology, that love *is* subject to the will and can therefore be something that is consented to in marriage. There is nothing inappropriate about spouses committing themselves, at the time of marriage, to being loving persons.

3.   In that same 1979 article Bishop Grocholewski made another point which would certainly contradict my own position, so let me list that as objection three.

   Grocholewski first of all recognizes that the *ius ad amorem* is essential for a valid marriage. For him, however, the essential nucleus of love is not love as we have defined it, namely as an affective tendency which is dialogical in nature. For Grocholewski, the essential nucleus of love includes no affectivity and no receiving, but only giving, non-affective giving.[26] By love, in other words, he means, if I understand him correctly, benevolence or, at the very most, caring (though he does not use that word). When people marry, according to Grocholewski, they give each other the right to benevolent acts and to a benevolent disposition, that and nothing more.

   I would answer that objection, I think, by briefly recapping my earlier remarks about benevolence or goodwill. Benevolence, as Aquinas noted, is not love and it should not therefore be dignified with the title of love. Grocholewski calls benevolence love by confusing, as I see it, *benevolentia* with *amor benevolentiae*, which, as I tried to point out earlier, are two entirely different things. Benevolence, indeed, is not even friendship but only the *principium amicitiae*. In itself benevolence is an impersonal thing. It would

215

seem, therefore, that benevolence by itself could not constitute the essential element of the *bonum coniugum,* which is generally regarded today not just as an interpersonal relationship but as an interpersonal relationship of some intimacy.

4.   This brings me to the fourth objection and it is this. The 1983 Code of Canon Law studiously avoided incorporating Vatican II's well known description of marriage as an "intimate community of life and love." The studious avoidance of the phrase strongly suggests that the legislator found notions like intimacy and love to be unacceptable or unworkable within a legal framework. It suggests, in other words, that love might be grand in real life but that it has no legal relevancy and is out of place in a legal setting.

This objection first of all smacks of legal positivism in that it implies that the written law is all important, certainly more important than justice or what is right and suitable for the community. But beyond that the fact is, I think, that the code simply wanted to leave the issue open. If it had included Vatican II's phrase, then it would at least to a large extent have closed off discussion; we would all be expected to accept the essentiality of love to marriage. Clearly, however, the world of canon law was not ready to do that in 1983, nor is it in 1986. The whole subject needs lots more thought and discussion. But the point is that we should not read more into the code's non-inclusion of the phrase than it merits. It means only that the subject is open to development, or non-development - through jurisprudence, books, articles, and so forth.

5.   One last objection is the one proposed by Monsignor Palazzini in his Rotal decision of June 2, 1971, namely that if love were regarded as essential, how would jurists ever figure out what degree of love would have to be lacking before nullity would result? Would nullity result from a partial lack of love or only from a total lack? Would the defect have to be absolute or might relative suffice? How severe would the limitation have to be on the intensity of love before it would result in nullity? These, said Palazzini, are the "absurd consequences" of recognizing love as essential to marriage, and they demonstrate how illogical such a position is.[27]

The point is well taken but perhaps exaggerated. On almost all grounds, after all, judgment calls are needed. That is what judges are for. In a force and fear case, for example, how much force is required before nullity results? In a *contra bonum prolis case,* how intense must the contraceptive intent be before it is considered to have prevailed over the marriage covenant? In a lack of due discretion case, how much discretion is "due" discretion? And so forth.

If the *ius ad amorem* comes to be regarded as essential to marriage it will no doubt be difficult for judges at first. But a sound jurisprudence will soon develop and we will soon be able to make reasonable judgments about what it means exactly when we say that, in order to enter a valid marriage, the parties must intend to be loving spouses to each other.

E. Practical Implications

If the *ius ad amorem,* the right to a loving relationship, came to be accepted as essential, the implications for jurisprudence would, I suppose, be rather obvious. Basically it would mean that the three grounds of lack of due competence, lack of due discretion, and simulation would all be expanded by one notch. If a person were judged to have lacked the capacity at the time of marriage to be a loving person to his or her spouse, that person would be considered to have lacked due competence. Or if a party did not maturely evaluate and freely accept love as one of the essential rights and duties of marriage, that person would lack due discretion. Or if, finally, a party excluded by a positive act of the will the *ius ad bonum coniugum* (having love as its essential ingredient), then that person would simulate marriage.

But even beyond the somewhat narrow tribunal implications of this position, there is also a broader implication here; it would bring into harmony the *lex orandi* and the *lex credendi.* In *Mediator Dei* (nn. 46-48) Pius XII warned against possible abuses of the "lex orandi, lex credendi" axiom but he also noted that the liturgy is very definitely a "locus theologicus" and a legitimate criterion of faith. The liturgy, in short, is a teacher of doctrine.

There is no question, it seems to me, but that the marriage liturgy (the prayers of the wedding Mass and the wedding rite itself) portrays love not just as important to marriage, but as essential to it. Love is at the core of the wedding liturgy. The wedding rings are said to be a sign of the bride and groom's love and fidelity, and throughout the ceremony God is implored over and over again to bless their love and to make them one in their love for each other. Furthermore, canon 1063, 3º (a very significant canon, it seems to me) specifically notes that the wedding liturgy should clarify "that the spouses signify and share in that mystery of unity and fruitful love that exists between Christ and the Church."

If, therefore, the *ius ad amorem* came to be generally recognized in law as essential to marriage, then law and liturgy (not to mention sacramentology) would finally come together, and that, it seems to me, is right and just, *dignum,* and above all, *iustum.*

ENDNOTES

[1] A. C. Jemolo, *Il Matrimonio nel Diritto Canonico* (Milano: Casa Editrice Dr. Francesco Vallardi, 1941), p. 76.
[2] *S R R Dec.* 61 (1969) 184. For an English translation see Lawrence G. Wrenn, *Decisions,* 1st ed. (Toledo: CLSA, 1980), p. 100. See also Thomas Aquinas, *ST,* Suppl. Q. 41, a. 1, especially ad 3; Q. 42, a. 2 and Q. 65, a. 2.
[3] *ST,* IIa-IIae, Q. 27, a. 2, sed contra.
[4] C. S. Lewis , *The Four Loves* (New York: Harcourt-Brace-Jovanovich, 1960), pp. 95-96.

[5] *CLD* 8: 778-781, under VI, a.

[6] *ST,* II^a-II^{ae}, Q. 27, a. 2, obj. 3

[7] Lewis, pp 91-92.

[8] Milton Mayeroff, *On Caring* (New York: Harper and Row, 1971), p. 8

[9] Rollo May, *Love and Will* (New York: W. W. Norton, 1969), p. 290.

[10] Martin Heidegger, *Being and Time* (New York: Harper and Row, 1962), p. 242.

[11] Mary McDermott Shideler, *The Theology of Romantic Love* (New York: Harper and Brothers, 1962), pp. 36-37.

[12] *ST,* I^a-II^{ae}, Q. 22-28.

[13] Ibid., Q. 26, a. 1.

[14] Ibid., Q. 26, a. 2.

[15] Ibid., Q. 28, a. 3.

[16] Ibid., Q. 28, a. 1.

[17] Ibid., Q. 26, a. 4.

[18] Karl Rahner, *Theological Dictionary* (New York: Herder and Herder, 1965), p. 266.

[19] Shideler, p. 126.

[20] *ST,* I^a-II^{ae}, Q. 28, a, 1.

[21] Theodore Mackin, *What Is Marriage?* (New York: Paulist Press, 1982), pp. 332 ff.

[22] Urbanus Navarrete, "Structura Iuridica Matrimonii Secundum Concilium Vaticanum II" *Periodica* 57 (1968) 208.

[23] *CLD* 8: 790-795.

[24] Zenon Grocholewski, "De 'communione vitae' in novo schemate 'de matrimonio' et de momento iuridico amoris coniugalis," *Periodica* 68 (1979) 474.

[25] *ST,* I^a, Q. 83, a. 1; I^a-II^{ae}, Q. 6, a. 8; Q. 17, a. 7; Q. 24, a. 1; Q. 26, a. 1 and 2; Q, 28 a. 3; and II^a-II^{ae}, Q. 26, a. 11.

[26] Grocholewski, p. 469.

[27] *SRR Dec.* 63 (1971) 471.

Propositions On The Doctrine Of Christian Marriage

Issued in 1977 by the International Theological Commission

1. MATRIMONY AS AN INSTITUTION

1.1. The Human and Divine View of Matrimony

The matrimonial pact is founded upon pre-existent and permanent structures which constitute the difference between man and woman, and is "instituted" by the spouses themselves, even though in its concrete form it is very subject to different historical and cultural changes as well as, in a certain sense, to the particular way in which the marriage is carried out by the spouses. In this, marriage shows itself to be an institution of the creator himself, both from the point of view of mutual help in conjugal love and fidelity, as well as through the rearing of children born in marriage within the heart of the family community.

1.2 Marriage in Christ

As is easily shown in the New Testament, Jesus confirmed this institution which existed "from the very beginning" and cured it of its previous defects (Mk. 10, 2-9, 10-12) by restoring all its dignity and its original requirements. He sanctified this state of life (*Gaudium et Spes*, n. 48, 2) by including it within the mystery of love which unites him as redeemer to his church. This is the reason why the task of regulating Christian marriage (1 Cor. 7, 10 f) has been entrusted to the church.

1.3 The Apostles

The epistles of the New Testament say that marriage should be honored in every way (Heb. 13, 4) and in response to certain attacks, they present it as a good work of the creator (1 Tm. 4, 1-5). Rather they exalt matrimony among the faithful because it is included in the mystery of covenant and love which unites Christ and the church (Eph. 5, 22-23, *Gaudium et Spes*, n. 48, 2).

They ask, therefore, that marriage be contracted "in the Lord" (1 Cor. 7, 39) and that matrimonial life be lived in accordance with the dignity of a "new creature" (2 Cor. 5, 17), "in Christ" (Eph 5, 21-33), putting Christians on guard against the pagans' habits (1 Cor. 6, 12-20, cf. 6, 9-10). On the basis of a "right deriving from faith" and in their desire to assure its permanence, the churches of apostolic times formulated certain moral orientations (Col. 3, 18ff, Ti. 2, 3-5, 1 Pt. 3, 1-7) and juridical dispositions that would help people live matrimony "according to the faith" in different human situations and conditions.

1.4 The First Centuries

During the first centuries of church history, Christians contracted marriage "like other men" (*Ad Diognetum* v, 6) with the father of the family presiding, and only with domestic rites and gestures, as, for example, uniting hands. Still they didn't lose sight of the "extraordinary and truly paradoxical laws of their spiritual society" (Ibid., v. 4): They eliminated from the home liturgies every trace of pagan cult. They placed special importance on the procreation and education of offspring (Ibid., v. 6), they accepted the bishop's vigilance over matrimony (St. Ignatius of Antioch, *Ad Polycarpum* v. 2), they showed in their matrimony a special submission to God and a relationship with their faith (Clement of Alexandria, *Stromata*, iv, 20), and sometimes at the marriage rite they enjoyed the celebration of the eucharistic sacrifice and a special blessing (Tertullian, *Ad Uxorem*, ii, 9).

1.5. The Eastern Traditions

From very ancient times in the Eastern churches the shepherds of the church themselves took an active part in the celebration of marriages in the place of the fathers of the family or even along with them. This change was not the result of a usurpation, but was brought about to answer the requests made by the family and with the approval of civil authority.

Because of this evolution, the ceremonies formerly carried out within the family were little by little included within liturgical rites. As time passed the idea took shape that the ministers of the rite of the "mystery" of matrimony were not only the couple alone, but also the shepherd of the church.

1.6 The Western Traditions

In the Western churches the problem of what element constituted marriage from a juridical point of view arose with the encounter between the Christian vision of matrimony and Roman law. This was resolved by considering the consent of the spouses as the only constitutive element. The fact that, up until the time of the Council of Trent, clandestine marriages were considered valid is due to this decision. Still, the blessing of the priest and his presence as witness of the church, as well as some liturgical rites, had already been encouraged by the church for a long time. With the decree *Tametsi,* the presence of the pastor and witnesses became the ordinary canonical form of marriage necessary for validity.

1.7 The New Churches

According to the desires of Vatican Council II and the new rite for celebrating matrimony, it is to be hoped that new liturgical and juridical norms will be developed, under the guidance of ecclesial authority, among peoples who have recently come to the Gospel, to harmonize the reality of Christian marriage with the authentic values of these peoples' own traditions.

This diversity of norms, due to the plurality of cultures, is compatible with basic unity and therefore does not go beyond the limits of legitimate pluralism.

The Christian and ecclesial character of the union and of the mutual donation of the spouses can, in fact, be expressed in different ways, under the influence of the baptism which they have received and through the presence of witnesses, among whom the "competent priest" occupies the prime post. Today various canonical adapations of these various elements may seem to be opportune.

1.8 Canonical Adaptations

In the reform of canon law there should be a global view of matrimony according to its various personal and social dimensions. The church must be aware that juridical ordinances must serve to help and develop conditions that are always more attentive to the human values of matrimony. Nevertheless it must not be thought that such adaptations can bear on the total reality of matrimony.

1.9 Personalistic View of the Institution

"The beginning, the subject and goal of all social institutions is and must be the human person, which for its part and by its very nature stands completely in need of social life" (*Gaudium et Spes*, n. 25). As an "intimate partnership of life and conjugal love" (Ibid., n. 48), matrimony is a suitable place and way to improve the welfare of persons in line with their vocation. Therefore marriage can never be thought of as a way of sacrificing persons to some common good extrinsic to themselves, since the common good is the sum of "those conditions of social life which allow people, either as groups or as individuals, to reach their fulfillment more fully and more easily" (Ibid., 26).

1.10 Structure and Not Superstructure

While marriage is subject to economic realities at its beginning and for its entire duration, it is not a superstructure for private ownership of goods and resources. While, in fact, the concrete ways in which the marriage and the family subsist may be tied to economic conditions, still the definitive union of a man with a woman in a conjugal covenant responds to human nature and the needs which the creator put in them. This is the reason why matrimony is not only no obstacle to the personal maturation of couples, but rather is a great help to them.

2. SACRAMENTALITY OF CHRISTIAN MARRIAGE

2.1 Real Symbol and Sacramental Sign

Jesus Christ disclosed in a prophetic way the reality of matrimony as it was intended by God at man's beginnings (cf. Gn. 1, 27, Mk. 10, 6, Mt. 19, 4, Gn. 2, 24, Mk. 10, 7-8, Mt. 19, 5), and restored it through his death and resurrection. For this reason Christian marriage is lived "in the Lord" (1 Cor. 7, 39) and is also determined by elements of the saving action performed by Christ.

Already in the Old Testament the matrimonial union was a figure of the covenant between God and the people of Israel (cf. Hos. 2, Jer. 3, 6-13, Ez. 16 and 23, Is. 54). In the New Testament, Christian marriage rises to a new dignity as a representation of the mystery which unites Christ and the church (cf. Eph. 5, 21-33). Theological interpretation illuminates this analogy more profoundly: The supreme love and gift of the Lord who shed his blood and the faithful and irrevocable attachment of his spouse the church become models and examples for Christian matrimony.

This resemblance is a relationship of real sharing in the covenant of love between Christ and the church. From its own standpoint, Christian marriage, as a real symbol and sacramental sign, represents the church of Christ concretely in the world and, especially under its family aspect, it is called rightly the "domestic church" (*Lumen Gentium*, n. 11).

2.2. Sacrament in a Real Sense

In such a way matrimony takes on the likeness of the mystery of the union between Jesus Christ and his church. This inclusion of Christian marriage in the economy of salvation is enough to justify the title "sacrament" in a broad sense.

But it is also at once the concrete condensation and the real actualization of this primordial sacrament. If follows from this that Christian marriage is in itself a real and true sign of salvation which confers the grace of God. For this reason the Catholic Church numbers it among the seven sacraments (cf. *Denz.-Schon.*, 1327, 1801).

A unique bond exists between the indissolubility of marriage and its sacramentality, that is, a reciprocal, constitutive relationship. Indissolubility makes one's grasp of the sacramental nature of Christian matrimony easier, and from the theological point of view, its sacramental nature constitutes the final grounds, although not the only grounds, for its indissolubility.

2.3 Baptism, Real Faith, Intention, Sacramental Marriage

Just like the other sacraments, matrimony confers grace in the final analysis by virtue of the action performed by Christ and not only through the faith of the one receiving it. That, however, does not mean that grace is conferred in the sacrament of matrimony outside of faith or in the absence of faith. It follows from this - according to classical principles - that faith is presupposed as a "disposing cause" for receiving the fruitful effect of the sacrament. The validity of marriage, however, does not imply that this effect is necessarily fruitful.

The existence today of "baptized non-believers" raises a new theological problem and a grave pastoral dilemma especially when the lack of, or rather the rejection of the faith, seems clear. The intention of carrying out what Christ and the church desire is the minimum condition required before consent is considered to be a "real human act" on the sacramental plane. The problem of the intention and that of the personal faith of the contracting parties must not be confused, but they must not be totally separated either.

In the last analysis the real intention is born from and feeds on living faith. Where there is no trace of faith (in the sense of "belief" - being disposed to believe), and no desire for grace or salvation is found, then a real doubt arises as to whether there is the above-mentioned general and truly sacramental intention and whether the contracted marriage is validly contracted or not. As was noted, the personal faith of the contracting parties does not constitute the sacramentality of matrimony, but the absence of personal faith compromises the validity of the sacrament.

This gives rise to new problems for which a satisfactory answer has yet to be found and it imposes new pastoral responsibilities regarding Christian matrimony. "Priests should first of all strengthen and nourish the faith of those about to be married, for the sacrament of matrimony presupposes and demands faith." (*Ordo Celebrandi Matrimonium, Praenotanda*, n. 7).

2.4 Dynamic Interconnection

For the church, baptism is the social basis and the sacrament of faith through which believers become members of the body of Christ. The existence of "baptized non-believers" implies problems of great importance in this respect as well. A true response to practical and pastoral problems will not be found in changes which subvert the central core of sacramental doctrine and of matrimonial doctrine, but only with a radical renewal of baptismal spirituality.

We must view and renew baptism in its essential unity and dynamic interconnection with all its elements and dimensions: faith, preparation for the sacrament, the rite, profession of faith, incorporation into Christ and into the church, moral consequences, active participation in church life. The intimate connection between baptism, faith and the church must be stressed. Only in this way will it be clear that matrimony between the baptized is "in itself" a true sacrament, that is, not by force of some sort of automatic process, but through its own internal nature.

3. CREATION AND REDEMPTION

3.1 Marriage as Willed by God

Since all things were created in Christ, through Christ and in view of Christ, marriage as a true institution of the creator, becomes a figure of the mystery of union of Christ, the groom, with the church, the bride, and, in a certain way, is directed toward this mystery. Marriage celebrated between two

223

baptized persons has been elevated to the dignity of a real sacrament, that is, signifying and participating in the spousal love of Christ and the church.

3.2 The Inseparability of Christ's Actions

Between two baptized persons, marriage as an institution willed by God the creator, cannot be separated from marriage the sacrament, because the sacramental nature of marriage between the baptized is not an accidental element which could be or could just as well not be, but is rather so tied into the essence of it as to be inseparable from it.

3.3 Every Marriage Between Baptized Persons Must Be Sacramental

Thus between baptized persons no other married state can exist really and truly which differs from that willed by Christ in which the Christian man and woman, giving and accepting one another freely and with irrevocable personal consent as spouses, are radically removed from the "hardness of heart" of which Christ spoke (cf. Mt. 19,8) and, through the sacrament, really and truly included within the mystery of marital union of Christ with his church, thus being given the real possibility of living in perpetual love. As a consequence the church cannot in any way recognize that two baptized persons are living in a marital state equal to their dignity and their life as "new creatures in Christ" if they are not united by the sacrament of matrimony.

3.4 The "Legitimate" Marriage of Non-Christians

The strength and the greatness of the grace of Christ is extended to all people, even those beyond the church, because of God's desire to save all men. They shape all human marital love and strengthen created nature as well as matrimony "as it was in the beginning." Men and women therefore who have not yet heard the gospel message, are united by a human covenant in a legitimate marriage. This legitimate marriage is not without authentic goodness and values, which assure its stability. These goods, even though the spouses are not aware of it, come from God the creator and are included, in a certain inchoative way, in the marital love which unites Christ with his church.

3.5 Union of Christians Who Pay No Heed to the Requirements of Their Baptism

It would thus be contradictory to say that Christians, baptized in the Catholic Church, might really and truly take a step backward by being content with a non-sacramental marital state. This would mean that they could be content with the "shadow" when Christ offers them the "reality" of his spousal love. Still we cannot exclude cases where the conscience of even some Christians is deformed by ignorance or invincible error. They come to believe sincerely that they are able to contract marriage without receiving the sacrament.

In such a situation, on the one hand, they are unable to contract a valid sacramental marriage because they lack any faith and lack the intention of doing what the church wishes. On the other hand, they still have the natural right to contract marriage. In such circumstances they are capable of giving and accepting one another as spouses because they intend to contract an irrevocable commitment. This mutual and irrevocable self-giving creates a psychological relationship between them which by its internal structure is different from a transitory relationship.

Still this relationship, even if it resembles marriage, cannot in any way be recognized by the church as a nonsacramental conjugal society. For the church, no natural marriage separated from the sacrament exists for baptized persons, but only natural marriage elevated to the dignity of a sacrament.

3.6 Progressive Marriages

It is therefore wrong and very dangerous to introduce within the Christian community the practice of permitting the couple to celebrate successively various wedding ceremonies on different levels, even though they be connected, or to allow a priest or deacon to assist at or read prayers on the occasion of a non-sacramental marriage which baptized persons wish to celebrate.

3.7 Civil Marriage

In a pluralistic society, the public authority of the state can impose on the engaged a public ceremony through which they publicly profess their status as spouses. The state can furthermore make laws which regulate in a precise and correct manner the civil effects deriving from marriage, as well as rights and duties regarding the family.

The Catholic faithful ought to be adequately instructed that these official formalities, commonly called civil marriage, do not constitute real matrimony for them, except in cases when - through dispensation from the canonical form or because of a very prolonged absence of a qualified church witness - the civil ceremony itself can serve as an extraordinary canonical form for the celebration of the sacrament of matrimony (cf. Canon 1098). For non-Christians and often even for non-Catholic Christians, this civil ceremony can have constitutive value both as legitimate marriage and as sacramental marriage.

4.   INDISSOLUBILITY OF MARRIAGE

4.1 The Principle

The early church's tradition, based on the teaching of Christ and the apostles, affirms the indissolubility of marriage, even in cases of adultery. This principle applies despite certain texts which are hard to interpret and examples of indulgence - the extension and frequency of which is difficult to judge - toward persons in very difficult situations.

4.2 The Church's Doctrine

The Council of Trent declared that the church has not erred when it has taught and teaches in accordance with the doctrine of the Gospel and the apostles, that the marriage bond cannot be broken through adultery. Nevertheless, because of historical doubts (opinions of Ambrosiaster, Catharinus and Cajetan) and for some more or less ecumencial reasons, the council limited itself to pronouncing an anathema against those who deny the church's authority on this issue.

It cannot be said then that the council had the intention of solemnly defining marriage's indissolubility as a truth of faith. Still, account must be taken of what Pius XI said in *Casti Connubii,* referring to this canon: "If therefore the church has not erred and does not err in teaching this, and consequently it is certain that the bond of marriage cannot be loosed even on account of the sin of adultery, it is evident that all the weaker excuses that can be, and are usually brought forward, are of no value whatsoever. And the objections brought against the marriage bond are easily answered" (cf. *Denz.-Schon.* 1807).

4.3 Intrinsic Indissolubility

Intrinsic indissolubility of matrimony can be considered under various aspects and grounded in various ways:

- From the point of view of the spouses: Their intimate conjugal union as a mutual donation of two persons, just as their very marital love itself and the welfare of the offspring, demands that indissoluble unity. From this is derived the spouses' moral duty to protect, maintain and develop the marital covenant.

- From God's vantage point: From the human act by which the spouses give and accept each other rises a bond, based on the will of God and written in nature as created, independent of human authority and removed from the sphere of power of the spouses, and thus intrinsically indissoluble.

- From a Christological perspective: The final and deepest basis for the indissolubility of Christian matrimony lies in the fact that it is the image, sacrament and witness of the indissoluble union between Christ and the church that has been called the *bonum sacramenti.* In this sense indissolubility becomes a moment of grace.

- The social perspective: Indissolubility is demanded by the institution of marriage itself. The spouses' personal decision comes to be accepted, protected and reinforced by society itself, especially by the ecclesial community. This is for the good of the offspring and for the common good. This is the juridico-ecclesial dimension of matrimony.

These various aspects are intimately tied together: The fidelity to which the spouses are held and which ought to be protected by society, especially by the ecclesial community, is demanded by God the creator and by Christ who makes it possible through his grace.

4.4 Extrinsic Indissolubility and the Power of the Church over Marriages

Hand in hand with the practice, the church has elaborated a doctrine concerning its powers over marriages, clearly indicating its scope and limits. The church acknowledges that it does not have any power to invalidate a sacramental marriage which is concluded and consummated (*ratum et consummatum*).

For very serious reasons and with concern for the good of the faith and the salvation of souls, all other marriages can be invalidated by competent church authority or - according to another interpretation - can be declared self-invalidating. This doctrine is nothing more than an individual example of the theory, today more or less generally accepted by Catholic theologians, on the evolution of Christian doctrine in the church.

Neither is it to be excluded that the church can further define the concepts of sacramentality and consummation by explaining them even better, so that the whole doctrine on the indissolubility of marriage can be put forward in a deeper and more precise presentation.

5. THE DIVORCED WHO HAVE REMARRIED

5.1 Gospel Radicalism

Faithful to the radicalism of the Gospel, the church cannot refrain from stating with St. Paul the apostle: "To those now married, however, I give this command (though it is not mine; it is the Lord's): a wife must not separate from her husband. If she does separate, she must either remain single or become reconciled to him again. Similarly, a husband must not divorce his wife" (1 Cor. 7, 10-11). It follows from this that new unions following divorce under civil law cannot be considered regular or legitimate.

5.2 Prophetic Witness

This severity does not derive from a purely disciplinary law or from a type of legalism. It is rather a judgment pronounced by Jesus himself (Mk. 10, 6 ff). Understood in this way, this harsh norm is a prophetic witness to the irreversible fidelity of love which binds Christ to his church. It shows also that the spouses' love is incorporated into the very love of Christ (Eph. 5, 23-32).

5.3 "Non-sacramentalization"

The incompatibility of the state of remarried divorced persons with the precept and mystery of the paschal love of the Lord makes it impossible for these people to receive, in the eucharist, the sign of unity with Christ. Access to eucharistic communion can only be had through penitence, which implies detestation of the sin committed and the firm purpose of not sinning again (cf. *Denz.-Schon.* 1676).

Let all Christians, therefore, remember the words of the apostle: "Whoever eats the bread or drinks the cup of the Lord unworthily, sins against the body and blood of the Lord. A man should examine himself first; only then should he eat of the bread and drink of the cup. He who eats and drinks without recognizing the body eats and drinks a judgment on himself" (1 Cor. 11, 27-29).

5.4 Pastoral Care of the Divorced Who Have Remarried

While this illegitimate situation does not permit a life of full communion with the church, still Christians who find themselves in this state are not excluded from the action of divine grace and from a link with the church. They must not, therefore, be deprived of pastoral assistance (cf. Address of Pope Paul VI, Nov. 4, 1977).

They are not dispensed from the numerous obligations stemming from baptism. They ought to be concerned about the Christian education of their offspring. The paths of Christian prayer, both public and private, penitence and certain apostolic activities remain open to them. They must not be ignored, but rather helped like all other Christians who are trying, with the help of Christ's grace, to free themselves from sin.

5.5 Combatting the Causes of Divorce

The need for a pastoral action to avoid the multiplication of divorces and of new civil marriages of the divorced seems ever more urgent. It is recommended that future spouses be given a living awareness of all their responsibilities as spouses and parents. The real meaning of matrimony must be ever more adequately presented as a covenant contracted "in the Lord" (1 Cor. 7, 39). In such a way Christians will be better disposed to observe the command of God and to witness to the union of Christ and the church. And that will redound to the greater personal advantage of the spouses, of their children and society itself.

Origins, Vol. 8, No. 15
September 28, 1978

APPENDIX FIVE

Private Response On Canon 1098

Issued by the Code Commission - February 8, 1986

Prot. No. 843/86

Your Excellency:

By letter of March 23, 1985, under protocol number 485/86, Your Excellency was informed that the question posed by you to the Supreme Tribunal of the Apostolic Signatura regarding the possible retroactivity of Canon 1098 of the Code of Canon Law was, for reasons of competence, transferred to this dicastery and was under study by this Pontifical Commission.

I would like now to assure you that the question, after first being subjected to a special and profound study by several of our consultors, was then examined collegially in a Consultation held on December 13 of last year in which it was decided, given the doctrinal complexity of the question, to have the matter placed before a Plenarium of the Cardinal Fathers of the Commission who would decide on the opportuneness of giving an authentic interpretation in this matter.

The Consultation is inclined to regard the wording of Canon 1098 as of merely positive law and consequently as *nonretroactive*. Given, however, the great variety of cases which the canon could embrace, once could not a priori rule out the possibility that some of those cases could involve nullity deriving from the natural law, in which case it would be legitimate to render an affirmative decision. It is therefore the task of the judge, who is in possession of all the possible facts, to determine whether the case at bar involves a type of error invalidating the consent not by the positive disposition of Canon 1098 but by force of the natural law, as was the case in certain sentences that predated the promulgation of the Code.

To arrive finally at a clarification and investigation of these criteria and concepts is a task reserved to doctrine.[1] In spite of the risk that meanwhile there will be different doctrinal interpretations and therefore different judicial decisions, it still seems inappropriate to preempt the doctrinal task by an authentic canonical interpretation. At any rate, it will, as I have said, be incumbent upon the Plenarium to decide on the opportuneness of a decision clarifying the matter, a decision regarded by some as premature since a sufficient doctrinal investigation has not yet been conducted.

In the absence of an authentic interpretation which favors the nonretroactivity of Canon 1098, there obviously remains a doubt about the nature of the prescript of Canon 1098 - and consequently a doubt about whether the canon may or may not be applied to marriages celebrated before November 27, 1983. In view of this doubt one should, of course, keep in mind Canon 1060 which indicates that "in doubt the validity of a marriage is to be upheld."

Trusting that these observations will be of some use to Your Excellency, I am

Devotedly yours,

Rosalio Cardinal Castillo Lara
President

J. Herranz
Secretary

[1] Translator's Note: A definitive decision on this matter would presumably be issued not by the Code Commission but by the Congregation for the Doctrine of the Faith, as in the case of the Decree of May 13, 1977 regarding impotence. See next page.

APPENDIX SIX

Decree On Impotence

Issued By The Congregation For The Doctrine Of The Faith - May 13, 1977

The Sacred Congregation for the Doctrine of the Faith has always held that persons who have undergone vasectomy and other persons in similar conditions must not be prohibited from marriage because certain proof of impotency on their part is not had.

And now, after having examined that kind of practice, and after repeated studies carried out by this Sacred Congregation as well as by the Commission for the Revision of the Code of Canon Law, the Fathers of this S. Congregation, in the plenary assembly held on Wednesday, the 11th of May, 1977, decided that the questions proposed to them must be answered as follows:

1. Whether the impotency which invalidates marriage consists in the incapacity to complete conjugal intercourse which is antecedent, of course, and perpetual, either absolute or relative?

2. Inasmuch as the reply is affirmative, whether for conjugal intercourse the ejaculation of semen elaborated in the testicles is necessarily requisite?

To the first question: *In the affirmative;* to the second, *In the negative.*

And in the audience granted to the undersigned Prefect of this S. Congregation on Friday, the 13th day of the said month and year, the Supreme Pontiff, Pope Paul VI, approved the above decree and ordered that it be published.

Given at Rome, from the offices of the S. Congregation for the Doctrine of the Faith, the 13th day of May, 1977.

CLD 8, 676-677

SELECTIVE BIBLIOGRAPHY

Reference Works

Bartocetti, Victorius. *De Causis Matrimonialibus*. Romae: 1950.

Bogdan, Leonard A. *Renewal of Consent in The Simple Convalidation of Marriage*. Dissertation Excerpt, Rome, Pontificia Universitá Lateranense, 1979.

Brenkle, John J. *The Impediment of Male Impotence with Special Application to Paraplegia*. Washington: Catholic University, 1963.

Brooke, Christopher. *The Medieval Idea of Marriage*, Oxford, Oxford University Press, 1989

Brown, Ralph. *Marriage Annulment in the Catholic Church*. Third Edition Suffolk, B.E.P., 1990

Brundage, James A. *Law, Sex and Christian Society in Medieval Europe*. Chicago, University of Chicago Press, 1987

Congregatio Plenaria, Diebus 20-29, octobris 1981 habita, Vatican, 1991

Diagnostic and Statistical Manual of Mental Disorders. Washington: American Psychiatric Association. First edition 1952. Second edition 1968. Third edition 1980. Third edition revised 1987. Fourth edition 1994.

Documenta Recentiora Circa Rem Matrimonialem et Processualem, Vol. I edited by I. Gordon and Z. Grocholewski, Rome 1977; Vol. II, edited by Z. Grocholewski, 1980.

Documentation on Marriage Nullity Cases. First compilation by Germain Lesage and Francis Morrisey, Ottawa, St. Paul University 1971; Second compilation by J. Edward Hudson, 1979.

Duby, Georges. *The Knight, The Lady and The Priest*, New York, Pantheon Books, 1983

Fellhauer, David E. *The Consortium Omnis Vitae as A Juridical Element of Marriage*, Ottawa, University of St. Paul, 1979 (Vol. 13, n. 1, of Studia Canonica).

Frattin, Peter L. *The Matrimonial Impediment of Impotence: Occlusion of Spermatic Ducts and Vaginismus*. Washington: Catholic University, 1958.

Freedman, Alfred with Harold Kaplan and Benjamin Sadock. *Comprehensive Textbook of Psychiatry - II*, 2 vols., Baltimore: The Williams and Wilkins Company, 1975.

Gies, Frances and Joseph, *Marriage and the Family in the Middle Ages*, New York, Harper and Row, 1987

Grocholewski, Zenon. *De Exclusione Indissolubilitatis ex Consensu Matrimoniali Eiusque Probatione*. Naples: D'Auria, 1973.

Häring, Bernard. *Marriage in the Modern World*. Westminster: The Newman Press, 1966.

Hastings, Donald. *Impotence and Frigidity*. New York: Delta, 1966.

Holböck, Carolus. *Tractatus De Iurisprudentia Sacrae Romane Rotae*. Graz: Styria, 1957.

Hudson, J. Edward. *Handbook for Marriage Nullity Cases*. Ottawa: St. Paul University, First edition 1975; Second edition 1980.

Huels, John M. *The Pastoral Companion*, Quincy, Franciscan Press, 1995

Kaplan, Harold and Benjamin Sadock, *Modern Synopsis of Comprehensive Textbook of Psychiatry IV*, Fourth edition, Baltimore, Williams and Wilkins, 1985

Kasper, Walter. *Theology of Christian Marriage*, New York, Crossroad, 1977

Keating, John Richard. *The Bearing of Mental Impairment on the Validity of Marriage*. Roma: Gregorian University Press, 1964.

Lawler, Michael G. *Secular Marriage, Christian Sacrament*, Mystic, Twenty-third Publications, 1985

Lazzarato, Damianus. *Iurisprudentia Pontificia - De Metu.* Typis Polyglottis Vaticanis: 1956.
---------------- *Iurisprudentia Pontificia - De Causis Matrimonialibus Praeter Metum.* 3 Vols., Neapoli: M. D'Auria, 1963.
Mackin, Theodore. *What Is Marriage?* New York, Paulist Press, 1982.
------------------------------- *Divorce and Remarriage,* New York, Paulist Press, 1984
------------------------------- *The Marital Sacrament,* New York, Paulist Press, 1989
Marriage Studies, Washington, CLSA, Vol. I, 1980; Vol. II, 1982; Vol. III, 1985; Vol. IV, 1990
Masters, William H. and Virginia E. Johnson. *Human Sexual Inadequacy.* Boston: Little, Brown and Company, 1970.
Matrimonial Jurisprudence, United States. 5 Vols. covering years 1968-1976. Toledo: CLSA, published annually from 1973 to 1977.
Mendonca, Augustine. *Antisocial Personality and Nullity of Marriage.* Ottawa: University of St. Paul, 1982. (Vol. 16, n. 1 of Studia Canonica).
Mendonca, Augustine, comp. *Rotal Anthology: An Annotated Index of Rotal Decisions from 1971 to 1988,* Washington, CLSA, 1992
Navarrette, Urbanus. *Structura Iuridica Matrimonii Secundum Concilium Vaticanum II: Momentum iuridicum amoris coniugalis.* Roma: Pontificia Universitá Gregoriana, 1968.
Netter, Frank H. *The Ciba Collection of Medical Illustrations. Reproductive System.* Summit, New Jersey: Ciba, 1954.
Noonan, John T. Jr. *Power to Dissolve.* Cambridge: The Belknap Press, 1972.
Orsy, Ladislas. *Marriage in Canon Law.* Wilmington, Michael Glazier, 1986.
Pospishil, Victor J. *Divorce and Remarriage.* New York: Herder and Herder, 1967.
------------------------------- *Eastern Catholic Marriage Law,* Brooklyn, St. Maron, 1991
Sable, Robert M., coordinator and editor. *Incapacity For Marriage: Jurisprudence and Interpretation,* Acts of the III Gregorian Colloquium. Rome: Pontificia Universitas Gregoriana, 1987.
Schillebeeckx, E. *Marriage: Human Reality and Saving Mystery.* New York: Sheed and Ward, 1965.
Staffa, Dinus. *De Conditione Contra Matrimonii Substantiam.* Romae: Libraria Pont. Instituti Utriusque Iuris, 1955.
The Bond of Marriage. Ed. by William Bassett. University of Notre Dame Press, 1968.
The Future of Marriage as Institution. Ed. by Franz Böckle. New York: Herder and Herder, Volume 55 of the Concilium Series, 1970.
The Tribunal Reporter. Ed. by Adam J. Maida. Huntington: Our Sunday Visitor Inc., 1970.
Tobin, William J. *Homosexuality and Marriage.* Rome: Catholic Book Agency, 1964.
Understanding Alcoholism. New York: Charles Scribner's Sons, 1968.
Van Ommeren, William M. *Mental Illness Affecting Matrimonial Consent* (Canon Law Studies #415). Washington, D.C.: Catholic University of America Press, 1961.
Woestman, William, ed. *Papal Allocutions to the Roman Rota,* Ottawa, 1994
Wrenn, Lawrence G. *Decisions,* Washington, D.C., CLSA, First edition, 1980. Second edition 1983.
------------------------------- *Law Sections,* Washington, CLSA, 1994

Articles

Ahern, Maurice B. "The Marital Right to Children: A Tentative Reexamination. *Studia Canonica* 8, 1974, pp. 91-107.
-------------- "Error and Deception as Grounds for Nullity." *Studia Canonica* 11, 1977, pp. 225-259.

Arena, Aldo. "The Jurisprudence of the Sacred Roman Rota: Its Development and Direction After the Second Vatican Council." *Studia Canonica.* 12, 1978, pp. 265-293.

Bauer, Francis, M.D. "Relative Incapacity to Establish a Christian Conjugal Union." *CLSA Proceedings.* 1974, pp. 36-44.

Bernhard, Jean. "The Evolution of Matrimonial Jurisprudence: The Opinion of a French Canonist." *The Jurist.* 41, 1981, pp. 105-116.

Bogdan, Leonard A. "Simple Convalidation of Marriage in the 1983 Code of Canon Law." *The Jurist* 46, 1986, pp. 511-531.

Bolen, Darrell W. "Gambling and Sex." *Medical Aspects of Human Sexuality.* May, 1969, pp. 60-65.

Braceland, Francis J. "Psychoneurotic Interpersonal Reaction: Incompatibility and the Tribunal." *CLSA Proceedings.* 1970, 63-70.

——————— "Schizophrenic Remissions." *The Jurist.* XXI. pp. 362-374.

Brown, Ralph. "Inadequate Consent or Lack of Commitment: Authentic Grounds for Nullity." *Studia Canonica.* 9, 1975, pp. 249-265.

——————— "Total Simulation - A Second Look." *Studia Canonica.* 10, 1976, pp. 235-249.

——————— "Non Inclusion: A Form of Simulation?" CLSA *Proceedings.* 1979, pp. 1-11.

——————— "Essential Incompatibility: Researches and the Present Situation." *Studia Canonica.* 14, 1980, pp. 25-48.

——————— "Simulation versus Lack of Commitment." *Studia Canonica.* 14, 1980, pp. 335-345.

Burke, Raymond L. "Canon 1095: Canonical Doctrine and Jurisprudence. Part I: Canon 1095, 1° and 2°." *CLSA Proceedings.* 1986, pp. 94-107.

Campbell, Donald M. "Canon 1099: The Emergence of a New Juridic Figure", *Quaderni Studia Rotale,* 5 (September 1990) pp. 35-72.

Cavanagh, John R. "Sexual Anomalies and the Law." *The Catholic Lawyer.* Vol. 9, No. 1, Winter, 1963, pp. 4-31.

Coburn, Vincent P. "Homosexuality and the Invalidation of Marriage." *The Jurist.* XX. 1960, pp. 441-459.

Coleman, Gerald D. "Can a Person With AIDS Marry in the Catholic Church?" *The Jurist* 49 (1989) pp. 258-266.

Cuneo, J. James. "Lack of Due Discretion: The Judge as Expert." *The Jurist.* 42, 1982, pp. 141-163.

——————— "Deceit/Error of Person as a *Caput Nullitatis.*" *CLSA Proceedings,* 1983, pp. 154-166.

Cunningham, Richard. "Recent Rotal Decisions and Today's Marriage Theology: Nothing Has Changed - Or Has It?" *CLSA Proceedings.* 1976, pp. 24-41.

Curran, Charles E. "Divorce: Catholic Theory and Practice in the United States." *The American Ecclesiastical Review.* 1974, pp. 3-34 and 75-95.

De Luca, Luigi. "The New Law on Marriage." *The New Code of Canon Law: Proceedings of the 5th International Congress,* 1986, pp. 827-851.

Doyle, Thomas P. "A New Look at The Bonum Fidei." *Studia Canonica.* 12, 1978, pp. 5-40.

Faltin, Daniel "The Exclusion of the Sacramentality of Marriage with Particular Reference to the Marriage of Baptized Non-Believers", *Marriage Studies 4,* 1990, pp. 66-104.

Felici, Pericle. "Juridical Formalities and Evaluation of Evidence in the Canonical Process." *The Jurist.* 38, 1978, pp. 153-157.

Fellhauer, David E. "The Exclusion of Indissolubility: Old Principles and New Jurisprudence." *Studia Canonica.* 9, 1975, pp. 105-133.

——————— "Psychological Incapacity for Marriage in the Revised *Code of Canon Law.*" *The New Code of Canon Law: Proceedings of the 5th International Congress,* 1986, pp. 1019-1040.